Praise for *Modern Hermeticism*

"An excellent introduction and thoroughly readable overview of aspects of Hermeticism most important to the study and practice of modern ritual magick."
—**LON MILO DUQUETTE,** author of *The Magick of Aleister Crowley*

"A helpful, down-to-earth primer that covers the essentials of practical magic in the Western Esoteric Tradition."
—**CHIC CICERO AND SANDRA TABATHA CICERO,** authors of *Golden Dawn Magic* and *Self-Initiation into the Golden Dawn Tradition*

"A thoughtful and artfully presented introduction and overview of Western ceremonial magick traditions. The authors skillfully cover both theory and practice in a way which is approachable for a beginner but detailed enough for those wishing to dig deep. Recommended!"
—**DAVID SHOEMAKER,** PsyD, author of *Living Thelema*

M·O·D·E·R·N HERMETICISM

© Photo by Bob O'Lary

About Erich Brown

Erich Brown, a.k.a. Frater Anubis, has been studying ritual magic since he was a teenager. He started self-training in the Golden Dawn tradition and was later initiated into the Order of the Gnostic Star (E.S.S.G) by its founder, Frater Barabbas, in his twenties. Erich currently coleads the Temple of Limitless Light, a magical school dedicated to raising spiritual development in the community, with his wife. He studies elemental, planetary, and Enochian magic and the inner order teachings of the E.S.S.G. Visit him at YouTube.com/@WhirlingChinaCat.

About Alannah Brown

Alannah Brown cofounded and coleads the Temple of Limitless Light, a magical school dedicated to raising spiritual development in the community, with her husband Erich Brown. Learn more at YouTube.com/@WhirlingChinaCat.

M·O·D·E·R·N HERMETICISM

· A BEGINNER'S GUIDE TO CEREMONIAL MAGIC ·

ERICH BROWN AND ALANNAH BROWN

LLEWELLYN
WOODBURY, MINNESOTA

First Edition
First Printing, 2025

Book design by Samantha Peterson
Cover design by Shannon McKuhen
Interior illustrations by Llewellyn Art Department
Tarot Original 1909 Deck ©2021 with art created by Pamela Colman Smith and Arthur Edward Waite. Used with permission of Lo Scarabeo.

Library of Congress Cataloging-in-Publication Data (Pending)
ISBN: 978-0-7387-7902-7

Llewellyn Publications
A Division of Llewellyn Worldwide Ltd.
2143 Wooddale Drive
Woodbury, MN 55125-2989
www.llewellyn.com

Printed in the United States of America

contents

List of Rituals, Practices, and Exercises ... ix
Acknowledgments ... xi
A Prayer to Begin ... xiii
Foreword by Frater Barrabbas ... xv
Introduction ... 1

part one: foundations

Chapter 1: As Above, So Below ... 11
Chapter 2: Hermetic Qabalah, the Tree of Life ... 17
Chapter 3: Your True Will ... 33
Chapter 4: The Three Veils and Shadow Work ... 41
Chapter 5: Elemental Energies, Angels, Gods, and Archetypes ... 55
Chapter 6: The Four Elements ... 65
Chapter 7: Enochiana ... 71

Part Two: Developing a Practice

Chapter 8: Tools ... 85
Chapter 9: The Tarot ... 93
Chapter 10: Breathing and Meditation ... 105
Chapter 11: Sigils ... 115
Chapter 12: Pentagrams and Spirals ... 125
Chapter 13: The Art of Scrying ... 133
Chapter 14: The Art of the Eidolon ... 139

Part Three: Rituals and Rites

Chapter 15: The Lesser Ritual of the Pentagram ... 151
Chapter 16: The Middle Pillar ... 161
Chapter 17: Temple Consecration ... 167
Chapter 18: The Rose Ankh Vortex ... 179
Chapter 19: Godforms ... 189
Chapter 20: The Greater Ritual of the Pentagram ... 199
Chapter 21: The Pyramid of Power ... 217
Chapter 22: The Concourse of Forces for the Pyramid of Power ... 229
Chapter 23: The Elemental Octagram ... 243
Chapter 24: The Concourse of Forces for the Elemental Octagram ... 255
Chapter 25: The Gate of Transformation ... 281

Conclusion: Final Thoughts ... 289
Appendix: Enochian Calls ... 291
Recommended Reading ... 307
Bibliography ... 309

Rituals, Practices, and Exercises

Ritual: Adoration to the Lord of the Universe ... 14
Ritual: The Qabalistic Cross ... 29
Practice: Liber Resh ... 37
Ritual: Ex Tenebris Lux, From Darkness Comes Light ... 51
Practice: Choosing a Personal Archetype ... 62
Practice: Exploring the Elements ... 68
Practice: Exploring Enochian ... 81
Ritual: Consecrating Your Tools ... 89
Practice: A Study of Tarot ... 103
Exercise: Basic Pore Breathing ... 108
Exercise: Mindfulness Meditation ... 110
Practice: Dedication of Merit ... 111
Practice: How to Make a Sigil ... 118
Practice: Drawing Pentagrams in the Air ... 128
Practice: An Experiment with Scrying ... 137
Practice: Fire Meditation ... 141

Practice: Water Meditation ... 142
Practice: Air Meditation ... 143
Practice: Earth Meditation ... 145
Practice: Spirit Meditations ... 146
Ritual: Lesser Banishing Ritual of the Pentagram ... 156
Ritual: The Middle Pillar ... 163
Ritual: Temple Consecration from the Temple of Limitless Light ... 171
Ritual: Egyptian Rose Ankh Vortex ... 185
Ritual: Godform of Ma'at ... 193
Ritual: Godform of Thoth ... 195
Ritual: Greater Ritual of the Pentagram ... 206
Ritual: The Pyramid of Power ... 221
Ritual: The Egyptian Elemental Octagram ... 247
Ritual: Gate of Transformation: Journey to the Underworld ... 284
Ritual: Gate of Return: Coming Forth by Day ... 286

Acknowledgments

Erich Brown

I would like to thank Frater Barrabbas, who initiated me into high magic and gave me the keys to unlock the heavens. I would like to thank my wife, Alannah, who created our temple where we teach and learn; and I would like to thank our students, especially Sebastian Whal, who forced me to get my ideas straight and taught me more than I thought there was to know. I would also like to thank Dr. Justin Sledge for his excellent YouTube site ESOTERICA. His work has been profoundly helpful in my research into the history of what I have spent a life practicing. I would also like to thank Lon Milo DuQuette for his daily free teachings, his many books, and his excellent reading that helped guide my spiritual practice.

Alannah Brown

I would like to thank the Great Holy Source, who saved me from certain doom more times than I would like to recall. I would like to thank my teachers and guides, both living and ethereal, for their wisdom, presence, and friendship. And I would also like to thank my friends who come to my parties, even when they don't understand what we are doing.

A Prayer to Begin

It is our belief that every book of sacred mysteries—every holy book—should begin with a prayer. When the book is opened, the prayer can be read and considered before the rest of the text is examined. We believe this practice helps the reader to enter the right state of contemplation. We've written this short poem as a prayer and road map of the mysteries to follow in this book. Let us pray:

Three are the veils that obscure the Bornless One,
Four are the letters of the name of the Infinite Thought,
Seven are the rays that emanate from the Cosmic Jewel,
Twelve are the citadels of the Secret and Unknowable Inner Kingdom,
Sixteen are the forces that express the Ultimate Feeling of Eternal Bliss.
Twenty-eight are the Mysterious Mansions of the Moon.
All for the miracle of the One.

foreword

I have known Erich Brown for decades, and I first met him when I was living in Tallahassee in early 1993. He was just beginning his magical path, yet he was also keenly intelligent, creative, and very magically precocious. I had no hesitation taking him on as a student, for I could see that he was eager for the work and thirsty for magical wisdom. I initiated him into the magical order that we called the Order of the Gnostic Star and began exposing him to the entirety of the ritual and occult lore that had been created by the members of that organization and added considerably thereunto by my own work. Erich took on the lore of the order and made great progress in a matter of months. By the time that I had to leave Tallahassee in the summer of 1994, he had already mastered the basic work of elemental magic and was quickly advancing to the study of talismanic magic and the art of spirit conjuration. He even took the rites written up from my first book, *Pyramid of Powers*, which was never published, and performed a Lunar Mystery rite. He documented his experience in a diary that I published in the book *Mastering the Art of Ritual Magick* under his assumed magical name of Frater Anubis.

Years after that occurrence, Erich continued his practice and study of ritual magic, and I gave him the entire library of the Order of the Gnostic Star because I knew that he would make good use of it and to help to grow and expand his occult horizons. I also knew that he would share that lore with those whom he deemed suitable. In the passage of the years, Erich has adapted the lore of the Gnostic Star along with other sources of lore, such as the Golden Dawn, to produce his own distinct and unique methodology of performing magic. He has, over the decades, become something of a master magician, having built his ritual lore from these many different sources but remaining faithful to precepts and teachings of the Order. Erich has become the embodiment of all that the original members of the Gnostic Star sought to emulate, and he has shown abilities and insights that represent the ideals of an approach to magic in the Western Mystery Tradition. Of all the students that I have trained or initiated, only Erich has continued on the path using the knowledge and wisdom that the Order and others have provided him.

This is Erich and Alannah's first book, and it is a distillation of all that they have practiced, learned, and mastered over the last thirty years. *Modern Hermeticism* is product of many years of faithful study and practice, and it is a brilliant representation of what someone might seek to accomplish having multiple sources of ritual and occult lore. Despite the multiple sources, the lore presented in this book appears seamless and has a definite continuity that is both impressive and accessible to even the beginning student. The occult philosophy of Hermeticism and the actual source texts that were originally translated in the fifteenth century, the Hermetic Corpus, are the intellectual foundation for the work that Erich and Alannah have sought to merge with their magical practices. They have successfully accomplished this task in their first book, which is likely to be followed by future works that will employ more complex Hermetic insights with more complex ritual lore.

The real substance of Erich and Alannah's book is the rituals that they have made an integral part of their Hermetic practice. Their approach is twofold, where they have a formal rite that is elaborate, detailed, and performed in sacred space and an informal approach that is mostly internalized and can be performed anywhere. Erich and Alannah believe that we should practice magic both in the temple and out in the mundane sphere. In this manner, the magician has a life that is filled with magic and is not limited to work that is done in sacred space. Erich and Alannah have used this perspective to formulate a formal and informal approach to Hermetic practices, where the formal approach are the actual ritual practices and the informal are the macro rites that build a continuity between sacred space and the mundane world. Through this twofold process, they have shown how to make one's life a full expression of sacred magic.

All of the rituals in *Modern Hermeticism* list the materials required and the mind-state needed to perform them. They also progress from the most basic operations that establish a foundation of spiritual and magical practice to working with elemental powers. Whether it is the Qabalistic Cross, the Lesser Invoking Ritual of the Pentagram, or the temple consecration rite or the more advanced lore associated with the Qabalah, tarot, or Enochian magic, the reader will find useful, practical, and helpful insights that make the approach to this art of ritual magic more accessible and readily adaptable. Complex rituals, such as the Rose Ankh Vortex, the Pyramid of Power, and the Elemental Octagon are explained and presented in a manner that makes them understandable to a wider audience than what might have been with the rituals alone.

Erich and Alannah Brown have produced the definitive modern study of the philosophies and practices of ritual magic, under the aegis of a modern formulation of Hermeticism. This book, *Modern Hermeticism,* contains everything that a knowledgeable practitioner might need to advance their knowledge of ritual magic. It is also accessible and a friendly introduction to this art for those who have only vague notions about ritual magic but who wish to inaugurate a more definitive practice. There is something in this book for both novice and experienced practitioner that makes it a unique contribution to the materials available to the student who seeks to be a practitioner of this sacred art.

—Frater Barrabbas

Introduction

While many people may be familiar with and feel comfortable practicing various forms of magic or spiritual modalities, such as meditation, Hermeticism is not universally practiced. This may be because it seems unapproachable, even though it is a wonderful and fulfilling spiritual path.

Hermeticism combines psychology, religion, and physical practices. This secret path of enlightenment in the West reaches all the way back to ancient Egypt in an unbroken tradition. Around 300 BCE, the first Hermetic teachings began when the Greeks discovered the wisdom of the Egyptians and combined it with their own ideas. The Hermetic tradition has been passed from generation to generation in secret because it gives an individual or group self-knowledge and power. Secret societies such as the Freemasons and the Rosicrucians used these teachings for the benefit of their initiates but held back these secrets from the general public.[1]

While Hermeticism has been steeped in secrecy and held in awe, it is worth the effort to get behind the veil. Today, what was once secret is now available with better scholarship than at any time in history.

1. Salaman, *The Way of Hermes*.

Erich's Journey

Erich has been studying ritual magic since he was a teenager. In fact, he has followed this path for more than thirty years now, and it has been an amazing journey of self-discovery with revelations that really have to be experienced to be believed.

As a teen, he started self-training in the Golden Dawn tradition. In his twenties, he was initiated into the Order of the Gnostic Star (the E.S.S.G.) by its founder, Frater Barrabbas. After taking the title Frater Anubis, Erich, along with his wife, established and currently coleads the Temple of Limitless Light. This magical school is dedicated to raising spiritual development in the community.

Since stepping onto this path, Erich has sought out the most effective ways of creating specific spiritual experiences at will. This is an important point that is often lost; rituals and practices create spiritual experiences that lead to our growth and help us to discover our authentic self. The Hermetic Path is a journey to find the real you—the wonderful, magical, powerful you that is already here now.

Alannah's Journey

Alannah Brown is a mystic. At about eight years old, she started a forty-year span of martial arts training and teaching, attaining the title of Master in the Shinjimasu tradition from Charles Dixon and the rank of teacher, or sifu, in Chen-style Taiji from Zhang Xu Xin. Being a martial artist also came with the study of Buddhist meditation. She focused her studies on mindfulness and Tibetan Dzogchen and is an initiated Ngakma, a householder yogini, in the Tibetan Vajrayana tradition. She continues with a daily Buddhist practice and currently focuses her studies on the mystical paths of Six Yogas of Naropa, dream yoga, and tummo with Glenn Mullin, in the tradition of the Dalai Lama. She is particularly interested in the integration of magical and Buddhist traditions.

Alannah holds a bachelor's degree in religion and psychology, a master's degree in counseling psychology, and a post-master's educational specialist degree. Here are the letters: Alannah Brown, MS, EdS, LMHC! She is a certified EMDR practitioner and member of EMDRIA. She has been in private practice for twenty-five years and specializes in difficult-to-treat, complex post-traumatic stress disorder and dissociation and works extensively with diverse communities, including the LGBTQIA+ community, providing her unique style of depth psychotherapy. She calls herself a depth psychotherapist, a shadow worker, and a skydancer.

Alannah's formal journey into the world of magic began in 2010 after a near-death experience from a tick bite. In a search for understanding the experiences of being in that liminal state for two years, she picked up her husband Erich's practice, and together they began focusing on magical study and practice. It was during this time that she became certified in herbology through Rosemary Gladstar and healed herself from what the doctors had called multiple sclerosis.

In 2016 Alannah and Erich established the Temple of Limitless Light as a study group and publicly practicing Hermetic temple of the ESSG, the Egregore Stella Sancta Gnostica, a tradition developed by Frater Barrabbas. Since then, Alannah has received initiations in the E.S.S.G., O.T.O., and Alexandrian traditions. Alannah and her husband host a community event called Swamp Mystics, featuring local and regional practitioners of the mystical arts. She and Erich offer weekly Zoom study groups and monthly in-person rituals.

What Is Hermeticism Exactly?

Our Limitless Light practice of Hermeticism springs directly from the Golden Dawn, a hugely influential organization of the late nineteenth and early twentieth century. The Golden Dawn was dedicated to Renaissance forms of mystical alchemy and Qabalah as well as astrology, tarot, and geomancy. Manuscripts and early modern printed texts provided much of the source for the organization's practices. These texts were supplemented by the magical knowledge unlocked through archaeological discoveries of the time from the ancient Egyptian and Hellenistic worlds.[2]

Hermeticists of the past were always searching for the best and most effective spiritual technology to quickly achieve gnosis and empowerment. One of the more recognizable members of Hermeticism is William Butler Yeats, a great poet and Nobel Prize winner of 1923, a member of the Hermetic Order of the Golden Dawn. Jack Parsons, the founder of the Jet Propulsion Laboratory that led the United States to the moon landing, was also a Hermeticist and a member of the order called the Ordo Templi Orientis, or the O.T.O.

As these famed Hermeticists have shown, an empowered individual can change the world. Consider that many great authors, musicians, and scientists have one thing in common: the ability to see the world clearly, through the obscurement of social programming telling them who to be. Empowerment means you are free to be the best you and not just accept who society tells you it is safe to be. When a person wakes up from the social programming of the prevalent culture or a subculture, they are hard to control and can disrupt the social hierarchy. Once awake and aware, we can no longer be hypnotized by the continuous stream of noise and advertising that seeks to divide and control us.

We have to awaken to our true nature to be really free and in control of our own destiny. Then we can develop our own narrative. In this way, the Limitless Light Hermetic path has evolved from

2. Davies, "The Hermetic Order of the Golden Dawn and the Origins of Wicca."

the Golden Dawn. We believe in innovating to create more effective and efficient spiritual technology, as this is a Hermetic practice.

The Principles

While Hermeticism can be traced back to the second or third century BCE, the term is often interpreted in a very loose fashion.[3] This is understandable considering the process of transformation it has been through over the last two thousand years.

Let's define *Hermeticism*, as we will be using the term to lay a foundation for your study and to avoid confusion. For this, we turn to the ideas of Antoine Faivre.[4] He was a French scholar of Western Esotericism; he played a major role in establishing Western Esotericism as a serious academic subject for study. Faivre offered a list of four intrinsic characteristics of Western Esoterica, an area of study which Hermeticism is a part of. They are intrinsic because all of Western Esotericism contains these ideas. These four principles are:

- Sympethea, or Correspondence
- Living Nature
- Imagination as an Organ of Perception
- Transformation

Faivre then added two nonintrinsic principles, which are found within most of Western Esotericism and always found in Modern Hermeticism: Concordance and Transmission.

We are going to add a seventh principle to complete the identification of what we call the Seven Principles of Modern Hermeticism.

The First Principle of Modern Hermeticism: Sympethea, or Correspondence

The first principle is that all things are linked through similar nature or vibration. Since all things are linked together, many have similar energies or vibrations and can be used to attract the energies of a similar thing. These energies and vibrations can be used in healing or rectifying an imbalance in someone's energy field.

3. Fowden, *The Egyptian Hermes*, page 2, footnote 11; Hanegraaff, *Western Esotericism*, 5, 183.

4. Hanegraaff, *Western Esotericism*, 5, 183.

For example, silver, the physical metal here on earth, is attributed to the moon and lunar energies. This correspondence is both because of silver's color and reflective properties and because of the subtle energetics of silver. Some people can feel the connection if they hold a silver mirror or piece of silver jewelry while looking at the moon. There are long lists of correspondences out in the world. We won't be using those so much in this book. Rather than using a lot of material substances, such as herbs, stones, and metals, we will be using symbols and archetypes to attract and control the forces that shape reality instead. However, the principle is worth mentioning because it still applies, as there are symbols and archetypes that do have similar effects cross culturally.

The Second Principle of Modern Hermeticism: Living Nature

The second principle is that all of creation is considered to be alive and going through some process of transformation and change. Everything has a life or an incarnation. The trees, the microbes, the rocks, the atoms—literally everything is having a life in a way that you are. All forms arise, exist, and then transform into something else, all with their own adventures and experiences.

The Third Principle of Modern Hermeticism: Imagination As an Organ of Perception

The third principle is that imagination can be used as a screen to view the contents of our unconscious and the collective unconscious mind. The Higher Self, the Eternal Self, speaks in images and feelings. Words are instead part of the conscious mind. Your dreams are meaningful—not always super profoundly meaningful, but they are not random.

We will be using trance and vision work to find wisdom and answers to our questions. This principle is a bit tough to follow when you first encounter it. But rest assured that we will develop our imaginations to be tools for the wisdom of our Higher Selves and spirit guides.

The Fourth Principle of Modern Hermeticism: Transformation

Principle number four is the transformation of the individual. You are not the person you were yesterday, and tomorrow you will be someone else as well. We are all going through a process of change and hopefully growth. Why not take control of the process and steer it so you can become more of the person you want to be?

Initiation is part of the process, but the work of magic as well as daily practice will enliven the best parts of yourself. This transformation will bring them to the forefront of your awareness and personality.

The Fifth Principle of Modern Hermeticism: Concordance

The fifth principle states that all esoteric studies are linked. The Qabalah joins together astrology, numerology, tarot, and many more spiritual technologies. Enochian magic is linked to the Qabalah in some ways as well. Under the hood, all of the esoteric practices are linked, so knowledge and skill in one area will give understanding in another. There is a synergy to studying multiple topics.

The Six Principle of Modern Hermeticism: Transmission

There is a tradition of transmitting knowledge from generation to generation and also the experiences of the practice, which is the sixth principle. Huge leaps of progress can be made by working with a group, not just because others can explain things you may not know but also because there is an effect of transmission of energy by being in ritual with more experienced people. Just as a piece of steel can be charged by being near a magnet, you can experience the energy of magic and can open your energy channels and awareness of those channels very quickly.

The Seventh Principle of Modern Hermeticism: Nonduality, the Pleroma

In the Limitless Light system of Hermetics, the seventh and final principle is that literally everything is divine in nature. There is no duality, only an illusion of duality. In the axiom "as above, so below," the above and below are contained within each other much like a fractal repeating the pattern of creation from the very large to the very small. In Hermeticism, we call this unity or nonduality the pleroma. The word *pleroma* literally means "fullness or completeness" in Greek. What the concept is trying to convey is that the fullness of being—all that could be, all that is, and all that ever was—is connected in a manner so intimate that it can only be described as an unbreakable unity. This pleroma is emanated by the Creator contemplating, or perhaps dreaming, about itself.

The transcendent aspect of creation is just the aspects that are beyond your present level of attainment. This will change as you experience the practices in this book and expand your awareness.

Getting Started

The rituals and practices found in this book can be selected to fulfill what you need at the moment. The practices in this book are at once approachable and also very powerful. Using the rituals and practices outlined in this book, there are times we have entered ritual in one state and left it changed at a very deep level. This path can cause a very rapid evolution of consciousness, and this can and will facilitate huge changes in your life. When you have a deep connection with the process of creation, it is possible to remove obstacles to your goals and achieve better relationships, wealth, skills, or whatever your goals are. Your goals will become clear to you once you awaken to who you truly are.

In this book, we have striven to distill this complex path to just the essentials, making it more accessible and effective without removing any of the majesty and mystery of the journey. During our time leading a magical lodge, we have used these teachings in our temple, refining them continually for clarity and usefulness for and by our students.

• • • • • • •

The aim of this book is to awaken you to your true nature and free you to become the very best version of yourself. But remember that awakening to your True Self is really just the beginning of an amazing adventure, the first step to liberation and the freedom to live your best life. Once awake, you can claim the knowledge and personal power and freedom that is your birthright.

We hope to guide you on this path and beyond and help cultivate within you a deep understanding of the tradition. This will allow you to develop an authentic connection with the true you and the wider universe, which you will come to see is just more you.

PART ONE
Foundations

— CHAPTER 1 —
As Above, So Below

"As above, so below, as within, so without." This famous quote comes from the Emerald Tablet of Hermes Trismegistus, a famous Hermetic document that is cryptic and highly regarded by Islamic and European alchemists as the foundation of their art. The Emerald Tablet's enigmatic words describe the very essence of the Hermetic tradition.

The name Hermes Trismegistus comes from when the Greeks were studying in Egypt. The Greeks encountered the Egyptian god Thoth and recognized Thoth as being similar to their own god Hermes. So, they combined the two god forms into one, creating a god or archetype representing all knowledge.[5]

Let us examine this famous quote. "As above, so below, as within, so without." It means, basically, that everything in the universe is in intimate contact with everything else in the universe. What happens outside of us affects how we are internally, and the opposite is true as well but harder to see. What happens within us affects the larger world. Our inner world is called the microcosm, and the larger world is called the macrocosm. Both are intimately connected, and what happens in one reverberates through the other. In effect, this is how magic works. Creating an inner change can reverberate through your life and change reality around you.

5. Fowden, *The Egyptian Hermes*, 22.

This concept can be hard to visualize. Let us illustrate this idea using the big bang theory as a metaphor. In 1929 Edwin Hubble observed that all galaxies seem to be moving away from our position here on Earth. Hubble had discovered the expansion of the universe. He found that all stars and planets—everything including space itself—is expanding as time moves forward. It then stands to reason that if you were able to run time backward, then everything would contract all the way back to the beginning of time when everything was compacted in a single point. This point contained literally everything, or the potential for everything. All space was also compacted to this singularity, a state of absolute unity. In this state of absolute unity, all the potential for stars and people and flowers and an infinite number of things and events was in a state of potential, like a seed for all that could ever possibly be.[6]

If we run time forward again, this point expands into three dimensions of space and one of time. As space expands larger and larger, it cools and atoms form, then stars and galaxies, then planets, then eventually you. The underlying unity of all *still* pervades all of creation. The pleroma is the name for this in the Hermetic teachings and in Gnostic theology.

The Pleroma of You

This process of creation is ongoing, as the universe is still expanding and building more complex forms. The universe is not an artifact; it is a process that you are an important part of. You couldn't be here without everything that happened before your birth, without all those distant stars and galaxies and billions of years required for all the myriad forms in the universe to come into being. It is harder to see, but the rest of the universe is also dependent on you being here in existence. All that is would unravel in an instant without you here now, reading this little story of creation.

Everything in heaven and earth is dependent on everything else in heaven and earth. Your role is to wake up and become conscious of this process so the universe can know itself and consciously evolve. As within, so without, and as we become aware and fully present, we can consciously affect the world around us.

This realization begs a question. *If we are the universe, then why are we not shaping reality now?* Well, we are, just not with intent. If we are unaware of our active role in shaping reality, we then shape it unconsciously, as do all sentient beings. Reality is a group project.

When you are born, you are a great magician full of power and imagination. However, there is a problem. To live in a house with people, you need to be domesticated, but we are all born a bit

6. Ferris, *Coming of Age in the Milky Way*, 207.

feral. The process of civilizing us creates a sense of self, an "I." This is an important process so we can function in society, but it often goes too far. Soon, we start to identify with this created identity and forget our true, innate nature.

We have to rediscover our Higher Selves, which are in effect floating over us and guiding us through life. We call the Higher Self the Holy Guardian Angel, and this name is taken from a book called *The Book of the Sacred Magic of Abramelin the Mage*, which has a detailed process for contacting your angel.[7] The magician starts by summoning their angel; only then are they ready for practicing magic. This process of summoning the angel takes a year and a half, with lots of praying and fasting. The concept that a part of ourselves is perfect and wise and in touch with the Creator is very ancient.

One of our favorite books, *Rebel in the Soul: An Ancient Egyptian Dialogue Between a Man and His Destiny*, is a translation from an ancient Egyptian sacred text some four thousand years old. It is a conversation between an initiate priest and his soul. The initiate wants to sacrifice his body and send his spirit to live with the gods, but his soul disagrees. His soul speaks to him, saying, "Only through the living Nifa can the intellect reach the heart and become a haven for the upstream struggle, then by my hand it will arrive blissful at the beyond."[8] The *Nifa* is the composite *incarnated* soul of the Egyptian belief system; it is layered like an egg. His soul is telling him that only an incarnated being can learn the lessons of life and become enlightened. But his soul will guild him to the bliss that awaits. We can't imagine a more perfect example of someone gaining knowledge and conversation of their Holy Guardian Angel. This is one of the goals of a Hermeticist, to gain this awareness, then its name, and then be able to tap into its knowledge and wisdom at will.

In book one of *The Corpus Hermeticum*, there is a conversation between Hermes Trismegistus and a person named Poimandres.[9] In a dreamlike state, Hermes encounters Poimandres and asks, "Who are you?" And the answer was, "I am Poimandres the *Nous* of the Supreme." *Nous* is an untranslatable word that means something like "the ability to comprehend what is truly real," although it is often translated simply as "mind." Poimandres then proceeds to school Hermes on Hermetic doctrine. We view this conversation as happening between Hermes and his angel. At first this angel can seem like a separate being; this is until we identify with this Inner Self and move our consciousness and identity to this Truer Self.

---

7. Von Worms, *The Book of Abramelin*, 37.

8. Reed, *Rebel in the Soul*.

9. Salaman, *The Way of Hermes*, 17–24.

The Fool

In the standard Rider-Waite tarot deck, the Fool card is numbered 0. It represents the Creator skipping blindly toward the cliff to fall into creation and start everything. The Fool has a little dog yapping at his feet. This little dog is the intellect, or really, it is better to think of it as the I or little self, which is a great companion but a very poor master.

Hermetic ritual work is designed to break down the internal blockages and get your creative energies flowing. Scholars divide the ancient Hermetic writings into two broad groups: the Technical Hermetica and the Philosophical Hermetica. The Philosophical Hermetica describes the philosophies of the tradition. Within the Technical Hermetica, there are the arts of astrology, medicine and pharmacology, alchemy, and magic. Within the magic group, there is natural magic, which is focused on the magical properties of plants, stones, and so on, and theurgy, or literally god-doing. Theurgy is what we will teach here. The other form of magic, natural magic, has been extensively covered by other authors. If natural magic interests you as well as theurgy, then I suggest you start by reading book one of *The Three Books of Occult Philosophy* (*De Occulta Philosophia libri III*) by Henry Cornelius Agrippa.

R•I•T•U•A•L
ADORATION TO THE LORD OF THE UNIVERSE

Your first practice is a simple prayer acknowledging the Source, or Creator. This divine force is beyond duality. What appears to be light and dark is largely the result of our own cultural and social programming that enables us to live in our world. While this can provide us with the structure of reality, it is also the appearance of duality that separates us from the Source and our own enlightenment.

The Adoration to the Lord of the Universe is a prayer used in the Neophyte Initiation of the Golden Dawn as part of the opening of the temple and in many other rituals to initiate or reinforce a connection to this Source beyond duality.[10] Lon Milo DuQuette is one of our favorite occult authors, and in addition to his books and vast experience in Western Esotericism as a practitioner and lineage holder, he is a genuinely

10. Regardie, *The Golden Dawn*, 18.

nice human being. At the start of his book on Enochian work, DuQuette says, "It's ok to pray."[11] If we can't acknowledge that there is a higher power than our current state of consciousness, even if it is ultimately our Higher Self, then there really is no room to grow and evolve spiritually. Consider this when you look at the night sky.

We have spent much time contemplating why it is traditional in many Hermetic prayers and writings to refer to the Creator as *Lord*. It never quite fit well with either of us. Other than "it's tradition," which is correct but not helpful, we have come to the conclusion that we call the Creator the Lord of the Universe because when we identify Source with the Holy name of Lord, we are referring to it as the creative process. In Hermeticism, we often think of things as verbs rather than nouns. The Lord of the Universe is the creative process that unfurls according to a pattern or will that is the sum of all our collective wills. Therefore, it is greater than our present incarnate self. I invite you to contemplate this prayer as well. It has several interesting pieces—some taken straight from the Golden Dawn. Consider the line "whom nature hath not formed." This comes directly from a Hermetic prayer.[12]

Things You Need

A quiet space

Your journal and your writing utensil

View of the stars or night sky

Directions

At night, in a place where you can see the stars, sit or lie on the earth. If possible, view the stars not as distant specks but as close to you as your own heart. When you are ready, say the Adoration to the Lord of the Universe:

Holy Art Thou, Lord of the Universe
Holy Art Thou, Whom Nature hath not Formed
Holy Art Thou, the Vast and the Mighty One
Lord of the Light and of the Darkness

---

11. DuQuette, *Enochian Vision Magick*, 30.

12. Salaman, *The Way of Hermes*, 24.

Sit and allow your imagination to connect you with the Lord of the Universe and receive what it has to say through the lens of your perceptions. This can come as an image, as if watching a screen, a thought, a recollection, or a body sensation. With this particular prayer, pay attention to the heart and the sensations that arise there. Consider that this feeling that arises in your heart is resonant with the pleroma. Often people will feel an expansion of their sense of self, a feeling of love, and a general sense of goodness and well-being. It is from this openhearted place that we begin our workings, setting and reinforcing that openheartedness in our consciousness.

It may be helpful to call into mind your place in the universe and how your atoms came into being and, after billions of years, arranged in a pattern that could look back and be aware of the beauty and majesty of the universe. You and all of the stars, galaxies, black holes, and other unknowable forms out there in space all came into being together as an unbreakable unity of being. Sit in devotional openheartedness for fifteen to twenty minutes, longer if you wish. When you are done, say a few words of gratitude, whatever comes to mind. Record your experience in the journal.

• • • • • • •

By learning the practices of theurgy, you will start to see the self you created to live in this world more as a tool of your Higher Self. Don't worry; you will keep your I (your ego), but it will become your beloved yapper dog pet rather than your master. Theurgy is soteriological magic; it causes an internal spiritual transformation that gives you the powers to transform the world around you. Once you are centered in your Higher Self, your actions are a result of your conscious will rather than instinctual responses, triggered emotional responses, or social programming. Your actions will be in line with your true will and will be conscious, enlightened, and very powerful because they will be in alignment with the intentions of your Higher Self.

Fortunately, there is a long tradition of mystics and mystery schools that can guide us in our journey.

— CHAPTER 2 —
Hermetic Qabalah, the Tree of Life

As we begin the journey to our Higher Self, we are going to need a map—and preferably several, as we don't want to get locked into only one perspective. The Hermetic Qabalah is both a map of creation and a description of the creation of the universe. Encompassing all of the various paths and practices of Hermetic thought, the Hermetic Qabalah allows us to relate all the concepts and practices together into a singular system. It is a metasystem that contains all we will be studying.

The Qabalah is a vast subject, and we will not fill these pages with information that is not immediately useful. If you are already familiar with the Qabalah, hopefully we can show you some new ways to use your knowledge. To learn more about the Qabalah, please see the recommended reading at the end of this book for suggestions of resources you can use at your own pace.

What Is the Qabalah?

The Qabalah is a mystical tradition inspired by the Kabbalah of Judaism. During the Renaissance, there was a split in the tradition. Mystical Judaism continued to develop on its own, and a separate non-Jewish group split off and became part of the Hermetic tradition. In 1517, Johann Reuchlin published *De Arte Cabalistica,* which made Qabalah accessible to Christian scholars. In the early sixteenth century, Henry Cornelius Agrippa published his landmark book *Three Books of Occult*

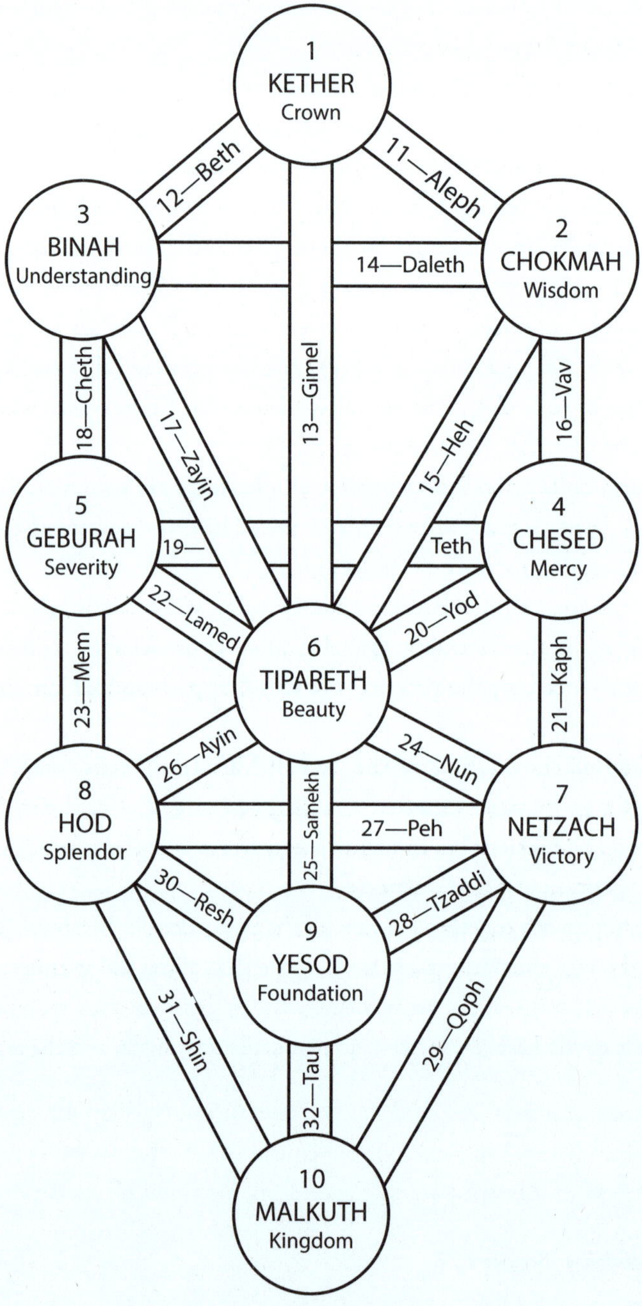

Basic Tree of Life

Philosophy, which cemented Qabalah in the Hermetic tradition.[13] We will study the Hermetic Qabalah, with great respect to the Judaic tradition.

The value of the Qabalah to unite all of nature and the spiritual world into one coherent pattern was immediately recognized by scholars in many fields of study; having a map of the universe that showed how everything was connected was too powerful a tool to ignore.

For example, Paracelsus, whose full name was Philippus Aureolus Theophrastus Bombastus von Hohenheim, was a physician, alchemist, lay theologian, and philosopher of the German Renaissance. He was a pioneer in several aspects of the medical revolution of the Renaissance, emphasizing the value of observation in combination with received wisdom. Paracelsus would trust the cures of the local county herb grannies more than what was considered medical knowledge in his time. He is credited as the father of toxicology. He was also a Hermetic philosopher who incorporated the wonderful system of the Qabalah into Hermeticism.[14]

Qabalah is the grand unification theory uniting all Hermetic philosophies. Tarot, astrology, and many forms of advanced practices are informed and united by this diagram. The Hermetic Qabalah has become ubiquitous throughout occult philosophies.

We truly believe everyone who encounters the Qabalah will become a better person, but the system is complex. To make the Hermetic Qabalah more approachable, we'll present it in layers, focusing only on what we need for the practice. For this first pass, simply familiarize yourself with the diagram.

The Qabalistic diagram shown is called the Tree of Life. The Tree is composed of ten spheres, called sephiroth, connected by twenty-two lines, called paths. These are the stages of creation and the elements of the mind and soul. It is a model of the universe and of the mind, as we are approaching all of creation as a process of consciousness.

The paths and the sephiroth together contain all the basic ideas in Hermeticism. The sephiroth, or the counting, are the ten emanations of the Creator that allow the manifest universe to form. The twenty-two paths that connect the sephiroth are the major arcana, or trumps, of the tarot. The paths have attributions to the Hebrew letters, elements, planets, signs, and the alphabet of creation.

---

13. Barrabbas, *Magical Qabalah for Beginners*, 77.

14. Hargrave, "Paracelsus."

The Spheres

The first sphere, Kether, is the point of first creation at the beginning of the universe. It is where all that could be is held in a state of absolute unity and potential. This is the highest state of being we can even imagine. Beyond this is the great unknowable or nothing. Called the Crown, it sits at the top of the tree diagram as the radiant source of all.

The second sephiroth, called Chokmah, is pure force or chaotic energy, like the first expansion of the early universe. The title Wisdom seems a bit strange, but if we consider the meaning of wisdom is the ability to act productively using knowledge and insight. Chokmah is the potential of Kether in action, the first thought of creation.

The third sephiroth is called Binah. It is the potential for form and often referred to as the great mother. It can be likened to the state of creation, where some sense of order can begin, forming the basic rules for subatomic particles. We believe the title Understanding is referring to an openness or ability to take in a concept and completely comprehend or merge with it. Binah can also be considered as the realization of the first thought.

Together these first three spheres are called the Supernals, and they are considered too abstract for a human mind to really comprehend. We can talk about them and consider their nature, but we can't capture their nature in words. They are referred to as the thinker, the thought, and the realization of thinking. Together they lie above a line called the abyss, a vast gulf the Hermeticist must cross on their way to enlightenment. But then, there are also many degrees of this experience of enlightenment, and in truth, we cross the abyss many times, at different levels.

When we reach the fourth sephiroth, we finally have the beginnings of a reality and consciousness we can relate to. If Kether is a point, Chokmah is a line, and Binah is a flat triangle, Chesed, the fourth sephiroth, is a cube. It represents three dimensions of space and one of time.

Chesed translates as loving-kindness and Mercy. That is the manifesting force that comes across the abyss from Binah, the great mother. This is the power we will use both for spiritual enlightenment and to manifest our will. Any act of creation or manifestation works best if we act out of love. It might sound corny, but it is undeniably true. Anything you love to do you will do well and willingly. Even a chore done out of love will be more enjoyable and better done than if done out of duty. This is similar to the Buddhist concept of *bodhicitta*, or the mind that strives toward awakening, empathy, and compassion for the benefit of all sentient beings. We should follow our spiritual practice for the benefit of all. Without this connection to the all, our spiritual work and knowledge will be empty and useless.

The fifth sephiroth is Geburah, meaning Severity, or the will. We must act out of love but temper and direct that force with our will. While you may direct unconditional love to a person, you might not want to loan them your car. Understanding is the title of Binah, the third sephiroth that lies just above Geburah, and we must manifest our love wisely. This is intended as the complement of Mercy. A more modern interpretation could be setting good boundaries.

The sixth sephiroth is called Tipareth, and it means Beauty. It is the very heart of the tree and balances all the forces of the sephiroth. Just as the sun is the center of the solar system, Tipareth is the center of the tree. This is the seat of the Higher Self that we are moving toward on our journey upward and back to the Source. Tipareth is also called the lesser countenance, meaning it is a reflection of Kether.

The seventh sephiroth is Netzach, the sphere of emotions and all the artistic creativity and imagination that is not ruled by logic and reason. Most of our basic motivations come from this inspiration, as do our pleasures and feelings that create the imperative for art, music, and invention. I think of Netzach as our intuitive intelligence, as it is a nonrational source of awareness.

The eighth sephiroth is Hod, and it is the seat of intellect. This is the center of logic and reason, which give form and function to the passions of Netzach. Math and science, planning and design give form and reality to the dreams and desires of the intuitive world of Netzach.

The ninth sephiroth is called Yesod. It is the realm of the unconscious mind, where all the information that our senses gather that we are not aware of resides, as well as the things we deem to be unimportant or too painful to be aware of. It is the world of dreams and is called the foundation of the physical world and the treasure house of images. Like the moon, which reflects the sun's light, Yesod reflects the bright light of Tipareth down to the material world. As the treasure house of images, Yesod also contains the archetypes of all material things, the blueprints of all the things of the material world. This also include subjective things, such as love, fairness, and injustice.

The tenth sephiroth, Malkuth, is the kingdom—the material world we experience. This final sphere is the result of all the actions of the previous spheres. All the workings of the previous spheres exist to create the manifest universe so we have a place to live and grow. It is the playground and school for souls to grow and evolve and send the force back up the tree. The process of ascension back up the tree is called pathworking.

There is an additional sephiroth called Daath. It is the first reflection of Kether and is positioned in the center of the tree above the line of Chesed and Geburah but below the line of Chokma and Binah. Daath is at once the pattern of creation contained within Kether, and it is also the method the Hermeticist uses to cross the abyss between duality and unity. Through our practices, our own personal gnosis is revealed to us by the Creator so we can awaken back to our god-consciousness. Daath is not normally shown on a Tree of Life diagram since it is in a sense created or realized by the individual. Daath is also the revealed Torah or instructions for redeeming and repairing our universe to a more perfected state, but now we are getting into the deeper mysteries of Qabalah. Better to save that for when you are more familiar with the basics.

The Sephiroth in Review

1. Kether: Crown, a point of absolute unity, primum mobile
2. Chokmah: Expansive burst of divine potential energy, chaos, unbound potential, the Zodiac belt
3. Binah: The great mother, constriction leading to structure, time, practical application of wisdom, intellect in context, establishing patterns, Saturn
4. Chesed: Kindness, giving, unlimited benevolence and expansion, healing, Jupiter
5. Geburah: Power, restraint, limit on expansion and outflow, filtering, Mars
6. Tipareth/Tiferet: Harmony, beauty, truth, sun
7. Netzach: Emotion, intuitive knowledge, cyclical energy, circadian energy, Venus
8. Hod: Logic and reason, communication, Mercury
9. Yesod: Foundation, the sub- and unconscious mind, the treasure house of images, moon
10. Malkuth: Kingdom (also known as Shechinah, divine presence), source of the physical world, Earth
11. Daath: The method or guide to personal gnosis, the patterns contained within the reflection of Kether

The Paths

On the Tree of Life, twenty-two paths connect the sephiroth and represent the experience of the soul in its growth to full realization. Each path is a stage or initiation of the soul as it returns to the Source. The energies of creation flow down the tree until they reach Malkuth. Then they turn around and return up the tree back to Kether, full of experience and wisdom. Each path is related to a Hebrew letter as well as other concepts, such as a planet or an element. In this chart, you will find the keywords and associations for the twenty-two paths.

Number	Letter	Meaning	Association
0	Aleph	Ox	Elemental Air
1	Beth	House	Planet Mercury
2	Gimel	Camel	The Moon
3	Daleth	Door	Planet Venus
4	Heh	Window	Sign of Aries
5	Vav	Pin or Hook	Sign of Taurus
6	Zayin	Sword	Sign of Gemini
7	Cheth	Fence	Sign of Cancer
8	Teth	Snake	Sign of Leo
9	Yod	Hand	Sign of Virgo
10	Kaph	Fist	Planet Jupiter
11	Lamed	Ox Goad	Sign of Libra
12	Mem	Water	Elemental Water
13	Nun	Fish	Sign of Scorpio
14	Samekh	Prop	Sign of Sagittarius
15	Ayin	Eye	Sign of Capricorn
16	Peh	Mouth	Planet Mars
17	Tzaddi	Fishhook	Sign of Aquarius
18	Qoph	Ear	Sign of Pisces
19	Resh	Head	The Sun
20	Shin	Tooth	Elemental Fire
21	Tau	Mark	Planet Saturn

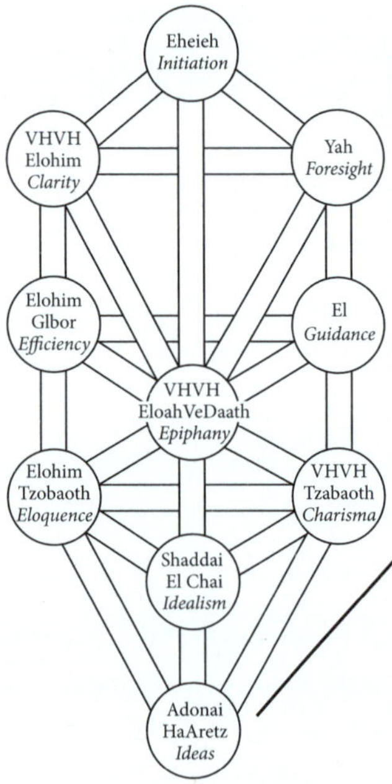

Atziluth
World of Emanation
Element of Fire
The Wand Cards in Tarot
Pure emanations of the source, powers of inspiration and bliss.

Key
Godname
Power

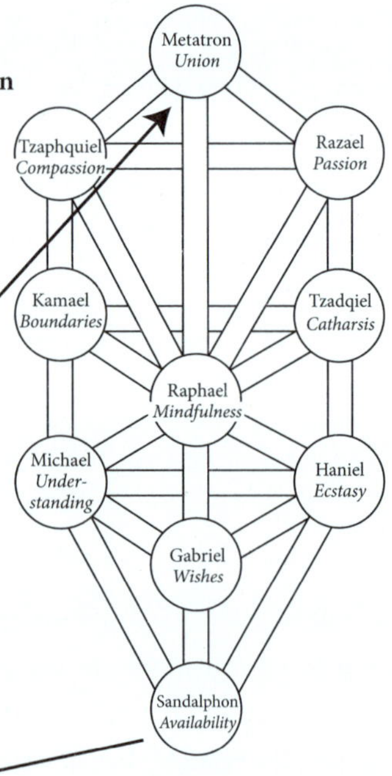

Briah
World of Creation
Element of Water
The Cup Cards in Tarot
Emotional reflection of inspiration, powers of feeling and imagination. Home of the Archangels

Key
Archangel Name
Power

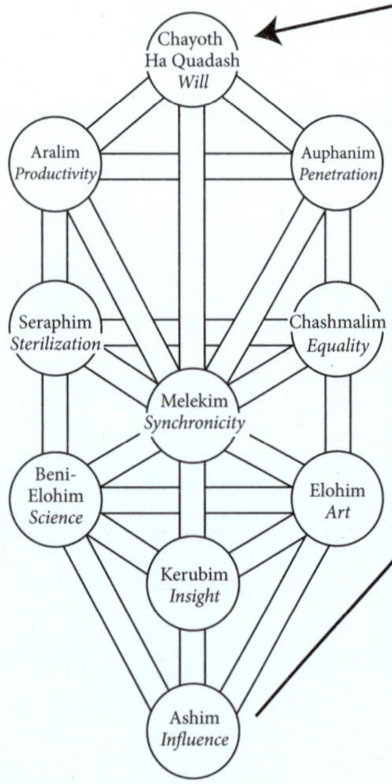

Yetzirah
World of Formation
Element of Air
The Sword Cards in Tarot
Where the one becomes the many, thoughts and plans on how to implement the inspiration of Fire and the intuition of Water. Power to plan, organize ideas.
Home to the Choirs of Angels who sing creation to being.

Key
Choir Name
Power

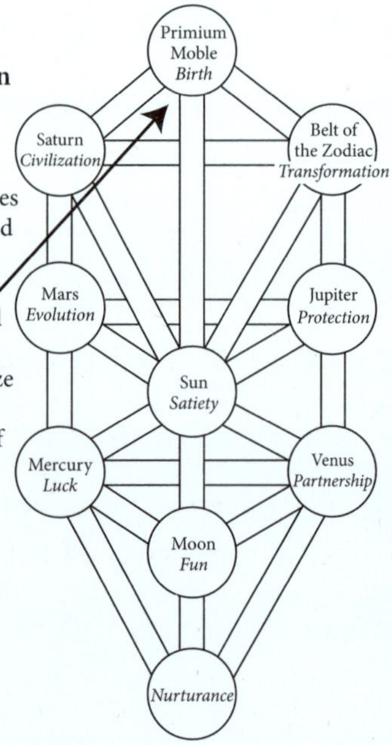

Assiah
World of Action
Element of Earth
The Pentacle Cards in Tarot or Suite of Coins
The material world, the resultant manifestion of the inspiration of Fire, intuition of Water, planning of Air and the embodiment of Spirit. Powers of manifesation, culture and society.
Home to the "Mundane Chakras" or Zodiac and Planetary elements that shape our reality.

Key
Zodiac Element
Power

Jacob's Ladder

The Worlds

There are also four Qabalistic worlds, each containing a tree. You can look at the Qabalah as one unified tree or as four—one in each world. In total, you have forty sephiroth in the four worlds.

You will find that in Hermetics, any time you have four of something, they will relate to the four classic elements: fire, water, air, and earth. So, too, do the Qabalistic worlds relate to the four classic elements. Here are the worlds:

Atziluth

The world of Atziluth relates to the fire element. Atziluth is the first inspiration of creation and has ten Hebrew god names assigned to it. It relates to the suit of wands in a standard tarot deck.

Briah

The world of Briah relates to water and is the response to the first burst of fiery inspiration. It is the world of feeling and imagination. Archangels are attributed to Briah, such as Michael, Raphael, Gabriel, and Uriel. Briah is expressed by the suit of cups in a standard tarot deck.

Yetzirah

Yetzirah is the world of air. It is where unity becomes the many. This world is the mind in action and relates to the suit of swords in a standard tarot deck. In Yetzirah, there is a group of angels attributed to each sephiroth, these groups are called choirs.

Assiah

The world of Assiah is related to the classic element earth. It is where creation is brought into focus and finally manifested as a grid of energy, thought, and meaning created by divine light. The tarot suit of pentacles is assigned to Assiah. Rather than having angels, each sephiroth in Assiah is assigned a mundane force, including the classic planets, the Zodiac, and the primum mobile, or literally the first mover, which is assigned to Kether of Assiah, as it imparts energy and movement to the manifested universe.

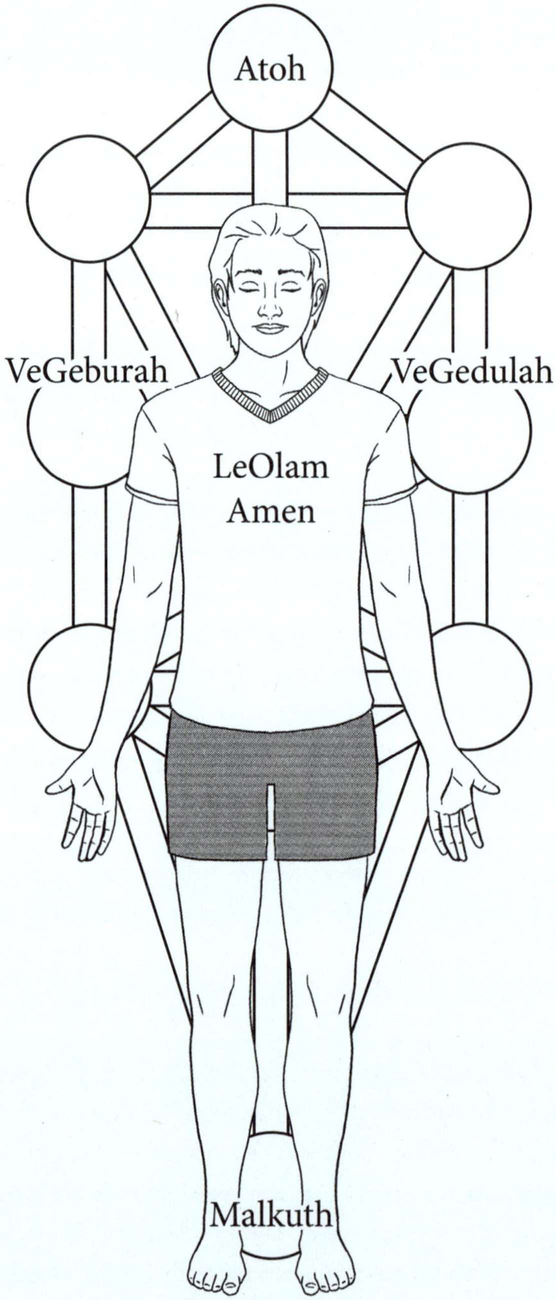

Qabalistic Cross

The Qabalistic Cross

The Qabalistic Cross is a very simple ritual that is foundational to learning the practice of theurgy. It is one method that will allow you to experience the wonder of the Tree of Life. It combines your basic knowledge of Qabalah with your goal of connecting with your Higher Self, and it also provides a grounding and balancing that we need so much in our daily lives. Basically, you are creating the Tree of Life within your aura as an exercise of grounding and empowering.

For almost every ritual in this book, there is both a formal practice and an informal practice. The formal practice is what we do in private when we have the time and space to fully perform a ritual. The formal practice will require you to do the full visualizations and powerfully vibrate the words to the full extent you are capable. The formal practice gives you the experiences, body sensations, and realizations so you can then do an informal practice. The formal practice is the main source of spiritual insights and makes the informal practice possible.

When you learn more advanced rituals and perform them, you gain the experience. This allows you to recall the energies and effects of that formal ritual when performing the informal version. Imagine for a moment that during a formal ritual you invoked a spirit or an angel for physical healing, then later, outside of the formal ritual, you recalled the experience of that healing and gained some benefit. We can create sigils, or symbols, that help to recall these energies or charge a token, such as a gemstone or a crystal. These objects can serve as reminders of the experience of doing the ritual work, taking us back to those spiritual experiences. Having such tokens will help you to integrate your practices into your everyday life.

The informal version of a ritual can be done anywhere. For example, you might want to do a quick Qabalistic Cross while sitting in a meeting or a class. You can quietly remember performing the formal version while mentally thinking about the words. This can have great benefits for grounding, centering, and much more. In time, we can instantly recall the body feelings and experiences we had in a complex ritual and use them for healing and insight in our daily lives. This is extremely practical.

When you perform the Qabalistic Cross, you are essentially sending a signal from your conscious mind to your Higher Self, asking to move to a higher, more balanced state of consciousness. First you connect to the Source of everything above you (Kether), then you ground the energy into the earth (Malkuth). You then balance the energy between your love (Chesed) and your will (Geburah). Finally, you seal this energetic state to preserve it. The words are in Hebrew, which in the occult is considered a sacred language. With practice, you can recite this ritual silently in your mind, which will enable informal practice.

Belly Breathing

Before learning the Qabalistic Cross, we need to discuss another foundational technique: belly breathing, or diaphragmatic breathing. This way of breathing promotes a calm state of awareness and helps the nervous system down regulate. Belly breathing can interrupt the fight-or-flight response or feelings of panic and is often taught as an emotional regulation technique.

To belly breathe, put the center of one hand on your belly button and the other hand on your chest. Slowly take a gentle, almost imperceptible breath in through your nose and guide the breath down into the belly. The hand on your chest will sink slightly and the hand on your belly will rise with the inhalation. Although air is not actually filling the belly, it seems that way. Use your imagination and feel the air go all the way down, press against your seat, and expand outward from the sides of your waist and back. The ball of air that you are directing into your belly will not seem to expand evenly. Play around with the tone, volume, and vibration until you experience something that feels comfortable for you. Just maintain a sense of gentle relaxation. After inhaling in this way, simply allow the body to exhale on its own.[15]

Practice this until it becomes your natural way of breathing, as it is very good for your health and mood and helps to relax the nervous system. At the beginning of any ritual, it is always good practice to belly breathe for a few moments to center and become calm and grounded.

Vibrating Words of Power and Divine Names

Vibrating a divine name or word of power refers to a method of speaking in a manner that causes your whole body to vibrate. To do so, first inhale from your belly and keep your throat open. Then slowly exhale and speak the word in a tone that vibrates your whole body. For Erich, this is a very low tone. Alannah's tone is more like a midrange singing voice. For others, it can be a high pitch.

This is a very individual skill. We all vibrate at different rates, so you will need to find your own frequency. As you speak the word, visualize the sound as filling the universe with its vibrations. Powerful words need to be spoken in a powerful voice. There is incredible power in moving past the difficulties in speaking the divine names with the firmness needed to experience a whole-body vibration. Try to notice any discomfort or tension that comes up for you in this practice; it will decrease over time. Allow yourself to feel these words of power in your whole being and in your body. The somatic or body sensation is very important, as much or more so than the visualizations.

15. Yang, *Qigong Meditation Embryonic Breathing*, 317–18.

If your situation does not afford you the privacy you need to speak loudly, you can still belly breathe and vibrate the words in a quieter voice. Still visualize your words filling the universe.

You will see the instructions to vibrate a divine name or word frequently. It is a technique you need to become comfortable with. If needed, you can vibrate the word in your mind, but at some point, you must find your frequency so you can imagine and feel it internally later.

R • I • T • U • A • L
THE QABALISTIC CROSS

It is very important that you practice the Qabalistic Cross at regular intervals. Once you have memorized the ritual and feel comfortable performing it, set an alarm to do the practice three or four times a day. You can perform the ritual in the morning, at noon, at sundown, and before you go to sleep—or whenever you have the privacy. It is important to avoid only performing the ritual when you are stressed and need grounding, as that can set up a negative association. If you only do the ritual when you feel stressed, then you are training yourself to feel stress when you do the rite.

Things You Need

A private place that is calming and quiet

Directions

Always begin any ritual with a few rounds of belly breathing, consciously focusing on breathing deep into your lower abdomen for three to nine breaths. Put one hand on your belly just below your belly button and the other hand on your chest. Slowly and naturally, take a deep breath in through your nose, and let your belly push your hand out. Then breathe out through your nose; again, do this slowly and naturally. Feel your hand fall. When you feel centered and calm, begin.

First, visualize yourself growing larger and larger until the earth is a small ball beneath your feet. Then visualize a ball of pure brilliance above your head. Reach up and touch this ball of light, bring it down to your forehead, and vibrate the word *Atoh* (thou art).

Next, bring the light down the center of your body, forming a column of light. As you pass your heart, whisper the name of your Higher Self. If you do not know it yet, vibrate *Adonai* or the name of any spiritual teacher or guru you have the highest respect for. Bring the column of light down into the earth below you, to the very center of the planet, and vibrate *Malkuth* (the kingdom).

Then bring the light up from the earth to your left shoulder and visualize a ball of blue flame. This symbolizes the unconditional love of Chesed. Vibrate the word *Ve Gedulah* (and the glory).

Next, bring the light across your chest to the right shoulder. Visualize a ball of red flame, symbolizing the will of Geburah. Vibrate the word *Ve Geburah* (and the power).

Continue by folding your arms across your chest with the palms of your hands touching your shoulders. Vibrate the word *Le Olam* (forever and ever).

Finally, hold your hands in front of your forehead. Slowly pull them down to your chest and say *Amen* (so be it).

Stay for a moment in this cross of light, connected to the source of all, grounded in the earth, and balanced between love and will. Focus on the feeling in your body, as this is more important than the visualizations. This feeling of grounded empowerment and balance is what you want to cultivate. Spend a moment simply being mindful of how you feel now, without judgment or interpretation. Mentally scan your body. Try to see if there are any feelings, if you feel fizzy or energized, if the feeling has a location, like your solar plexus, for example. Does the feeling have a color, texture, temperature, flavor, or sound? Try to remember this feeling so you can recall it later when you want to do an informal version of this ritual. If there is no obvious body feeling, that's okay too. It can take a while to develop awareness of the body sensations of doing ritual work. It will come in time.

The informal version of the Qabalistic Cross would be to remember the rite and mentally say the words. Using just your imagination, perform the rite, and remember the bodily sensations of doing the formal rite. This could be done silently, even while in a meeting, for grounding and centering.

Application and Understanding

From this brief overview of the Tree of Life, you may glean a few points of advice for your spiritual and practical evolution.

- We can love people unconditionally. After all, we are a manifestation of the universe with a Higher Self, and everyone must also be the same.
- We must use our will and wisdom to set good boundaries with our space and time.

- While intellect allows us to plan and manifest, our emotional life gives us the creativity and ideas to feed the ever-hungry intellect.
- There are pairs of opposites on the left and right pillars of the tree, and they work together dynamically rather than being in opposition.
- The middle path of the tree leads to the Higher Self, through the unconscious mind. Our spiritual practice must take this into account.

Ultimately, the Tree of Life is a map of the universe and of consciousness with the ten sephiroth representing the stages of creation and the twenty-two paths connecting them and four Qabalistic elemental worlds. This is the grand unification theory of Hermetics, as it relates the elements, the planets, the Zodiac, and more into a coherent relationship. This is our map, our tool to see how ideas relate to each other and build mythic and ritual meaning.

This Qabalah is a lot to take in at once, as our conscious mind is limited in what it can hold at any given moment. These ideas will become imprinted on your subconscious mind fairly quickly by doing the practices in this book; don't worry about memorizing all this before you do the work. In time, it will become familiar when you apply it. Just take notes in your journal on what you feel is useful.

— CHAPTER 3 —
Your True Will

Imagine the following as a creation story that describes how the universe came into being. In the beginning, the Creator wished to achieve supreme enlightenment. To do this, the Creator needed to experience every possible manifestation, every possible possibility. So, the Creator went to sleep and dreamed it was an atom, and within this dream, the Creator went to sleep and dreamed it was a molecule. Within that dream, the Creator went to sleep and dreamed it was a single-celled organism. This went on and on, dreams within dreams, the Creator experiencing manifestation as all the forms in the universe. The Creator dreamed it was a bird, then a mammal, until the Creator fell asleep in its dream and dreamed it was you.

When we go to sleep, we dream, and we are surprised by our dreams. No matter how odd our dreams are, we take them very seriously. Whether it's the dreams where we can fly, the ones where we see old friends, or even frightening dreams, we almost never question the reality of the dream. We accept what our dream senses tell us without question—no matter how strange or ridiculous. We are both the dream and the dreamer, but we act as if they are separate. We accept what we see and who we think we are in our waking life in the same way.

We are sure you have heard of, or maybe experienced, lucid dreaming. Lucid dreaming is where you realize you are in a dream state and can then affect the outcome of the dream. To achieve lucid dreaming, you need to become aware of the fact that you are dreaming and wake up just enough to control the dream. The Hermetic path is similar. We must wake up in our normal waking consciousness just enough that reality itself becomes mutable. While no magic we know of can violate the laws of physics, there is a lot we can change in our lives, and we can even change our destiny.

The skill of manifesting change in our lives (e.g., generating prosperity, love, opportunities) does not hinge on probability or even magical skill so much as it is directly related to what famed occultist Aleister Crowley called our True Will.

Age of Horus

Crowley was a poet, a ceremonial magician, a painter, a novelist, a mountaineer, and the founder of the religion of Thelema. He saw himself as a prophet who would guide humanity into the age of Horus.[16]

This new age of Horus would be about the individual finding their true purpose. The preceding ages of Osiris and Isis were more about subverting the individual's will to help the group.[17] Our True Will is our essential nature that flows from our Higher Self, our life's purpose. It is what we reincarnated to do—to learn and to change this world for the better.

If we do rituals and work magic that is in line with our True Will, the results are immediate and powerful. However, if we try to work magic that is not in line with our True Will, it is ineffective and can even backfire. This backfire will manifest in a way that, if we are mindful, will give us clues on how we need to change our focus to be in line with our True Will. If we are not yet awakened enough to see the meaning of our life events, then the backfire will seem frustrating and even cruel.

When we are in harmony with our true nature, manifestation is easy and enlightenment flows to us. But how can we understand our life's purpose? Surely this must be a great mystery. Well, not really. There is much we can understand about our True Will, and it does unfold as we become wiser and center our consciousness more and more in the Higher Self.

To start, look at the things you enjoy doing the most and see if there is any commonality. When you were a child, what games would make time seem to pass without notice? Ask the people who know you the best what effect you have on people when you walk in the room. Very often, things that are obvious to other people are hard for us to see about ourselves. As you know, fire can't burn itself. Once you start to get a clue about your True Will, if you tell someone who knows you well what it is, they will not be surprised; they will think it is obvious.

---

16. The Editors of Encyclopaedia Britannica, "Aleister Crowley."

17. DuQuette, *The Magick of Aleister Crowley*, 16–21.

As long as your ritual work is in line with your True Will, manifestation is easy. Let us give you an example of how a working can have real effects in your life. Suppose you were to use the rites in this book to perform a ritual to enhance your health. Your health will always be essential to you being able to perform your True Will, so it's a good example. You pick a date, design a rite, and perform it. During the rite, you gain some insights on experiences and injuries in the past that have contributed to lifestyle choices that damage your health. Perhaps you were taught that a successful person devotes all their time to work, that sleeping eight hours a night is for lazy people, or an unhealthy process for managing stress, such as smoking. You write down your insights in your journal and go about your life. Quite soon after, a friend sends you a link to a movie about detoxing your life with healthy foods and exercise. You watch it rather than just delete it, which you might have done a week ago. The video impresses you, and you actually consider trying this as a lifestyle change, just for a bit. You mention that you are considering walks, better food, and steam baths to your cousin. They say, "My apartment complex has a gym and steam room you can use a couple times a week." So suddenly, almost by accident, a series of lucky coincidences occur, and you find yourself eliminating unhealthy choices for healthier ones—something you would never have even considered before you did the ritual work. You become stronger, your skin improves, you have more energy, and smoking cigarettes becomes completely unappetizing. No laws of physics were broken, but it works.

Larger changes are possible as well, of course, but the pattern is basically the same. You gain some new insights, a series of lucky coincidences occur, and you are no longer living your life and seeing the world in the same way. A working will bring your life more in tune with your True Will by the changes and insights it brings. Carl Jung, a psychiatrist and psychoanalyst who founded analytical psychology, was a brilliant and controversial figure. He called these lucky occurrences synchronicities, an acausal connecting principle, which are meaningful coincidences.[18] Jung defined a synchronicity as having three qualities. First, it must be acausal. Second, there must be two events, one internal and the other external. Third, these events must happen at the same time. Jung gives many examples of synchronicity in his book of the same name. In one example, he was working with a patient who was telling him of a dream they had where they were given a golden scarab. Jung heard a tapping on the window beside him. He turned and saw a very scarab-like beetle tapping on the glass. Jung opened the window, caught the beetle, and handed it to the client. The client's problem related to their inability to see beyond the mundane; they could not see the magic in life. The production of the beetle from

18. Hanegraaff, *Western Esotericism*, 24, 124.

their dream broke through this blocking belief and made therapy much more effective for the client.[19] In this example, the inner and outer events are the discussion of the beetle and the appearance of a similar beetle. They happened simultaneously, and there was no obvious cause.

We don't think we have ever had a beetle tap any of our windows—seems very strange behavior. This is a meaningful coincidence, and our lives are frankly full of them; yours will be as well. This is an example of how the pleroma connects everything, even our inner thoughts to outer actions. As within, so without. These seemingly lucky coincidences are nothing of the sort; rather, they are strategically orchestrated and aligned events to guide us on our spiritual path. When we are aware and mindful, we can see the pattern unfold before us. These synchronicities are the guideposts that we should expect to find as the result of a spiritual practice.

Seeking Wisdom

Of course, larger, more profound realizations and rites will cause much greater shifts in you and your life. If you pursue wealth magic, you might find yourself going back to school to learn a new profession. You might even feel the need to spend hours and hours writing a book, but who knows? The adventure never ends. It's never boring. That's for sure.

The most profound and most powerful magic is always done out of love and asking for wisdom. This is what we really ask for from the gods and angels and other archetypal forces we encounter. In the legend of King Solomon, God came to him and said he could have anything he wanted. Solomon asked for wisdom, for a knowing heart. Then God said to Solomon, "Since you have asked for wisdom and not for a long life, wealth, or the removal of your enemies, you will have all of these things and more."[20]

Asking for wisdom is like wishing for more wishes. You are humbly admitting you need to grow and asking for guidance and teaching. This request cannot be ignored, as the entire purpose of the spiritual realms and indeed all of creation is for the Creator (you) to find a certain enlightenment. Also, if you just ask for money or intimacy, it will manifest but then fade. When we gain insight, it is permanent. We change and grow toward our true potential.

Eventually, all sentient beings will find this enlightenment, and then the universe will return to the Source. Think of it like the breath flowing in and out. Seeking wisdom, or enlightenment, is your True Will. While you may be seeking certain specific spiritual experiences at the moment, spiritual growth is a constant.

---

19. Jung, *Synchronicity*, 22.

20. *Holy Bible*, 2 Chronicles 1:11.

Erich once was exploring the Enochian Table of Union, which holds the names of many powerful entities that signify forces that are very close to the Source. He was invoking an entity named Hcoma, which has a correspondence to the Ace of Cups and can be viewed as the watery part of spirit. When he opened the final barrier to scry this force, he was completely overwhelmed. He had a vision of absolute consciousness. He was in a very old and huge forest, and somehow Erich's mind could perceive every drop of dew on every leaf and the sunlight reflecting off them.

Just the experience of this level of consciousness should have been enough for him to feel that the ritual was successful; Erich never understood that it was even possible. Erich pressed onward to find his spirit, Hcoma. Eventually he made contact, but holding on to the vision was like holding on to the ears of a tiger. He could be consumed by the vision, which would not cause him any harm, but he was eager, hungry for the wisdom and a vision of this powerful spirit. Erich meekly managed to mentally send his questions, "Who are you? What is your purpose? Can I have your wisdom?" The answer was forthcoming, and it seemed to fill all of creation.

"You know me, I am the *jadnah*, the unity of all beings. I am love and all things live within me. Those are your words. As for our wisdom, we have given it to you, but you don't believe any of it. Well, now you can."

At that point, something within him melted away. Ideas he once thought were corny suddenly became true. He could accept all the truths he had rejected. All the truths he'd tolerated as true but sentimental or trite suddenly became undeniably true. He was unashamed to think that all is love and love is the power that moves the universe. What followed was a series of powerful visions and finally a vision of the image of Hcoma herself.

That day, Erich walked into the temple, waved his hands, and said stuff. He sat down one person and stood up as a completely different person. He was permanently changed for the better, as a useless limitation was removed. He thought his cynicism made him tough, but it was just a protection mechanism that limited his ability to feel. What he gained was part of himself that he had hidden away to keep safe. He used the received vision to write more personal versions of the rituals he had received.

P•R•A•C•T•I•C•E
LIBER RESH

This practice will attune you to the flow of the day and the position of the sun in the sky. This practice can be invigorating at dawn and calming before sleep. We include the Qabalistic Cross in our practice of the Liber Resh because we feel the Qabalistic Cross is essential in any spiritual practice. Originally created by Aleister Crowley for his magical order, the Ordo Templi Orientis, it uses a simple visualization of the four forms of Ra, the Egyptian sun god.

In Egyptian mythos, many gods had several forms depending on which aspect of their archetype was most active. Ra is the primary sun god, representing the power of the sun. Hathor is the Egyptian Aphrodite, a goddess of beauty and the benevolent aspects of the sun. Tum is the god of the setting sun and crossroads. Kephra is the scarab beetle, representing rebirth of the sun. The other two Egyptian gods in the practice are not forms of Ra but are very important in the mythology of Egypt and the O.T.O. Tahuti is the same as Thoth, the god of writing and all knowledge. Tahuti is acting as the navigator of the celestial bark, or ship made of papyrus reeds. Rahoor is a bit more complicated, as this archetype represents Crowley's new age of humanity where the individual is exalted but not at the expense of the common good. Rather, when each person can attain their unique potential, all of society benefits. Rahoor steers the celestial bark on its new path across the heavens.

You will need to do some research on your own on the listed Egyptian gods. There is plenty on the internet, and there are many books available to help you understand these four aspects of the sun. Here is a quick list:

- Ra, at or close to sunrise, is the main sun god representing the power of the sun.
- Hathor, at or close to high noon, is the Egyptian Aphrodite, a goddess of beauty and the benevolent aspects of the sun.
- Tum, at or close to sundown, is the god of the setting sun and crossroads.
- Kephra, at midnight or before sleep, is the scarab beetle, representing rebirth of the sun as it passes through the corridor of night.
- Tahuti or Thoth is the god of all knowledge and inventor of science and magic.
- Rahoor is a version of the god Horus, the child of the new age of the self-actualization of the individual.

Things You Need

A private place that is calming and quiet

Directions

At sunrise, noon, sundown, and midnight or before you go to bed, perform this practice. Begin by performing belly breathing. Perform the Qabalistic Cross (chapter 2). Then say the appropriate text as follows, and visualize yourself as the deity mentioned riding in an Egyptian boat, or bark, through the heavens.

At Sunrise

Hail unto thee who art Ra in thy rising, even unto thee who art Ra in thy strength, who travelest over the heavens in thy bark at the uprising of the sun. Tahuti standeth in his splendor at the prow and RaHoor abideth at the helm. Hail unto thee from the abodes of the night.

At Noon

Hail unto thee who art Hathor in thy triumphing, even unto thee who art Hathor in thy beauty, who travelest over the heavens at thy bark at the highest point of the sun. Tahuti standeth in his splendor at the prow and RaHoor abideth at the helm. Greetings from the abode of the morning.

At Sundown

Hail unto thee who art Tum in thy setting, even unto thee who art Tum in thy joy, who travelest over the heavens at the down going of the sun in thy bark. Tahuti standeth in his splendor at the prow and RaHoor abideth at the helm. Greetings from the abode of the day.

At Midnight or Before Sleep

Hail unto thee who art Kephra in thy hiding, even unto thee who art Kephra in thy silence, who travelest over the heavens at the lowest point of the sun in thy bark. Tahuti standeth in his splendor at the prow and RaHoor abideth at the helm. Greetings from the abode of the evening.

Once you have completed the Liber Resh, perform the Qabalistic Cross again. Sit mindfully for a few moments. This practice is quite empowering, and it will help to organize your day. It is important to note that it does not need to be performed exactly at the times specified. Close is better than not at all.

• • • • • • •

There is nothing wrong with you now, so give up on the idea of fixing yourself or anyone else. You can increase your capacity for awareness, compassion, intelligence, and so much more. Just as a weightlifter can become stronger, you can become more aware and enlightened and achieve anything you desire—including knowing exactly what you want to be happy.

The key to manifesting what we want is knowing what we truly want—what our True Will is. Once we determine what our life's purpose is, manifesting is easy. Personal growth will bring more long-term satisfaction than manifesting little material things. While you can't break the laws of physics, you can change your life path for the better and become the best possible version of yourself. The Liber Resh will help organize your day, focus your will, and bring a practice into your daily life, making it more conscious and magical.

— CHAPTER 4 —
The Three Veils and Shadow Work

When we begin any spiritual practice, we encounter resistance. There is the ordinary inertia of changing our habits, and then there are the blocking aspects of our inner personalities. Aleister Crowley once said, "The whole and sole object of all true Magical and Mystical training is to become free from every kind of limitation."[21]

To become free of imposed limitations on ourselves is one of our first goals. There are three main obscurants, or veils, that come up when people first approach the path. These include religious trauma, difficulty in being in the body and being mindful, and overcoming social programming.

Religious Trauma Veil

Many occultists who are drawn to esoteric paths are seeking something that is separate from the negative associations with patriarchal and monotheistic religions. The strictness of orthodoxy comes from a time and place that is no longer in synch with modern diversity. A lot of people can feel like they are not represented within various religious communities. The sets of rules laid down may seem to go against our own natural instincts and desires. Often, we are expected to accept as absolute fact the stories that are part of the lore of these traditional monotheistic religions. If we are treated with exclusion when we question this lore, then we feel even more rejected. When Erich was

21. Crowley, *Little Essays Toward Truth.*

a child, he would ask, "How did they get all of those animals in the ark?" and other similar questions. This did not go over well, and he was severely chastised.

Religious trauma can even be caused by well-meaning people who will use the most beautiful spiritual path as a way to control others. Some people believe that we must all behave in a certain way, then things will be good. This way of thinking can turn into a very oppressive, fear-based system of control. Of course, this system of control is intended to prevent one from wandering into other spiritual practices, as this implanted fear comes up when we try something new or different. This religion-based trauma is designed to keep you from finding your own personal connection to the Divine. We are no longer reliant upon religious authorities. If you are seeking orthodox training and initiation into a specific established religion, then find a good teacher with a good connection to the lineage. In Modern Hermeticism, we offer a method of using the powerful spiritual technologies of ancient religions in modern ways that make sense to us now, this forging our own spirituality.

We have observed that people are often initially intimidated by the first spiritual practice: the Qabalistic Cross. Often there is resistance to trying the practice, as it seems like something they were told not to do by previous religious authority figures. It helps to talk about it and bring these discomforts to light and not let them remain unexamined. Discussing concerns about certain symbols and patterns, such as the pentagrams drawn in these rituals and other practices, can be very healing, as it brings our fears to consciousness where can work with the veil. Also, mindfully sitting with the discomfort helps as well; it can diffuse the negative emotional associations and help you to work through things that come up.

Mindfulness and Being in the Body Veil

Similarly, many people have difficulty with mindfulness, which is defined as moment-to-moment nonjudgemental awareness of the present. We like to encourage practicing ritual as a mindfulness practice. Maintaining a clear, focused awareness during the process of a trance-inducing ritual will intensify and maximize the power of your working. Learning to be present in the moment and holding on to an anchor is the key here. There are a number of ways this could be accomplished. One practice is to maintain an awareness of your feet and breath simultaneously and continuously as you perform the actions of ritual. You can also bring clarity, intention, and focus to your ritual movements and the use of your implements. Many people will rush through the ritual as if it were a chore to be completed or something they have seen so many times it holds nothing new. Taking your time with each of the pieces can open the way for much deeper experiences and greater transformation. Sink in slowly to the feelings as they arise and savor them. We like to pay attention to our hearts in particular as an object of focus for our ritual mindfulness practice, but the entire body will vibrate with an enjoyable sensation. Tune into that. It is worth addressing that some may prefer to use trance more fully and release a sense of control that mindfulness utilizes. There are spaces the conscious mind cannot fully enter. You may find the techniques of mindfulness and full trance useful at different times and even within the same ritual. Experiment with the different ways that consciousness can be used and find fluidity with what works for you. You may even find that you can do both things with your conscious awareness: stay in the present and do a deep dive into the depths of the subconscious.

It can be difficult to introduce mindfulness to your magical practice. It is a very challenging skill and by its nature will bring up various discomforts. You may find that past experiences you thought were resolved resurface. It can be very difficult to be in the body, especially if bad things have happened in the body or you do not like your body. Similarly, it can be difficult to remain aware of your heart when your heart has been hurt. Seemingly, all the things that distress us in life come up during a mindfulness practice and ritual only intensifies this. This intense and transformative process is what we seek.

Eventually, as your practice ripens, there are various powers, or *siddhis,* that you can develop, as you will develop a greater capacity for introspection. These are natural powers that every person has, yet they are obscured by the veils. By clearing these veils of what is not true for us, we are able to access our inner divine nature. The senses will bloom, and the siddhis will rain down from the clouds.

Social Programming Veil

Probably the most universal blocker is the aforementioned domestication, or social programming, we all went through to some degree. We were told to walk and talk and then to sit down and be quiet by our primary caregivers and parents. Further social rules were enforced by our siblings and friends in order to fit in. This social programming—some of it helpful, some of it harmful—can prevent us from developing more naturally into who we are.

Social programming provides us with guidelines for living in relation to others. Basic important programming involves elements of self-control, personal hygiene, safety, and the skills we use for daily living. But it can also include ideas and perspectives about people, situations, and things. These perspectives tend to be very old ways of thinking, and we pick them up by being around people who hold those perspectives. As we mature as people and magicians, it is necessary to examine the way these impressions influence us and reevaluate their effectiveness based on new information and our experiences. Not all social programming is harmful, and much of it can be a big help while we are learning and developing our identities. But recognizing when they are influencing us can help us to reevaluate and choose a path that is more congruent with the underlying authenticity of our true selves.

A spiritual path requires us to unpack many parts of ourselves that we have put away and hidden. We may find that we have different feelings toward our roles and the masks we wear for social conformity. There may be parts that appreciate the safety of the veils. But there are also parts within our subconscious that want to align with the Higher Self and achieve the transformation that magic promises. It is worth listening to our feelings of awkwardness around breaking social conventions. This is how we lift the veils and discover who we really are. Again, it is not easy work. These veils can feel more like unforgiving walls. But when we release this programming and discover who we really are, life starts to become a whole lot easier. It's actually more effort to go against your nature than it is to find it, as difficult as that may seem.

The Veils of the Qabalistic Cross

Now we see three ways to identify the action of a veil, working in our subconscious and limiting our ability to access the fullness of a self connected to the pleroma. There are many more that you may find as you continue to do the work. Having examined the three main types of veils, let's look at how they show up in ritual practice. As an example, let's walk through some of the ways a veil can appear when we are doing one of the core daily practices.

If you examine the Qabalistic Cross, you can see how it breaks so many of the rules you were most likely given without much explanation during your childhood domestication. First in the ritual, we imagine we are becoming larger. This goes against the teaching to not go beyond our boundaries. We were told we should be humble and stay small within our limitations.

Next, we are moving our arms about but not accomplishing any work. This is definitely not allowed or normal, as we are told we must be productive at all times—or at least have our hands at our sides. When our child was in a public school in first grade, he was told by teachers to hug himself and put a bubble in his mouth. In other words, don't talk and keep your hands to yourself. We got him out of there as soon as we could.

Using the imagination is often discouraged, so imagining balls of light is simply not approved of. Speaking words in another language can be considered weird or offensive. We've known people who would become upset if a language other than their native English was spoken in their presence. All of these rules are broken in a practice that is at worst harmless and potentially very beneficial.

The breaking of a social taboo can release a flood of mental energy, which can be quite helpful, as it frees up our minds and opens possibilities of new thoughts and behaviors. This catharsis can also be quite blissful.

This breaking of taboo is not really the goal of the Qabalistic Cross ritual or any of the other more complex practices of Hermeticism. The real goal is to create a set of practices that improve your inner communication and empower you to be the best you. The techniques are supposed to seem odd at first to separate our spiritual practices from our mundane routine. In time, however, the practice ripens and seems as natural and fun as anything else, and the veils become more and more transparent until they fade like mist in the morning sun.

Shadow Parts

The first three veils, or obscurations, are the ones that most students encounter in some combination. The next important element that can function as a veil and inhibit the magician's progress is the parts of the self they do not want to see, which are often called shadows because they remain outside of the light of awareness. These shadows are hidden, often very deeply, within our sub- and unconscious. These can be very personal and unique to us individually. But through ritual practice, they will arise. Learning to recognize these as they come up is the first step.

In the novel *Zanoni*, published in 1842, Edward Bulwer-Lytton refers to the spectral image that is encountered when the student begins their spiritual journey as the dweller on the threshold. In his introduction to the 2012 edition, Lon Milo DuQuette mentions how he was encouraged to read *Zanoni* by the head of his chapter of the Ancient Mystical Order Rosae Crucis (AMORC).[22] The more modern terms *shadow parts* and *shadow self* are probably more familiar to most people, as those terms come from modern psychology. When we turn our awareness inward, we are often confronted by aspects of ourselves that we have long ignored or forced to the back of our consciousness. Ignoring these aspects only works for a time. These parts that have been forced out of consciousness will still affect our behavior—often in negative and unpredictable ways.

It is good to remember that these shadow parts, even when they are causing us discomfort, are trying to help. Often, they are trying to protect us from a situation that was previously harmful. However, when they act without our conscious intent, they can cause chaos. Our energy is tied up in these forgotten parts, blocking the free flow of creative energies and our own healthy vitality.

Ignored, these shadow parts create cognitive distortions. When we are unaware of these hidden aspects of ourselves, we can act unconsciously on their biases. This may lead to misinterpreting people's actions, projecting negative expectations on them, or setting unrealistic expectations. Both types of distortions can prevent healthy relationships of any kind. They can also cause us to miss out on opportunities in life. Bringing these distortions into conscious awareness opens up many possibilities that we have shut ourselves out of.

22. Bulwer-Lytton and DuQuette, *Zanoni: Book One: The Musician.*

There are several types of shadows, but here we will look at personal shadows, family shadows, cultural shadows, and collective shadows.

Personal Shadow

Shadow parts are almost always created by some form of personal trauma we encounter while developing our sense of self as we grow up. When we open ourselves to spiritual growth, we will need to address and be aware of our blocking thoughts and habits. Our practices will help with this healing by unblocking our personalities and connecting us with the uninjured Universal Self. At that time, we can become freer and happier in our lives.

Family Shadow

In addition to your personal shadow, or dweller on the threshold, you will have a shadow from your family of origin. An example of this would be like language like "We don't like to talk about Uncle Bob…." Be aware of any things your family wants to ignore, but don't judge. Your family of origin may have not wanted to talk about mental health, for instance, or a family member who had such problems or addictions. Your family may have suffered discrimination. There may have been good reasons to ignore certain subjects. Just be aware so you are not also ignoring these subjects.

Cultural Shadow

There is also a cultural shadow from your culture of origin. This may also show up as avoiding a certain subject or as issues relating to assimilating into a new culture if your family of origin immigrated. If you are integrating into a new culture, you may be urged to ignore aspects of your culture of origin in order to fit in. Doing so might make it easier in the short run, but it can cause distortions in your perceptions of your culture of origin. Likewise, if you are a member of the dominant culture, then you may have been trained to ignore certain problematic aspects of your family history, such as the oppression of marginalized peoples. Look for moments of feeling defensive about things like social justice, history, and cultural differences, especially when it has nothing to do with you personally. Don't judge your feelings as right or wrong; just notice and be aware.

Collective Shadow

The collective unconscious of all humanity has a shadow as well, full of things we humans don't want to deal with. We cling to thoughts such as "We are not really animals; we're specially created beings apart from nature...." These concepts are packed-away parts of our culture that cause all sorts of cognitive distortions and neurotic behavior, such as our tendency to abuse the natural world and damage our environment, which, again, harms us.

Shadow Work

When you begin a spiritual path of almost any sort, you will probably encounter some parts of yourself that you put away and hid long ago. This is normal and natural. There are methods we can use to work with these shadows and have the process benefit us. By bringing the shadows to the light of our conscious awareness, we undergo a gnosis, a sacred transformation.

Mindfulness

The first method that can be used to approach our shadow parts and begin to work with them is a simple technique called mindfulness. Alannah was one of the initial pioneers of mindfulness research in the mid-nineties and published two academic theses. Mindfulness forms the foundation of her therapy and her daily practice.

Mindfulness is moment-to-moment, nonjudgmental awareness of the present. We can apply this to our shadows when we notice that they are arising within us. We can then notice what we feel in our bodies, what thoughts come up, our emotions, and any recollections that may arise as we maintain our shadow in our conscious awareness. By doing this, we will begin to psychologically process the shadow aspects of ourselves. We may notice that the stuckness of thought begins to release and new insights will occur, which will lead to acceptance of our shadows and then integration.

We can sit with this shadow and be mindfully aware of it. The awareness of these shadow parts can be very helpful in understanding ourselves and our accepted limitations so we can overcome those limitations when we are ready. These Hermetic practices will bring these parts and more to light, allowing you to become whole and in charge of the utter vastness that is you.

If you notice any of these obscurations coming up as you do the practices, try not to judge the shadows that you unpack. To call them good is to align with them; to call them bad is to push them away. Both choices cause us to get caught up in the drama. Simply be aware and make good decisions on how to act on the impulses that spring from these parts. Remember to act, not react. Simply be with them, mindfully, noticing how they present to your senses

When one begins to open up to greater awareness or achieve some new level of initiation, these shadows will become apparent, even obvious. It is a well-known occurrence for a beginning or even advanced practitioner of Hermetic magic to encounter their own personal dweller on the threshold.

These shadow parts must be integrated in some way for progress to be made and the tremendous power they contain released for our benefit. The work done to reintegrate these parts is commonly called shadow work.

While simply sitting with your uncomfortable shadow parts is good and maybe even enough, what if you want to go deeper, faster? Psychotherapy with a professional will always be best. An expert can guide you through the process of creating a container and then approaching and communicating with these parts of you.

That being said, and if you are not in too much distress, there is some shadow work you can do that can bring those parts into the light alone or alongside therapy. This shadow work can lessen the distress and chaos created within us and free up the power they are consuming, thus releasing the light trapped within the darkness.

Solomonic Magic

One method of the Hermetic tradition of shadow work is Solomonic magic, or Grimoire-style magic. This tradition works with the Geotic or chthonic earthbound spirits. It is a very popular way to get your internal demons under control and working for you instead of against you. From one point of view, the demonic spirits listed in these old grimoires are shadow aspects of your own personality, so getting them in line and working for you is very attractive as a methodology. For someone in great distress, the idea of quickly forcing the chaotic, untamed aspects of our unconscious to behave sounds great. But the problem is you are working with shadow parts from someone else in a different culture long past. In addition, using force to get your shadow parts to behave productively will only work for a while, as you are not addressing the root cause of the distress.

We personally would rather work with our own personal shadows or daemons, and we would rather employ a strategy of power with rather than power over. There is much to gain from working with our shadow parts, and it's better to go that route than to use methods that further traumatize them.

The word *demon* comes from the Greek *daemon*, originally a divine spirit sent to advise us. We choose to see these shadows in their more original form, as parts of ourselves that have something to offer if we can integrate or accept them. A messenger from our own inner divinity is a more productive way of looking at these parts.

Tibetan Chod Method

This method comes out of a very rare and highly sought after Tibetan method that was not widely taught until recently. Now, it has become modernized and introduced to audiences outside of formal, dedicated Tibetan practices. Alannah has received these initiations multiple times, along with her son. The first time her son received this, he was an infant, still breastfeeding. This is considered very auspicious.

Traditionally, Chod practice involved visualizations while singing sacred prayers. This is accompanied by special instruments: a Tibetan bell called a *ghanta* and a drum called a *damaru*. Through the visualizations, shadow parts are brought forth to be faced and then fed. The objects of visualization are quite graphic and unpleasant, and traditionally this ritual is performed in a graveyard. The offering bowl from which we feed our demons is a real human skull. However, these are illegal in most places and people generally use a replica made of resin. You can also visualize your own skull, cut from your head, inverted, and filled with the nectar of your essence. This nectar is your fears, shadows, demons, and other parts you want to work with, but it is also every part of you as well. In Buddhism, we seek nonduality, and so everything that we are, our entire energy stream of thoughts, emotions, sensations, recollections, and efforts are offered. In this method, you do not try to control or banish your shadow parts. You actually feed them.

A modern method we enjoy and find easier to use is one taught by Lama Tsultrim Allione.[23] As a living master, she teaches a simplified method of Tibetan Chod practice that enables us to cut through the obscurations that prevent us from achieving enlightenment. Lama Tsultrim's method is available for a lay practitioner and does not need to have all the traditional elements. She cuts right to the essence of the teaching and presents the ideas in a way that non-Tibetans and lay people can easily begin using right away.

It can seem counterintuitive to our modern minds, as we think if we feed these shadowy demons by paying attention to them we will make them stronger or fall into unhealthy rumination. However, shadows gain strength when we fight them. To paraphrase Jung, what we resist persists. The more you push away or try to forcefully control or block your shadow, the more control it will have over you. The more you struggle, the tighter the bind and the more your power is tied up in the distress of the inner conflict. When we fight against the parts of us that we don't like, we end up reinforcing an opposite part. To do this, we use our active imagination skills and invite our daemons in for tea using any kind of vessel you like. It doesn't have to be a skull cup. As an example, in Alannah's psychotherapy practice, she works with folks who have all sorts of traumas. She might ask her

23. Allione, *Feeding Your Demons*.

client if it is okay to invite in a part that stores the memory of a particular event. The body will have a pattern of tension associated with this recollection stored within the nervous system. This tension can be brought into awareness and meditated upon. Then we see the demon sitting outside of us, and we can begin to have a conversation with it. We can ask it to tell us its story and then ask it to tell us what it needs. More often than not, what it needs is to have its story heard, recognized, and validated. These forbidden voices are just wanting to be accepted and not pushed away or judged. Then, we invite the demon to come into us as a conscious, mindful part.

In order to feed the demon, Lama Tsultrim recommends asking the demon to sit near you. You mentally imagine that your entire body dissolves into light streams of nectar and flows from you into the demon. By providing this, we feed them with our energetic essence and awareness and start to integrate the separated power back into our psyche. The shadow part will then transform and become integrated into consciousness, thereby losing the negative impact on us emotionally.

Determining Your Shadow Parts and Your Veil

In order to determine your shadow parts and begin shadow work, we have to first consider if we have enough personal awareness to identify our blockers or shadow parts. We need to have enough clarity to be able to identify what our blockers are. This is the most difficult part for many.

Here is the best tool for identifying your shadows: Notice what is happening in your body. Using the skill of mindfulness, which we have described, note if there is tension arising. If so, then there is almost certainly some shadow part at work. Be sure to rule out other obvious factors, such as climate, that might be causing tension. But in the absence of those, there are patterns of tension people tend to use to guard themselves from the shadow. These patterns of bodily tension are unique to every person. If you learn to examine these when they come up, you will begin to recognize them. At this point, just hold the patterns in mindful awareness.

We may have emotions, such as anger or frustration, and those are bundles of unresolved experiences and emotions that have been stored physiologically.

Another word for shadow is *daemon*. A daemon could be a behavior we have a hard time resisting, a critical voice that comes up often, or an uncomfortable mood state, such as depression or anxiety. It is anything that creates tension and unhappiness within you rather than relaxation and joy.

To start, pick something that blocks you from doing the practices of this book or perhaps prevents you from doing something else you want to do. Keep it simple to start. Examples of good practice targets could be a minor pain, such as a headache or sore joint; the annoyance you feel about a coworker (not the person, just the annoyance); or a household task you dislike, such as emptying the recycle bin. The idea is that this first daemon is a stressor but not a major one. Start with little daemons and work your way up.

R • I • T • U • A • L
EX TENEBRIS LUX, FROM DARKNESS COMES LIGHT

The following practice has been profoundly useful in clearing our own mental obstacles that were limiting us. We spend a lot of our time and energy trying to get out of our own way.

After performing the ritual, you may notice that the shadow causes you less distress right away. However, you may need to repeat the visualization several times until you can be with the part and feel no distress at all. This is assuming the part is problematic but not so stressful that you can work with it on your own. Just remember that it's okay to get professional help; in fact, it is the best thing to do if you need it.

We have provided both the formal and the informal version of this practice. As always, begin with the formal.

Things You Need

A private place that is calming and quiet

Directions for a Formal Practice

Begin by performing the Qabalistic Cross (chapter 2). This will create the container and context for this practice. Then sit and breathe mindfully to calm and center yourself.

Once centered, bring up the discomfort you want to work with. Try to identify where in your body you can feel it. Is it in your stomach, chest, or head? What color is it? Does it have a smell or a texture? Does it make a sound? What else can you feel about the discomfort? Is it a dull or sharp sensation? Hot or cold? Try to feel it first; the body sensation is the first identification.

After feeling the shadow part, imagine the shadow part that you are focusing on is sitting before you. Let it appear in your mind in whatever form it comes in. Mindfully notice its nature and appearance. Is it animal or humanoid? How big is it? Is it solid or transparent? What sort of covering does it have—fur or skin, rough or smooth? What color is it? How does it smell? Does it make a sound? It is hot or cold? Notice all these things, but do not engage in conversation. Just observe.

Now move your awareness to the shadow part. Through its eyes, observe yourself. How does it see you? What age are you? Do you look like yourself or another person or creature? From its point of view, ask all the same questions as the previous step so you can understand its point of view. Once you feel you understand how this part sees you, return to your body.

Next, you can ask for its name if you don't know it already, but do not engage in conversation. Conversation can devolve into a spiral of a storyline that is not helpful and just repeats the story of the original injury. Remember that these shadow parts are information and experiences that you were not able to process and integrate, so going into the storyline is a trap. You will just spin around in the memory, and you have done enough of that already.

Ask the daemon what it needs. It may ask for something odd or seemingly silly. For example, Erich has a part that likes blue snow cones. Then ask what it will give you in return for what it needs. Erich has a part that gives him physical energy and alertness and another that gives him the ability to pause before reacting. The shadow's gift will be very useful, even if it does not appear to be at first.

When you are ready, imagine your body becoming whatever stuff the daemon needs and feeding it. Imagine your body slowly becoming a sort of holy nectar or whatever the shadow part wants and streaming over to the shadow part. Feed it until it is completely full and satisfied. You should see the shadow part becoming smaller or less distressed as it is fed.

Finally, sit with the part for a moment, and then allow it to dissolve. Perform the Qabalistic Cross again and ground yourself.

Directions for an Informal Practice

Once you have success with this formal practice, you can also do an informal practice. First perform the Qabalistic Cross, and then go through the visualizations, but do so in a simplified manner that works for you. We find this can be done in a few minutes in almost any situation to lower any distress we are feeling from a shadow that has come up. This technique is surprisingly powerful and permanent in taming these shadows.

• • • • • • •

Three veils, or blockers, can prevent our success in spiritual work. Religious trauma can make it difficult to open to spiritual experiences. Difficulty being in the body can block our deeper spiritual experiences. Social programming can keep us from experiencing our True Self. Becoming aware of our blocks and sitting with them can bring them into the light. You may want to seek professional help if you have a lot of distress. If you can, use shadow work to help resolve many issues.

Shadow work allows us to lessen the emotional impact of our parts that are not fully integrated. We can work with little shadows and big ones. By becoming aware of our stressors and feeding them rather than resisting them, we diffuse the emotional tangles that have built up over our lifetimes. We should strive to be more aware of our daemons and what they can offer us, whether that is advice and insight or a release of energies tied up in an internal conflict. Getting professional help is always a good idea.

— CHAPTER 5 —

Elemental Energies, Angels, Gods, and Archetypes

We have examined our shadow parts, so now we should look at the light. Hermeticists believe that the universe is made of divine light, and we must become aware of the divine light within us in order to be aware of our own divine nature.

This practice can be called theurgy, or god-doing. Theurgy involves contacting angels, gods, and other archetypes that exist in our inner divine light and the outer, or shared, divine light. This contact spurs our own spiritual revelations and spiritual growth. Let us define what we mean by *elemental energies*, *archetypes*, *gods*, and *angels* as these terms can have many meanings.

Elemental Energies

In order to make contact with the forces of creation, we need a spark to raise our energy field to match that of the higher, more spiritual forces. For work in our personal world, or microcosm, we will employ the elemental energies and sacred geometry. Our immediate world is called the microcosm, while the greater universe is called the macrocosm. This distinction is useful in that it allows us to understand how our personal view of the universe is a fractal image of the larger pleroma or universe.

The elemental energies are the power source for sacred geometry and other advanced ritual work. The elements of fire, water, air, and earth as well as spirit active and spirit passive can be used to create fields of energy that raise our own energetic levels and allow communion with the higher spiritual forces of the universe.

Sacred geometry, in this context, means drawing meaningful geometric shapes with energy and focused spiritual forces. These shapes are three-dimensional, and we build them around ourselves in the sacred space that we create. The shape we draw has an effect on the expression of the energies as well. For instance, if I draw a pyramid shape around myself and fill it with fire energy, the shape will tend to focus the elemental fire energies at the upper point, concentrating the spiritual energies in the same way that the sharp point of a knife focuses physical energies, thus allowing you to make a clean cut in some substance too hard for you to shape with your bare hands. An inverted pyramid shape would tend to ground the energies into the earth, and combining both shapes creates a ten-pointed star. This star acts as a sort of vehicle to travel to and communicate with spiritual beings. There is also a circle or sphere for defining sacred space and the triangle for creating gateways. These will all be explained in detail in the coming chapters.

There is an underlying energetic structure that forms the foundation of physical reality. This provides a powerful gridwork that we can align our consciousness toward. The underlying structure can be expressed as geometric shapes. With Modern Hermeticism, we can ritually connect to these basic templates by drawing symbols, using imagination, and connecting intellectually and emotionally with the correspondences. Thus, we tap deeply into a space where physical reality is created and insert a pattern based on our magical intention. The more the practitioner can be in alignment with the structural gridwork that underlies space and time, the more effective the magic can be and the more transformational it is to the psyche because the unconscious mind developed evolutionarily in the context of these energies.

One element can also be combined with another, creating other kinds of elemental energy fields that have very different energy signatures and effects. If, for instance, we wanted to make contact with a spiritual force that was very emotional, we might create an elemental of water. This would vibrate in harmony with the force we are calling and make it easy to contact. We could also create an elemental of air, which would be very mental and rational, then add the elemental of water and fuse them together. This would be the watery part of air, a very powerful and creative force, perhaps very artistic in nature.

This method ensures we get the results we are seeking. By accurately tuning the space with elemental energies and sacred geometry, we are guaranteed success in creating the spiritual experience we are seeking.

Archetypes

While the elemental energies and sacred geometry are effective and powerful in their own right, to really tap into the powers of the pleroma we need a tool that can directly access it. The psychologist Carl Jung was, among other things, an expert on both myth and religion. Jung noticed that his patients had themes in their dreams and their fantasies that were very similar to themes found in myth and religion from other cultures and times. Even the children he worked with would produce imagery and themes found echoed in world religion and mythology.

A case brought to Jung by a fellow psychologist illustrates this very well.[24] The fellow psychologist was given a book by his young daughter that she had created from scratch, telling of her dreams. While the child was only ten years old, the dreams contained motifs and themes that could also be found in an adult's dreams. There were dreams about the origin of the world, moral relativism, and destruction and restoration, and they contained ideas such as the sacred four cardinal directions. The girl's father could not place any of these dreams into a personal context, and the oddness is why he took the book of dreams to Jung for analysis. The girl's family members were mildly Protestant and not very religious, and it was long before television. How could have the ten-year-old girl been exposed to these profound philosophic ideas? What influences contributed to her dreams with common motifs that are found cross-culturally?

This and countless other experiences led Jung to believe that the psyche contains elements that are not the product of personal experience and are instead arising from a universal source that is common to all consciousness and with us from birth. We are not born a blank slate; we are born unconscious. We come preloaded, not just with simple instincts but universal psychic structures that influence our thinking and behaviors. Jung divided our psyches into three broad areas. These areas do interact but work differently. These three areas are as follows:

Personal Conscious Mind: Immediately accessible and identifiable, the personal conscious mind is responsible for the narration of our lives, plans, and intrusive thoughts. This is the inner narrator and running dialogue that we are very aware of. This is often considered the self. The personal conscious mind emerges from the personal subconscious mind.

Personal Subconscious Mind: The personal subconscious mind holds things we think are unimportant or too painful to remember, our personal shadow parts, and forgotten memories that still affect our perceptions. By compartmentalizing complex experiences, we can focus on the work in front of us and get back to those experiences later, or we can choose to

24. Jung, *Man and His Symbols*, 57–63.

avoid something painful we would rather not think about. Things stored in the subconscious can be easily accessible and readily understood aspects of one's inner dynamics, or they can be very deeply buried and forgotten, only recognizable by the patterns we notice in our lives.

This is a storage area for the mind. We can choose to place ideas, emotions, thoughts, and recollections of experiences here for later processing. The personal unconscious mind emerges from the collective unconscious mind.

Collective Unconscious Mind: The collective unconscious mind holds transpersonal mental structures common to all, including the archetypes and the collective shadows, both of which we encounter symbolically as they point to the ineffable. This is the place where all conscious beings are connected and have a universal experience in this reality. We have to enter this very soup to find the Source.

The conscious mind is the tip of the iceberg and a very focused and specialized offshoot of the other two areas of consciousness. The personal conscious mind contains the intimate and personal things we are aware of, think about, and experience. The conscious mind is an offshoot of the personal unconscious mind. Here are all the things we know and experience but do not hold in our day-to-day awareness. However, they do come up in the conscious mind with regularity. The subconscious mind contains the shadow elements mentioned before along with other elements that we deem to be unimportant but can still affect our thinking and behavior. It also contains unprocessed experiences, often held as trauma. These can be stored so deeply that they only rarely enter the conscious mind and exist very separately from how we understand our conscious self.

The third and largest area is the collective unconscious. It contains the psychic structures, cognitive categories, and universal energetic templates that are not unique to the individual but are also influencing an individual's thoughts and behaviors. These are called the archetypes. The collective unconscious contains other elements, such as our collective shadows, evolutionary opportunities, and much more. At this place of shared human experience, we connect to a universal transcendence characterized by trance, bliss, and a connection to and receptivity from the source of creation, the pleroma. Merging our conscious intention with the subconscious and the unconscious using archetypes, symbols, and sacred geometry as tools is how we create personal and collective transformation.

The archetypes create a similarity of experience and representation cross-culturally and across time. Unlike an idea in the conscious mind, an archetype cannot be directly observed. An archetype can only be pointed to by symbols that group around the concept they are trying to express, like so many fingers pointing toward the moon. This is because an archetype represents something that is ineffable and transcendent. The conscious mind cannot realize its meaning since our minds rely on clearly defining concepts using the tools of physical reality. Archetypes are the language of the subconscious and require a different set of tools. How can we tap into the vast collective unconscious mind and its connection to the pleroma? Modern Hermeticism gives us a method.

Gods and Goddesses

To Jung, the central archetype was the self-archetype. This archetype represents the unification of the conscious and then unconscious and represents the divinity within. Jung believed that the representations of gods and goddesses in art and religion were representations of the self-archetype. This is not so much to say that god is a product of our minds or of the collective unconscious but rather that the archetypes are the medium through which religious experiences flow. By invoking various deities as archetypes, we can communicate with the personal and collective unconscious and tap into its limitless power for personal change and evolution.

In the Modern Hermeticism practice, we mainly work with Egyptian and Greek/Roman deities. Egypt and Greece are the ultimate source of Hermetic thought, so it seems only fitting to use their archetypes. We like Egyptian gods because they have attributes that lend them to ritual design, such as cardinal directions. For instance, the god Anubis is a god of the underworld, a psychopomp and guide of the soul in the afterlife. He also has the direction north as one of his attributes. When we go to design a ritual, we know that we can place Anubis in the north. The gods of Egypt are also not as human as the Greek gods yet not so abstract as a Gnostic god. They occupy a nice middle ground. There is also the glorious artwork the Egyptians left for us in their tombs and temples, which can be used for powerful visualizations.

Erich's primary god is Anubis. Early in his studies, he came upon an image from the *Book of the Dead* where Anubis was guiding the scribe Ani through the underworld. Anubis was holding Ani's hand to show him it was going to be okay. In Anubis's other hand was the ankh, the symbol of eternal life. Erich was moved by the idea of a god who was not abstract, a god who would hold your hand and guide you in times of darkness.

We also work with the Greek gods because they are familiar to most Westerners and correspond to planetary energies that cover most human needs. Hermes is the same as Mercury and corresponds to the planet of the same name. One would invoke Hermes for mercurial things, such as travel, communication, and commerce. There is a wealth of art, poetry, and accessible mythology available as well. The Greek gods are woven into Western culture so deeply that we hardly even notice it. Statues of Themis adorn many courthouses, and our movies and comic books are filled with Greek gods as well. If there are other pantheons you like to work with, then please rewrite the rituals using your personal mythology.

In the rituals in this book, we will invoke gods and goddesses as sacred archetypes to point to a deeper part of the collective unconsciousness—sometimes as many as twelve. But what are the deeper structures in the collective unconsciousness that we are trying to access? What are our archetypes pointing to? The very fundamental structures that determine reality itself.

Angels

In our opinion, *angel* is a problematic word, but our language is limited, so we are stuck with it. The word *angel* is steeped in meaning from the Abrahamic religions and can bring up images of powerful male beings from the glorious Renaissance art that has come down to us. We use the term *angel* because that is the tradition, and no other English word is better suited. An angel in this context is a conscious energetic field that is part of the synergistic aspect of creation. They are conscious energy fields that help create and build up the universe. Of course there are angels that help break things down as well; there is an entire ecology of angelic forces. They have intelligence, and by intelligence we mean that these forces know how to do certain things, how to manage what they are responsible for. Just as electricity is a force that knows how to follow Ohm's law, the angels know how to do what is in their nature and what they are responsible for.

For instance, one of Erich's main spirits is the Enochian angel that rules the earthy part of the earth table. It directs energies that have a deep connection to the life force and manifestation. It is his go-to for healing work, grounding, and quick manifestation. This angel appears in his visions as a young woman wearing clothes made of leaves and chunky jewelry made of uncut stones and raw mineral ores. The angel has no real physical gender; it's just how it appears to him. Someone else might see this entity as a ball of light or just feel the presence. This angel is great for healing work because that is its nature and specialty. However, if Erich were to invoke it for help with emotional healing, it would still attempt to help, but it would not be very effective. This angel would literally be out of its element. The angelic spirits are part of the circuitry or programming of our reality. Inserting your will on the inner worlds at the source will alter the entire flow of manifestation, and the changes you create will be much more durable.

A much higher angelic force is Hcoma, the watery part of spirit. Another way to put it is that she is the presence of the Qabalistic plane of Briah. Hcoma is the summation of the entire reality of watery energies. Communing with such a vast consciousness is rewarding just for the wisdom and spiritual attainment. There is no real need to ask for anything other than Hcoma's wisdom, as she will know what you need better than you do.

Angelic Hierarchies

The concept of angelic hierarchies is a difficult one to approach. Due to our society, the word *hierarchy* suggests imposition of one person over another, often for completely arbitrary and nonsensical reasons, such as order of birth or gender. That sort of hierarchy is not really what we are talking about here, but again we are stuck with the term.

For this practice, *hierarchy* refers to the evolution of an energy as it goes from being very simple near the source of creation to complex near manifestation. Traditionally, we might say the Archangel Gabriel is set over elemental water and rules over the elemental king, Nixsa, who then rules over the undines. But really, Gabriel is elemental water near the source. When the force of elemental water begins to manifest, it is more like the force we call Nixsa, which in manifestation is spread out in many forms that we call undines. All these forces would qualify as angelic. They are part of a continuum of intelligent energy that is creating our reality in cooperation with all of the sentient beings that are inhabiting it. Traditionally, Nixa and the undines are called elementals, and we will refer to them that way, but they are part of the pleroma of angelic energy that forms the circuitry of our reality.

This tradition of spiritual hierarchies is ancient, and people in the past tended to see things in terms of the social structures of their day, with kings, dukes, princesses, and so on. So, that is how they documented things. We now know that all is a unity, and the spiritual realms are not filled with separate beings bossing each other around. However, it is still useful to have these hierarchies so we can understand the spiritual ecology and how it works in order to be specific about which force we want to contact and experience.

Infernal Spirits

Lon Milo Duquette has said that the best way to get things done in the material world is to invoke the infernal spirits.[25] These spirits include those found in the grimoires that contain instructions for European sorcery, such as the ones we mentioned in the shadow work chapter (chapter 4). These earthly spirits are close to manifestation or even below it, and they do all the heavy lifting in the material world. These forces correspond to the instincts of survival and thus help to power and guide both our lower nature and animal life. There are even adverse Enochian angels and Qliphoth (adverse Qabalistic forces) we could use, but they all have the same problem. Without first mastering the light, the wilder, untamed forces are hard to control and like to pull the old monkey's paw

25. DuQuette, *Low Magick*, chapter 2.

shenanigans (e.g., you ask for a million dollars and next thing you know your favorite uncle dies and leaves you the money).

While there is a time and a place for working with the more entropic forces, we have found that the angelic intelligences are just as capable of manifesting spiritual evolution, which will lead to money, relationships, and whatever you need to fulfill your True Will. For example, if you ask for money from an infernal, or chthonic, spirit, you will probably get some small windfall. If you ask an angelic force for a career, money will never be a problem again. Remember that all the material benefits you can ever make use of will be the result of gaining a knowing heart. If you want to be a richer or wiser person, then you will need to become a different person. And you will. You are already not the same person who went to bed last night. You can't use the same methods you have used in the past and expect a different result.

P•R•A•C•T•I•C•E
CHOOSING A PERSONAL ARCHETYPE

In the adventures ahead of you, it will be useful to have a personal archetype to be the representation of the guide on the path. Erich's is Anubis, but yours can be any god, hero, saint, or guru you have encountered and would like to have as a guide on your journey. You can change your mind later; this is just an exercise so you can experience the sacred archetype in your life. If you already have one, then we suggest you select a new one as their assistant temporarily.

Explore gods and goddesses and heroes, and pick one to be your temporary patron. Once you choose your archetype, learn everything you can about them—what they like and what they don't like, favorite foods, clothing, colors, and so on. Build an altar to them. It can be as simple as a shoe box containing some objects or even drawings of objects your archetype would enjoy. Offer your patron archetype praise. Either compose it yourself or use something that is traditional. For instance, if you choose Hermes, you can look up the Orphic Hymns on the internet. These are traditional Greek hymns to the gods. Hermes's hymn is number twenty-seven. Finally, imagine what it would be like to meet and talk to your archetype. What advice would they have for you? Explore this over a couple weeks and make notes in your journal. It is fine to explore several different options to find one you really like.

• • • • • • •

We now have three spirit forces to work with: the elemental energies of the microcosm, the "angelic" forces of creation, and the sacred archetypes of the collective unconscious. To reach the exalted states of consciousness and magical power that is our goal, we will be using them together, synergistically. When we work with the magic of the macrocosm, we will add in the planetary forces as well. All are activated through the use of symbolism, trance, movement, mudras, mythology, and the imagination. The intellect gets to help with organization and planning.

— CHAPTER 6 —
The Four Elements

The microcosm is where we begin the process of taking conscious control over our spiritual trajectory. This is our world around us—our social and immediate world. Once this is in order, we can shift to the macrocosm, the larger universe. For now, let's focus on gaining awareness and control in our personal life.

To begin to understand how to use ritual to influence and shape your microcosm, you need to first grasp the most fundamental concept of the four elements. In chapter 2, when we made our first pass on the Qabalah, the first three sephiroth were a bit abstract. It was only when we got to the fourth sphere that we arrived at a level of reality that we can relate to, such as when the universe cooled enough to have three dimensions of space and one of time and became the universe we live in and are familiar with. The four elements are the microcosm divided by four: the universe itself in a relationship of fire, water, air, and earth. While the physical substances resemble the concepts, what we are really talking about is our experienced reality divided by four.

Fire

Fire Triangle

Energetically, fire is considered the first expansion of the universe. Its activity is explosive and expanding, consuming as it grows. Fire is the inspiration of our True Will, our purpose. In ritual, it is the heat of the noonday sun and corresponds to the south.

Fire is sudden like a lightning flash; it represents light, illumination, realization, understanding, and insight. It is electric, expansive, and volatile. Fire seeks to destroy boundaries in its creative expression. Fire cannot be contained. It either consumes its restrictions as it expands, or it dies. Fire is the most active and relentless of the elements, but its energies are soon spent if it is not nourished.

Fire consumes as it creates, and it is continually redefining itself through action. Fire reduces and refines ideas to their most essential essence, to their most basic truth. Fire rules decision-making. In magic we invoke the energies of fire to gain insight and inspiration but also to remove blockages in our lives and our thinking. Invoke fire when starting new projects or when you need clarity on an issue.

The first world of the Qabalah is called Atziluth, which corresponds to the element of fire. Each Qabalistic world contains its own tree of ten sephiroth, giving us forty in all. In Atziluth, the Divine exists in a continual state of unity and bliss. There are ten god names corresponding to the ten sephiroth of Atziluth.

Also, the Spring Equinox is the time associated with fire, as it is when the sun enters Aries, which is the cardinal fire sign. In the spring, the world of nature wakes up from its long winter slumber.

Water

Water Triangle

Every force invokes an equal and opposite reaction, making elemental water the natural response and the opposite of fire. Water is cooling and containing; it represents our emotions and imagination. It is the force of love that seeks to connect and corresponds to the west, the sundown and cooling off of the day. Water also represents sensation, feelings, emotions, empathy, and receptivity. It is contractile and stable.

Water is passive and receptive. Water conforms to the boundaries it encounters. It is not as active as fire, but it is enduring. Water has mass and weight, while fire does not. Given time, water can wear down the strongest stone and create wonders such as the Grand Canyon. Water is the element of feeling and reception. It is quiet and understands through empathy. It listens and reflects what it hears. Emotional intelligence can create wonders that do not conform to logic. Water also rules creativity, memory, and understanding. Understanding comes through the use and reflection of the insight of fire.

Invoke water for emotional healing and emotional clarity. Elemental water can also create connections between people and help them to understand each other on an emotional level; it also brings compassion and peace. Water energy can also help you to understand what you really want and how to manifest it.

The Qabalistic world of Briah corresponds to water. Briah is the home to ten archangels that receive the inspiration of Atziluth and direct it to creation.

At the time of the Summer Solstice, the sun enters the sign of Cancer, which is the cardinal water sign. At the height of summer, the elemental qualities turn to humid rains and thus the Summer Solstice is also related to the element of water.

Air

Air Triangle

Air is the combination of water and fire. It represents intellect, reasoning, planning, and logic. Air corresponds to the east and the rising sun. Much like the sunrise, elemental air helps us wake from sleep and allows our minds to become active.

Air is the most penetrating of elements, and it rules the realm of thought and reason. Air does not have quite the passion of fire nor the endurance of water, but it strikes a balance between the two. It is considered to be an active element. Fire supplies air with insight and direction; water provides reflection and creativity. Air seeks to explain through reason and form a plan of action. Reason gives names to things, defining them and setting limitations. It establishes order. Air also rules communication, learning, and strife.

Elemental air is invoked for practical problem-solving. As a computer programmer, Erich invokes it often. Air energy can also clear situations and people from your life who are troublesome; it can be very sterilizing. Gaining education and becoming a better communicator are also air effects that can be invoked.

The Qabalistic world of Yetzirah corresponds to the element air. Here ten choirs of angels carry out the design of the archangels, as it is in this world that the one becomes the many and a plan for creation.

At the Fall Equinox, the element changes again. Here the sun enters the sign of Libra, cardinal air, and it is the time of elemental air. The fall winds mark the change between the heat of summer and the cold of winter.

Earth

Earth Triangle

The element of earth is the combination of fire, water, and air with the addition of the fifth element of spirit, or life force. Earth is in the north and corresponds to midnight, when the sun is on the other side of the earth.

If fire inspires, water feels, and air thinks, then earth lives. Earth is the end product of the actions of the first three elements. The element of earth rules our activities in the world: our work, our health, and our practical projects that we hope to manifest and experience. Earth is the densest and most complex of the elements. It is considered to be a passive element; it is what you create of it. Earth can be refined, shaped, divided, and nourished into a myriad of forms. You get out of it what you are willing to put into it.

Earth energy is called upon first for physical healing and vitality as well as creating abundance of material goods, acquiring property, and resolving issues with inheritance and ancestors. Most of these material things come into our lives via our social group, and earth energy is influential in forming productive bonds between people for practical and purely social functions. It can help you find work or a career, as well as a fun group of people to play softball with or a book club.

Assiah is the Qabalistic world of earth, where the forces manifest as the signs and planets of the zodiac. These energies flow from the source down to solid manifestation. The ten mundane forces represent the qualities of the manifest universe, which are the forces of the zodiac and the planets of astrology. These astrological forces—along with the elements—are considered to be the transmitters or forces that form all creation.[26]

At the Winter Solstice, the sun enters the sign of Capricorn, which is cardinal earth. In winter the earth pulls its energies inward, and this is the time of earthly energies.

P•R•A•C•T•I•C•E
EXPLORING THE ELEMENTS

In this practice you will simply explore the elements. Before you begin, you will need to establish which way is east; use a compass or an app on your phone to do this. You can always just use the general direction of the sunrise. If all else fails, just decide which way is east for today.

26. Al-Kindi, *On the Stellar Rays.*

Things You Need

A quiet place

Your journal and writing utensil

Directions

Find a quiet place and sit down with your journal. Perform the Qabalistic Cross (chapter 2) as well as a few belly breathing rounds.

Face south and imagine in your mind a blazing fire in front of you. You can feel the heat and smell the smoke. Think about the heat of the day at noon, with the sun directly overhead. Contemplate the nature of elemental fire, how it illuminates and removes darkness, how it refines and expands. How do we use fire energy in our lives? Take just a few moments, and then write down your thoughts in your journal.

Now face west and imagine in your mind a vast pool of natural water, such as a lake or stream, maybe a saltwater lagoon full of plants and animals. Think about sundown and the cooling off of the day, the play of colors in the sky. Think about the feeling of rain, thunderstorms, and rainbows. Contemplate the nature of water energy contrasted to fire energy. Contemplate water's ability to hold things in suspension, its ability to wear away stone. Think about how you can see your reflection in water, its ability to act as a mirror. Write your thoughts about water in your journal.

Face east and imagine in your mind a sunrise. Picture the light and color coming over the horizon and the sky and clouds illuminated by the morning light. Consider air and the ceaseless motion of wind; like our thoughts, it never rests. Consider how fire needs air and water contains air for all the plants and animals to breathe. Even in the earth there is some air for the roots and bugs and worms. Consider how air is transparent. We can't see it, but we can see what it affects. Write down your thoughts in your journal.

Face north and imagine it is late at night. The sun is on the other side of the world and all is dark and cool and peaceful. Consider the stability of earth; feel your weight being supported by whatever you are sitting on. Contemplate the nature of earth energy and how it sustains and nourishes all life. Think about how the earth gives us everything we need to live and flourish. Write your thoughts down in your journal.

When you are finished, say the Adoration to Lord of the Universe (chapter 1).

• • • • • • •

The four elements correspond to the four directions, four times of the day, and the four seasons of the year. All things flourish in our own personal microcosm. The elements flow like fractals throughout all of creation. Even when we start working with the macrocosm and planetary archetypes, we will still work with the elements. It will simply be on a higher octave. The elements are some of the first words in your magical alphabet; you will use them over and over. Let's explore them experientially.

— CHAPTER 7 —
Enochiana

The system of magic that has come to be known as Enochian was channeled by John Dee and Edward Kelley in the late 1580s. There are many opinions on the right way to use the huge amount of material channeled by Dee and Kelley, but anyone who uses their material does agree that it is highly effective. The effects can be so obvious it can be almost startling. Working as a team, Dee and Kelley channeled three systems of magic; an alphabet and a series of magical prayers, called Calls; and a wealth of other material. Before going into details on the material and how it will be used, let us provide some historical context for its origination.

The History of Enochiana

The material that is now commonly called Enochian was received from archangels, including Raphael, Michael, Gabriel, and Uriel, and a number of their angelic assistants through the process of scrying (what today some call channeling). John Dee and his seer, Edward Kelley, worked for years as a team to scry and record a vast number of angelic communications in the 1580s.[27]

John Dee was a famous astronomer and a leading expert on navigation and mathematics. He was also an international spy for England's Queen Elizabeth I. Having absorbed all of the scientific

27. Leitch, "What Is Enochian Magic?"

knowledge of his day, Dee turned to more spiritual matters, although Dee would have made no distinction between scientific matters and spiritual ones.[28]

Dee's main goal, at least at first, was to deepen his understanding of natural philosophy by tapping into the knowledge of the angels, who assisted in the creation of the universe or at least witnessed it. From these angels, Dee sought out radical knowledge in the most literal sense: a fundamental understanding of creation.[29] Dee was a multitalented genius, but he was not good at scrying or channeling; for that he needed an assistant.

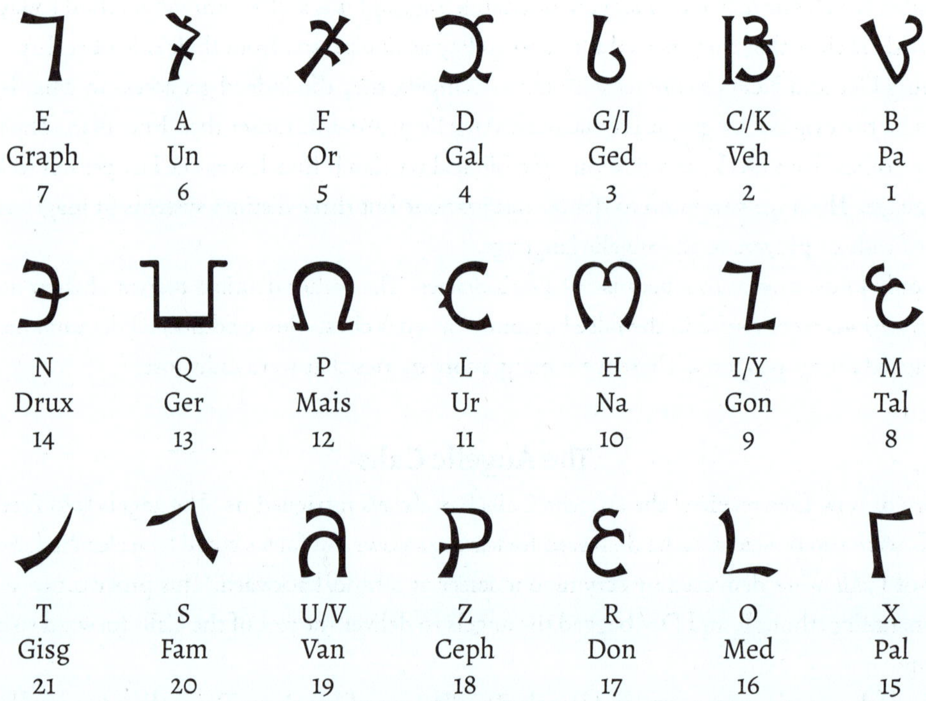

Enochian Letters

Edward Kelley comes down to us as a shady character. A trained alchemist and notary, he is said to have lost his ears as a punishment for being convicted of forgery. However, Kelley was an exceptional channeler; his ability to go into a trance and see and hear the angels is amazing to read

28. DuQuette, *Enochian Vision Magick.*

29. Leitch, *An Encyclopedic Lexicon of the Tongue of Angels*, 4.

about in Dee's surviving diaries.[30] Since Dee was a trained scientist, he kept very detailed records of the angelic communications. In trance, Kelley would produce complex methods and diagrams needed to create tools for further angelic communication as well as an entire language, which he spoke consistently throughout the angelic communications. While he was an imperfect person, the angels found in Kelley a perfect medium to transmit their wisdom.

Dee would conduct the rituals to make contact with the angels and question Kelley. Dee would then make detailed notes on the answers Kelley provided. Working as a team in this way, a seer and a controller, is a classic method of scrying or channeling, and it is still a common method today. The angels made it clear that they viewed Dee and Kelley as one person from their side of reality.

During Dee and Kelley's contact with the archangels, they did indeed get access to what is supposed to be the original language. Dee called it Angelic or Adamic rather than Enochian. The name *Enochian* comes from Dee's assertion that the biblical patriarch Enoch was the last person to know this language. The angels went on to deliver not just one but three distinct systems of magic as well as a set of calls or prayers in the angelic language.[31]

We only know any of this because of Dee's diaries. The rather detailed diaries of their angelic communications were found in the false bottom of a cedar chest. Some additional documents were found buried on his property. There were many more diaries that were sadly lost.[32]

The Angelic Calls

The story of how Dee received the Angelic Calls has always intrigued us. The angels told Dee that the Calls were too powerful to be delivered forward, as powerful forces could be unleashed. So, the first set of Calls were delivered by scrying one letter at a time, backward. This process proved too time-consuming, though, and Dee begged the angels to deliver the rest of the Calls forward to speed things up.

At first, the angels grew angry and knocked Kelley out of his chair. They refused to speak for a while. When the angels returned, they delivered the final Calls in a more normal forward manner that sped up the process. Only much later did Dee and Kelley receive the translations of the Calls from Enochian to English. When they did, words from the first calls that were delivered backward

30. Peterson, *John Dee's Five Books of Mystery*, 92.

31. DuQuette, *Enochian Vision Magick*, 17, 98.

32. Peterson, *John Dee's Five Books of Mystery*.

had the same meaning as words that were delivered later in the forward manner.[33] When they eventually received the translations, what they discovered was poetry—some of it pretty good too.

For example, here is an excerpt from the Second Call:

Can The Wings Of The Winds Understand Your Voices
Of Wonder? O Ye, The Second First: Whom Burning Flames
Have Framed In The Depths Of My Jaws; Whom I Have Prepared
As Cups For A Wedding, Or As Flowers
In Their Beauty For The Chamber Of Righteousness. Stronger Are
Your Feet Than The Barren Stone, And Mightier Are
Your Voices Than The Manifold Winds.[34]

This is a pretty amazing story, and it is just one of many recovered from Dee's diaries. There isn't enough material to say for sure if Enochian is a "real" language; there are only about two hundred and fifty translated words. A normal conversation requires about three hundred. We get to decide for ourselves if this is indeed a fragment of some original language used to create the universe. We believe it is a fragment of some original language filtered through the mind of a sixteenth-century Englishman.

One thing is certain, though, the Enochian material is powerful for creating specific trance states, and it is widely regarded as the most powerful tool in all of Hermeticism. The power of the Enochian language is that it can put a person into a predictable trance state in which they can commune with the forces of the universe. This is why we use it.

Also, as a magical language, it is clean of any prior associations. When a person speaks in their native tongue, each word they use has many prior associations and can have many meanings. If we ask you if you want an apple, you might think of the fruit or the phone or the computer. With Enochian, we all start with a clean slate, and if we use the language only for spiritual work, our subconscious is immediately primed and activated for spiritual work.

A Powerful Tool

While the whole Enochian system is quite vast and can be overwhelming, we will focus on teaching you to use the angels from what is called the Great Table. The Great Table is a grid of letters—twenty-seven by twenty-five squares that contain the names of hundreds of angels. The Great Table

---

33. DuQuette, *Enochian Vision Magick,* 110.

34. DuQuette, *Enochian Vision Magick,* 201.

can be broken down into four smaller tables, called watchtowers, and a central cross of letters. In the early 1900s, the Golden Dawn created an approach to the Great Table that gave it both elemental and planetary attributions. Briefly, the four tables correspond to the four elements, and on each table there are sections that correspond to the seven classical planets of astrology. The central cross corresponds to the element of spirit. On the original drawings, the central cross was painted in black, so it is often called the Black Cross. While this is not part of the original Enochian system, it has proven to be quite effective in understanding this marvelous system and transforming it into a workable system of spiritual attainment. We use the Golden Dawn's elemental and planetary attributions.

There are other approaches to the Enochian system. Some people reject the Golden Dawn system and attempt an originalist methodology. They want to use the material in a way that Dee might have used it. There is nothing definitive in the surviving diaries to show how or even if Dee and Kelley used the material though, and we think most people find the Golden Dawn methods reasonable and effective.

Paraoan

In Dee's conversations with the angels, he wished for a sort of political magic that he could use to influence the leaders of the world. The angels obliged him, but what they delivered was much more than that—they delivered a map of the circuitry of the mind of the Creator.

Through a series of visions, the scrying delivered a list of angels that governed parts of the earth along with some squiggly lines that were the sigils, or symbols, of the governing spirits. Next came a vision of four great castles with a number of royal figures marching out, carrying banners and trumpets. Then the Great Table of letters was received.

Dee and Kelley were told to place the squiggles on the Great Table so that none of the lines overlapped. When they placed the sigils on the table of letters, the only letters left over spelled out *Paraoan*, who is a secret spirit governing one of the inner planes. This spirit is still quite mysterious. We mention it only to impress on you how complex and amazing these scrying sessions were.

The Great Table

The table with all the angelic names reminds Erich of a toy he had as a child. It was a learning toy for electronics with a flat board with many holes in a grid pattern. You placed wires and electrical components, such as resistors and capacitors, in patterns to create effects, including blinking lights and buzzing, and even a crystal radio to receive signals from the ether. We imagine this is a pretty good metaphor for the Great Table, a learning tool for spiritual seekers.

	r	Z	i	l	a	f	A	y	t	l	p	a	e	T	a	O	A	d	u	p	t	D	n	i	m	
	a	r	d	Z	a	i	d	p	a	L	a	m		a	a	b	c	o	o	r	o	m	e	b	b	
	c	z	o	n	s	a	r	o	Y	a	u	b	x	T	o	g	c	o	n	x	m	a	l	G	m	
	T	o	i	T	t	z	o	P	a	c	o	C	a	n	h	o	d	D	i	a	l	e	a	o	c	
	S	i	g	a	s	o	m	r	b	z	n	h	r	p	a	t	A	x	i	o	V	s	P	s	N	
	f	m	o	n	d	a	T	d	i	a	r	i	p	S	a	a	i	x	a	a	r	V	r	o	i	
Air	o	r	o	i	b	A	h	a	o	z	p	i		m	p	h	a	r	s	l	g	a	i	o	l	**Water**
	t	N	a	b	r	V	i	x	g	a	s	d	h	M	a	m	g	l	o	i	n	L	i	r	x	
	O	i	i	i	t	T	p	a	l	O	a	i		o	l	a	a	D	n	g	a	T	a	p	a	
	A	b	a	m	o	o	o	a	C	u	c	a	C	p	a	L	c	o	i	d	x	P	a	c	n	
	N	a	o	c	O	T	t	n	p	r	n	T	o	n	d	a	z	N	z	i	V	a	a	s	a	
	o	c	a	n	m	a	g	o	t	r	o	i	m	i	i	d	P	o	n	s	d	A	s	p	i	
	S	h	i	a	l	r	a	p	m	z	o	x	a	x	r	i	n	h	t	a	r	n	d	i	L	
	m	o	t	i	b			a	T	n	a	n		n	a	n	T	a			b	i	t	o	m	
	b	O	a	Z	a	R	o	p	h	a	R	a	a	d	o	n	p	a	T	d	a	n	V	a	a	
	u	N	n	a	x	o	P	S	o	n	d	n		o	l	o	a	G	e	o	o	b	a	u	a	
	a	i	g	r	a	n	o	o	m	a	g	g	m	O	P	a	m	n	o	v	G	m	d	n	m	
	o	r	p	m	n	i	n	g	b	e	a	l	o	a	p	l	s	T	e	d	e	c	a	o	p	
	r	s	O	n	i	Z	i	r	l	e	m	u	C	s	c	m	i	o	a	n	A	m	l	o	x	
	i	z	i	n	r	C	Z	i	a	M	h	l	h	V	a	r	s	G	d	L	b	r	i	a	p	
Earth	M	o	r	d	i	a	l	h	C	t	G	a		o	i	P	t	e	a	a	p	D	o	c	e	**Fire**
	O	c	a	n	c	h	i	a	s	o	m	t	p	P	s	u	a	c	n	r	Z	i	r	z	a	
	A	r	b	i	z	m	i	i	l	p	i	z		S	i	o	d	a	o	i	n	r	z	f	m	
	O	p	a	n	a	l	a	m	S	m	a	P	r	d	a	l	t	T	d	n	a	d	i	r	e	
	d	o	l	o	P	i	n	i	a	n	b	a	a	d	i	x	o	m	o	n	s	i	o	s	p	
	r	x	p	a	o	c	s	i	z	i	x	p	x	O	o	D	p	z	i	A	p	a	n	l	i	
	a	x	t	i	r	v	a	s	t	r	i	m	e	r	g	o	a	n	n	P	A	C	r	a	r	

The Great Table

As mentioned, the table is divided into four smaller tables by a cross containing the spirit names: Bitom, Hcoma, Exarp, and Nanta. Spirit separates and unifies the four elemental tables, or watchtowers.

- Bitom is the fiery part of spirit and represents the entire fire table and the Qabalistic plane of Atziluth. The Ace of Wands is the tarot card that represents this power.

- Hcoma is the watery part of spirit; it represents the entire water table and the Qabalistic plane of Briah. The Ace of Cups is the tarot card that represents this power.
- Exarp is the airy part of spirit and represents the entire air tablet and the Qabalistic plane of Yetzirah. The Ace of Swords is the tarot card that represents this power.
- Nanta is the earthy part of spirit and the summation of the earth tablet and the Qabalistic plane of Assiah. The Ace of Pentacles is the tarot card that represents this power.

The spirit cross folds up like a carpenter's ruler to make a smaller table called the Table of Union.

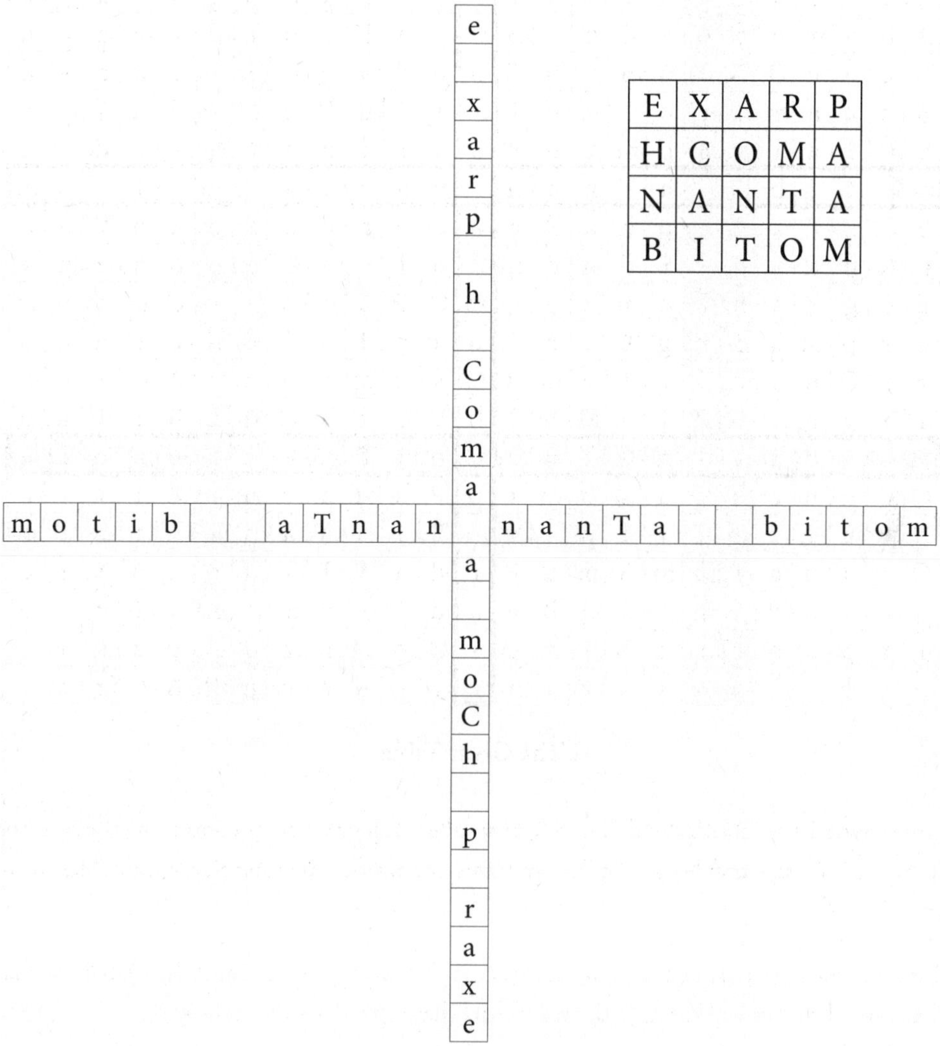

E	X	A	R	P
H	C	O	M	A
N	A	N	T	A
B	I	T	O	M

Table of Union

Reading the first column of letters we get *EHNB*, or spirit of spirit. This name sums up the entire Great Table. EHNB is used to call the energy of spirit active. BNHE is used to call spirit passive, representing the same force flowing in the opposite direction.

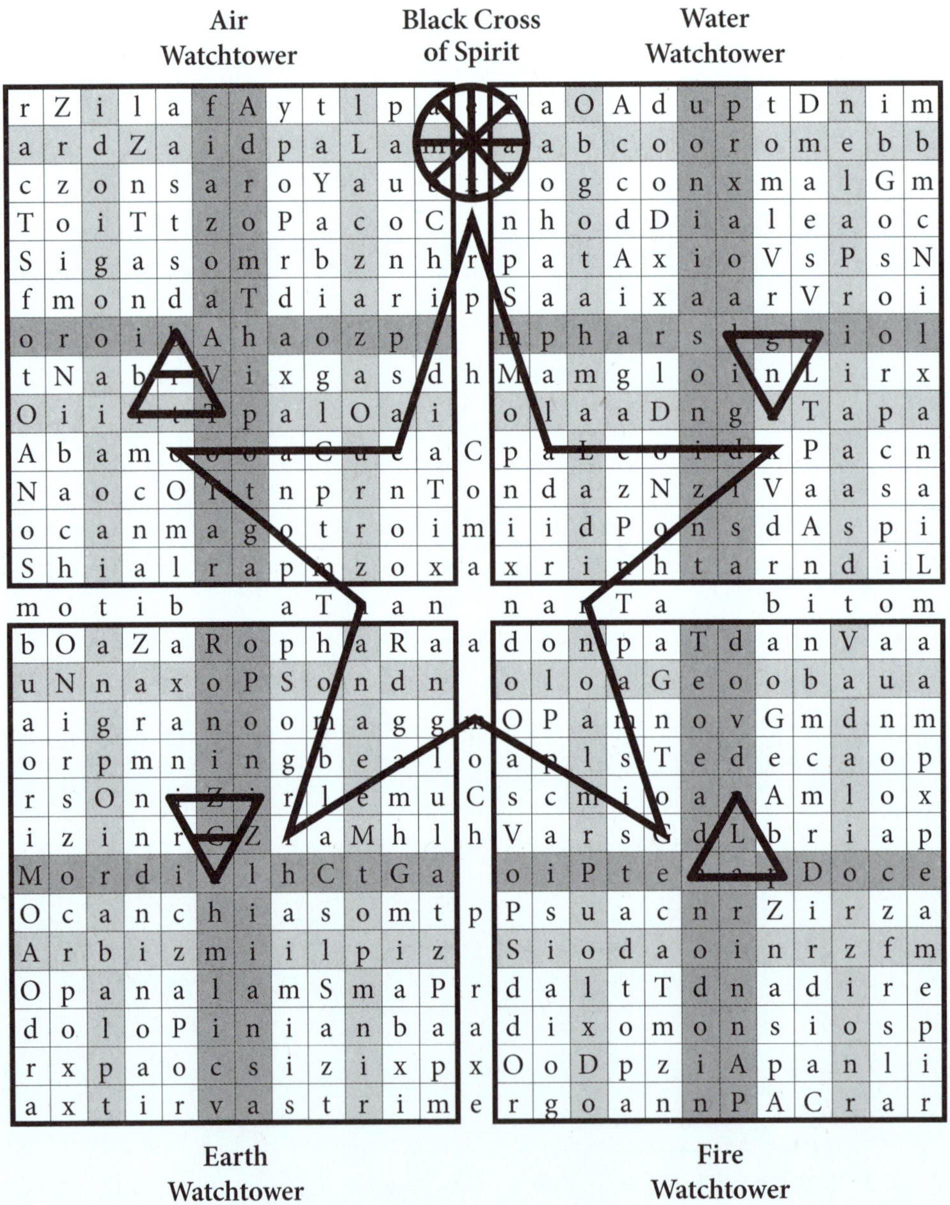

Great Table with Elements

If we overlay a pentagram on the Great Table, we can see how the four smaller tables get their elemental attribution. The upper left is attributed to air, lower left to earth, upper right to water, and lower right to fire. The wheel of spirit touches the cross that separates the four elemental tables.

Sephirotic Angels and the Holy Name

It is easy to get lost in the complexity of the system. There are many ways to spell out names of angels or circuits of creation on the tables, so for now let's focus on the forces we work with the most: the powerful sephirotic angels.

Air Watchtower with Elements

As we mentioned earlier, the Great Table can be broken down into four smaller tables and the Cross of Spirit. If we take the four smaller tables and place a pentagram on them, we see that each small table has four quadrants that have the same correspondences as the elements shown on the pentagram. These quadrants or tablets are called the sub angles. In the example shown, we have the air tablet. In the upper left area, we have the airy part of air; in the upper right, the watery part of air; in the lower left, the earthy part of air; and in the lower right, the fiery part of air.

In each sub angle, there are a number of names, but let's focus on the light gray crosses in each one. Each gray cross spells out the name of the quadrant's sephirotic angel, or the angelic ruler of that sub angle.

In total there are sixteen of these angels. The cross that spells out their name has ten letters, eleven if you count the cross letter twice when spelling out the two-part name of each angel. There is one name for the horizontal bar of the cross and a second name for the upright part. The first name is said to call the angel, and the second is said to command them. We think the idea of commanding them is from another time. To us, the names are more like a username and password to access functions deep within creation. As the Tree of Life symbol has ten sephiroth—eleven if you count Daath—thus these angels are sometimes called the sephirotic angels.

These sixteen angels will be the next group of beings we work with.

Secret Holy Name

The darker gray band across the center of each of the elemental tablets contains another name we will use: the Secret Holy Name. This name consists of three, four, and five letters. For instance, the Secret Holy Name of air is ORO IBAH AOZPI. The first three letters are ORO, the next four letters make the second name, IBAH, and finally there's AOZPI. These are read together as one name.

The four Secret Holy Names are Enochian words of power used to fuse the spirit and elemental pentagrams. These names are the highest of the elemental names from the elemental tablets. We have heard that these names refer to the signs of the zodiac, which makes sense, with three per element.

The first three-letter name refers to the cardinal sign of the element, which represents the first burst of the element coming into being. The second name, which is of four letters, refers to the fixed sign, which is the element cooling off and stabilizing. The final name, which is five letters, refers to the mutable signs, which is the element begging to change into the next element. You can imagine the first name as the element exploding into being, the second stabilizing, and the last changing. We like to say the first name with force, the second flatly, and the last quietly.

In the following list, I include how I say the names. However, you can come up with your own way of saying them as well. Enochian pronunciation is controversial, mostly you read the names as you would if it were English, throwing in a natural vowel sound where needed.

Air: ORO IBAH AOZPI (Oh-Roh IBah A-oh-Zod-Peh)
Fire: OIP TEAA PDOCE (Oh-Ee-Pay Tey-ah-ah Pay-Day-Oh-See)
Water: MPH ARSL GAIOL (Em-Pay Ar-Ss-El Gah-Ee-Ol)
Earth: MOR DIAL HCTGA (Mo-Are Dee-al Hec-teh-Gah)

P•R•A•C•T•I•C•E
EXPLORING ENOCHIAN

For your practice to be and feel authentic, you will need to create a connection to the names and words of power. In this practice, you will sit with the words of power and try to feel them and come up with your own way of pronouncing them, thus making the words your own.

Things You Need

A quiet space

Your journal and your writing utensil

A tarot deck if you have one; pull out the four aces and set them aside

Directions

Perform the Qabalistic Cross (chapter 2) and relax. In your journal, write out the names of the aces, putting each name at the top of a separate page. This will give you plenty of space to write about each name. At the top of one page, write "Bitom: The Ace of Wands," the next "Hcoma: The Ace of Cups," then "Exarp: The Ace of Swords," and finally "Nanta: The Ace of Pentacles." Then meditate or simply free associate on each name. Go one at a time. If you have a tarot deck, look at the ace card while you contemplate the meaning of each name. You should play around with the pronunciation as well and come up with your own way of saying each name. Put your thoughts down on the page under the name.

You can also do the same with the four Secret Holy Names. Give each of them a page in your journal, come up with your own way of saying them, and write down your impressions and ideas. In this way, you will become familiar with each of these powerful words, and they will become your own.

When finished, perform the Qabalistic Cross again. You may return to this practice several times if you like and work through all the names as you have the time for it. You don't need to do all of them at once.

• • • • • • •

Enochian is a powerful and clean tool. While it may seem complex at first, it does have its own logic and internal consistency. This self-referential logic enables us to use it creatively. The Enochian material was given to John Dee, we believe, to enable us to contact the angels and to spur on humanity's evolution. This chapter's practice, "Exploring Enochian," will help you build an authentic connection to this important tool.

P·A·R·T T·W·O
Developing a Practice

— CHAPTER 8 —
Tools

Now that we have covered some of the background of Hermeticism, it is time to develop some of the tools and skills needed to practice. One of the advantages of this tradition is that very little is needed as far as tools and equipment. We have had the good fortune to have an extra room to dedicate as a temple for all of our adult lives. It is full of talismans, swords, cups, robes, and all sorts of fancy, fun things Erich has made himself. However, none of it is really required.

Buy a copy of Crowley's *777* and have the right incense, colors, metals, and such if you wish.[35] It can make the rituals more engrossing, and there is an energetic effect to all the correspondences, as mentioned in the introduction as the principle of Sympethea. At times, we have made our own planetary incense, which is very nice. We even grow some of our own herbs and plants for use in ritual.

But never let the lack of a material or a tool keep you from the work, ever. If all you have is a small space where you can turn in place and quietly say the words, then that is enough. If you have physical limitations that make it difficult to move about, then imagining the rituals in your mind is excellent. In fact, it is considered superior. That is because performing the rites in your mind is called "in the spirit vision," and it is considered to be performing the rites on the inner or astral plane, which is much more powerful.

35. Crowley, *777 and Other Qabalistic Writings of Aleister Crowley.*

Some people may tell you that you must have special materials and go on some complex magical scavenger hunt to gather them, but you don't have to unless you want to. In addition, the old grimoires have complex instructions on special materials, but that is largely due to the extent people had to go through to get paper and ink before Amazon and art stores existed. In the end, the eye of newt turned out to be mustard seeds.

Required Tools

The tools we find ourselves always using are our cups and plates. There are portions of ritual that include making lustral water, which is holy water for blessings. To make it, you combine salt and water to create what is essentially the life-giving waters of the cosmic sea, combining the opposites of water and salt unites the polarities thus going beyond them.

Find a nice small dish you can put some salt on and a nice cup. Use them only for creating lustral water, and put them away when not in use. They can be something you made, or they can simply be any convenient cup and saucer you have. Secondhand stores often have very nice antique sets you can buy for little money. Have these two tools and make them the symbols of your practice, as the two sum up the totality of the great work better than any of the other tools.

Other Suggested Tools

There are a few other tools that are nice to have, but they are not totally necessary.

A Bell

A bell is nice to have for marking the beginning of a ritual. We have one of those chime bells that looks like a metal bar on a wooden stand, and it is rung before rituals instead of knocking. If a ritual says ring the bell *X* number of times, you can knock on the floor or table just as well.

Drawing Tool

It is often nice to have some sort of pointy implement for drawing pentagrams and spirals in the air. A dagger, wand, crystal point, or lit stick of incense may be used. We just use our fingers most of the time, and they work great. However, if you have a favorite wand or crystal, try using it for drawing the shapes in the air.

A Journal

There are many rites in this book. It is fine to read the rites directly out of this book. However, if you can copy them into a journal in your own hand, it may help you connect to them more. In time, you will memorize them if you find them of value and receive benefits from them. It is also important to keep a record of your ritual work, noting anything you find important. This will help you track your progress and will lead to many insights.

A Sword

A sword is used in a couple of practices for separating the mundane from the spiritual. Any sword will do, even a machete. If you decide to include a sword in your practice, you will want to use it only for your rituals. Don't use it to whack weeds after you use it in your sacred work.

Robe or Special Clothing

Wearing a robe or some other special clothing you only use in ritual can make the practice more symbolic. We have made a couple of robes from sewing patterns as a fun craft project. We don't always use them; only if it is a special ritual do we dawn our sacred vestments. When we do group work, everyone wears colors they think are appropriate. For instance, if we are doing something fire-related, everyone wears red and orange. You can also select from your clothing a special set of clothes to wear only in ritual. Even if you choose a certain t-shirt and pair of sweatpants, just keep them separate. You can add magical words and symbols to them too if you wish.

Incense

Incense is great, but it is often problematic. People have allergies, and not every location is suitable for smoke. If you can use incense (and you like it), research different varieties of incense to incorporate into ritual, or just use your favorite. We use both the charcoal resin incense and the stick kind; both have their advantages and disadvantages.

If you use the resin form of incense, you need will to use charcoal bricks as well, but you will then have access to a wide range of quality incenses that are pure; you can get pure frankincense for instance. You will also need something that can handle the heat of the charcoal brick, which is quite intense.

Stick incense is easy to burn, and you can use it like a wand to draw shapes in the air. Stick incense comes in many scents, but you might want a pure scent, such as myrrh, that can be hard to find as a stick but easy to find as a resin.

We use both kinds but favor the Japanese stick incense, which has no wooden stick in the middle. It's just a stick of pure incense. To start, use whatever you like or have on hand. Burn it at the beginning of a ritual to improve the atmosphere.

Tarot Deck

A seventy-eight-card deck is useful for this style of magic. It should be something standard, such as a classic Rider-Waite-Smith, Thoth, or Golden Dawn deck. We advise against getting a highly specialized deck for use in ritual, at least until you are familiar with the system. See chapter 9 for more information on tarot.

Enochian Tools

Many magical tools were used by John Dee and Edward Kelley during their practice. We have made them for ourselves using the instructions in DuQuette's book (see Recommended Reading). These tools include a set of seven talismans, called the Ensigns of Creation; a table to put them on, called the Table of Practice; and a large beeswax seal, which is called the Sigillum Dei Aemeth. These fit together to make a talismanic machine for talking to angels. It works like a magical antenna to improve your reception.

Other Enochian tools include a magic ring, a lamen (a type of talisman worn over your heart), and flags to place around the ritual area. We can assure you that those tools, rings, and tables are not needed for success in using the system. Crowley and the Golden Dawn didn't seem to use them, and for decades, neither did we.

If you find Hermeticism rewarding, you can create the tools later to enhance your practice. We did eventually make all the tools, and we have found that it's the process of *making* all the items that changes you to be better in tune with the system opposed to actually *having* them. Both of us would rather make a crude set of tools out of paper than buy them perfectly made of solid gold.

Storage of Your Tools

Ideally you want to keep your tools in a special place, such as a cabinet or chest, and wrapped in some silk cloth. This is to keep your sacred tools separate from your mundane tools, and silk is thought to have special properties that help contain the magical energy of tools. Always store your tools carefully when not in use. You don't want people picking them up and playing with them, as they are sacred objects.

Tool Consecration

It is traditional to consecrate your tools before using them. This process dedicates the tool to your practice and cleanses it of any prior energies and history. This is often a simple rite, where you bless the tool and cleanse it in some fashion. You can also consecrate through use. This is done just by using the tool. By treating it as a powerful, sacred object, it becomes just that. We consider any tool we create ourselves to be consecrated already, but objects that we buy need some sort of simple ceremony to dedicate them to the great work of our spiritual development.

R•I•T•U•A•L
CONSECRATING YOUR TOOLS

The following ritual can be used to consecrate your tools. During the ritual, you will be creating lustral water, or holy water. The water is sacred and will bless the tools. Gather your tools when you are ready to get started.

Things You Need

Quiet space
Your journal and writing tool
A candle and appropriate candleholder (or a lamp)
Lighter or matches
Stick incense if possible (a single stick is enough)
Salt (any kind will work; use whatever you have on hand)
A plate or saucer
A cup or chalice filled with water
New tool or tools
Optional: Mason jar or other container

Directions

When it's time, sit with your new tools and light the candle or use a lamp if that is not practical. Perform the Qabalistic Cross (chapter 2)

If you can use incense, light the stick and wave the smoke around the tools to purify them. Now welcome them into your home and sacred practice. Say something like: "*I*, (your name), *welcome you as sacred tools to my home and my holy practice. May we achieve success with the great work together*," and "*I bless you in the name of what I hold holy and dear, may you be renewed and reborn in the limitless light*." Feel free to use your own words to welcome and bless the tools.

Next you will create holy water. Place about a teaspoon of salt on the center of the plate. Next, place the cup or chalice of water on the dish, covering the salt.

Over the cup or chalice of water, recite:

Most pure substance, you are the first, without limits,
and without form. You are the basis for all that is.

Lift the cup off the dish and set it nearby, exposing the salt sitting in the middle of the dish. Then say:

Most perfect fractal, you are the second. You are found within all things but
have no substance of your own. You are the pattern of all creation.

Take the dish and carefully pour some of the salt into the cup. Set down the dish and place the cup back upon it.

While mixing the salt and water with your finger, say:

Motion is the child of time and space. All things move and all things change. This
holy elixir embodies the forces of Creation that it may sanctify this sacred space.

Lift up the chalice and say:

Let there be light!

The water in the cup is now holy water. Sprinkle some water over your new tool to bless and consecrate it to the great work. As you sprinkle the water on your new tool, say something to the effect of:

By these most sacred waters, I sanctify you and dedicate you to
the great work. May you be ever effective and pure.

Close by performing the Qabalistic Cross.

When the rite is finished, clean the tools and put them away. We like to leave the cup on the plate so the holy water can slowly evaporate. We normally make it fresh each time we need it.

If leaving the holy water out is not practical, then you can place it in a mason jar or some special container kept for this purpose. If you want to dispose of the holy water, the best thing to do is to pour it on the ground outside; don't just dump it down the drain.

When you bring new tools into your practice you can welcome them the same way.

• • • • • • •

Remember that ritual tools, including Enochian tools, are wonderful, and you are encouraged to use them, but they should not be an impediment to doing the actual ritual work. You can build your tool kit over time with things you find useful as you develop your practice. It is also acceptable to use your imagination where you lack the material object. To start, try to have these tools:

- Cup for water and creating holy water
- Plate to hold salt when creating holy water
- Something for drawing shapes and symbols in the air; a wand or a crystal will do, but you can also use a dagger if that suits you.
- Incense if possible
- A standard tarot deck

— CHAPTER 9 —
The Tarot

One of the tools often used during ritual is a tarot deck, but the tarot is more than just a tool. As we have explained, the Hermetic Qabalah is our main map of the universe on our spiritual journey, and every map needs a key to explain it. The seventy-eight-card tarot deck is just that. Many of the forces we will employ ritually can be expressed by individual cards of a standard tarot deck, and we can use them in ritual to symbolize the forces we are working with.

The first tarot card decks appeared around the early fifteenth century and had nothing to do with the Hermetic Qabalah. The original tarot cards were created from card games and later used for divination. Hermetics saw the potential in using the cards to expound on Qabalah and more easily teach the complex subject.[36]

In the 1800s, influential writer and ceremonial Hermetic magician Éliphas Lévi organized the tarot to better align with the Hermetic Qabalah. Then the Hermetic Order of the Golden Dawn made some final adjustments to the order of the cards, which created the common arrangement of the seventy-eight-card deck that is still most popular today. Aleister Crowley made some controversial but compelling changes for his Thoth Tarot deck, but these changes are not universally accepted.[37] Most seventy-eight-card decks use the Golden Dawn arrangement, and we will use that

36. DuQuette, *Understanding Aleister Crowley's Thoth Tarot*, 85.

37. DuQuette, *Understanding Aleister Crowley's Thoth Tarot*, 88.

arrangement as well. The most well-known and used deck is the Rider-Waite-Smith deck. It was the first popular deck to have an image on every single card. Prior to this, the lesser arcana cards, or small cards, just had wands or cups or swords or pentacles on them. This was similar to the numbered cards in a normal deck of playing cards, which just had a number of hearts, diamonds, clubs, or spades on them. Pamela Colman Smith designed an image for every single card; many of today's modern decks replicate her images in new styles of art.

The deck of tarot cards became a tool for explaining and—more importantly—using the Qabalah as a ritual tool, as well as an oracle. More than just a set of esoteric flashcards, the tarot represents the sephiroth and the paths in action.

The standard seventy-eight-card deck is divided into three sections: the major arcana, the minor arcana, and the court cards. If you wish to find in-depth explanations of the cards, there are numerous books on tarot you can consult. We list some excellent books in the recommended reading section, but one of our all-time favorite books is *The Qabalistic Tarot* by Robert Wang. Wang lists all of the important Qabalistic correspondences in great detail. Lon Milo DuQuette's book *Understanding Aleister Crowley's Thoth Tarot* deconstructs one of the most beautiful decks ever made. Both of these books will help you to understand the underlying structure of the tarot, making it much easier to understand the meanings of the cards. For now, let's look at the organization of the cards to see how we will use each section in ritual.

The Major Arcana

There are twenty-two cards in the major arcana. They correspond to the paths on the Tree of Life. For instance, the card called "the Fool" connects the first sephiroth, Kether, with the second, Chokmah. Each card also corresponds to a Hebrew letter. The Fool corresponds to *aleph*, meaning "the ox," the source of power in ancient times. We can tell from its place on the Tree that the Fool card is about beginnings, about the start of creation.

The image on the Fool card is a buffoon skipping and playing near a precipice. This image is trying to convey the innocence or purity of this force. The Fool is about to begin the journey of creation from which there is no way of knowing what will happen and no return to exactly where the individual started.

The following is a chart with the major arcana correspondences; these are pretty standard. We have taken them from our own personal notebooks and from Wang's *Qabalistic Tarot*.[38] It is an invaluable resource.

38. Wang, *The Qabalistic Tarot*, 49, 51, 126–35.

Title	Number	Letter	Meaning	Association	Path
Fool	0	Aleph	Ox	Air	Kether to Chokmah
Magician	1	Beth	House	Mercury	Kether to Binah
High Priestess	2	Gimel	Camel	Moon	Kether to Tipareth
Empress	3	Daleth	Door	Venus	Chokman to Binah
Emperor	4	Heh	Window	Aries	Chokman to Tipareth
Hierophant	5	Vav	Pin	Taurus	Chokman to Chesed
Lovers	6	Zayin	Sword	Gemini	Binah to Tipareth
Chariot	7	Cheth	Fence	Cancer	Binah to Geburah
Strength	8	Teth	Snake	Leo	Chesed to Geburah
Hermit	9	Yod	Hand	Virgo	Chesed to Tipareth
Wheel of Fortune	10	Calph	Fist	Jupiter	Chesed to Netzach
Justice	11	Lamed	Goad	Libra	Geburah to Tipareth
Hanged Man	12	Mem	Water	Water	Geburah to Hod
Death	13	Num	Fish	Scorpio	Tipareth to Netzach
Temperance	14	Samekh	Prop	Sagittarius	Tipareth to Yesod
Devil	15	Ayin	Eye	Capricorn	Hod to Tipareth
Tower	16	Pe	Mouth	Mars	Hod to Netzach
Star	17	Tzaddi	Hook	Aquarius	Netzach to Yesod
Moon	18	Qoph	Ear	Pisces	Netsach to Malkuth
Sun	19	Resh	Head	Sun	Hod to Yesod
Judgement	20	Shin	Tooth	Fire	Hod to Malkuth
World	21	Tau	Mark	Saturn	Yesod to Malkuth

The Hero's Journey

The cards of the major arcana are also tied to the Hero's Journey, the series of initiations that the soul encounters on its journey to enlightenment. Joseph Campbell, a professor of literature at Sarah Lawrence College, worked in comparative mythology and comparative religion. One of his most influential books is *The Hero with a Thousand Faces*. In this book, Campbell puts forth his theory that there is a monomyth or metamyth that is repeated cross culturally and across time. This is the human story—our story.

Basically, the hero is called, meets a guide, leaves the local society, faces challenges in some sort of other world, and then is transformed by the experience. The hero finally receives a boon, a solution to their problems, which they must bring back to their normal life to resolve the issue that initiated the journey to begin with.

In *The Hero with a Thousand Faces*, the journey has twenty-two stages, just like the major arcana. The cards can be attributed to the stages. In his book *Mastering the Art of Ritual Magick*, Frater Barrabbas relates the twenty-two major arcana to the stages of the Hero's Journey.[39]

Major Arcana	Hero's Journey
Fool	Refusal of the Call
Magician	Self as Exalted Being
High Priestess	Meeting with the Spirit Guide
Empress	Virgin Birth
Emperor	Rescue from Without
Hierophant	Master of Two Worlds
Lovers	Meeting the Goddess
Chariot	Ultimate Boon
Strength	Woman as Temptress
Hermit	Fierce Guardian
Wheel of Fortune	Lesser Ordeals

39. Barrabbas, *Mastering the Art of Ritual Magick*, 129–39.

Major Arcana	Hero's Journey
Justice	Refusal of Return
Hanged Man	Dissolutions
Death	Transformation
Temperance	Reoccurrence of the Boon
Devil	Atonement of the Father
Tower	Belly of the Whale
Star	Emanations from the Void
Moon	Magic Flight
Sun	Freedom to Live
Judgement	The Call to Adventure
Universe	World Navel

We will follow a simplified version of the Hero's Journey, which will inform how we perform our rituals and use the boons gained from them. It helps that the Hero's Journey represents the design of a good ritual practice.

Stage 1 is the Call to Adventure. There is some event or problem, and it calls you to seek answers outside of your normal social setting. The solution you seek is within, and it is there you must go. This stage corresponds to the card Judgement.

Stage 2 is Crossing the First Threshold and Meeting the Fierce Guardian. The threshold represents the limit of what is permitted by society or is capable of definition by the self. The guardian represents the obstruction that caused the transformative powers to be unleashed. Here we must use our wisdom to resolve the issues of our shadow. This stage corresponds to the Hermit.

Stage 3 is Supernatural Aid or Intervention and Meeting the Spirit Guide. Here you encounter the guide of the pathways, the teacher who directs the seeker through the ordeals of self-transformation by offering hope as a protective force. This corresponds to the card the High Priestess.

Stage 4 is the Ultimate Boon. This is when the secret knowledge of the soul is revealed. You receive from the Absolute Spirit a vision that consists of the secret knowledge of your soul, which is your place within the divine plan. This stage's card is the Chariot.

Stage 5 is the Magic Flight and Escape or Crossing the Return Threshold. Having received the boon, you must return and separate truth from illusion, holding on to the wisdom gained and leaving behind the patterns that no longer serve you. This stage corresponds to the Moon card.

Again, while this is a simplified version of the Hero's Journey, it is the pattern of a good ritual design.

The Minor Arcana

The forty small cards, or the minor arcana, deal more with everyday life events and tribulations. The minor cards are also more complex than the major arcana cards. While each major card represents a stage of initiation for our hero, each small card is a mixture of four worldly energies, representing the complexity of life here on earth. Each of these cards is a small world unto itself. The recipe for most of the minor arcana cards is one sephiroth, one element or Qabalistic world, one planet, and one zodiac sign.

Sephiroth

The Tree of Life gives these cards their structure. The small cards are numbered from one to ten and correspond to the sephiroth. In other words, all the ace cards correspond to Kether and are about beginnings or the source of something. All the cards numbered five are about boundary setting in some form because the fifth sephiroth is Geburah, our will or ability to set good boundaries. And so on and so forth.

Worlds

There are four Qabalistic worlds, one for each element. There are four suits in the minor arcana—wands, cups, swords, and pentacles—and each one corresponds to an element and, consequently, to a world. All the wands are related to the element of fire and the world Atziluth, so they will be about inspiration and initiation. They are very energetic cards. All cups will be related to the element of water and the world of Briah, so they will be emotional, creative, and imaginative cards. All the swords will be related to the element of air and the world of Yetzirah, so they will be about thinking, breaking things down, and analysis. There is often a sense of strife in all sword cards, as our process of analysis tends to deconstruct ideas into their components. All pentacle cards will be related to the earth element and the world of Assiah. These cards will all be practical, earthy, and focused on our social structure and activities. They are more outwardly focused than the other cards.

Sign and Planet

The sign and planet assigned to each small card gives further meaning and is why some cards are challenging while others are easier. The Five of Cups' planet and sign is Mars in Scorpio, a very emotional combination. Fiery Mars in watery Scorpio creates discontent and disappointment, which is the standard meaning for the card. As a note, the ace cards have no sign or planet. Only the cards two through ten do. The aces and the pages, which are court cards, are the alpha and omega of each suite, so they don't have this attribution; they are very pure in their energetic signature.

Minor Arcana Card Recipes

In the Pyramid of Power ritual (chapter 21), the cards of the minor arcana are used to create practical effects, as these cards focus on everyday occurrences. For this, we only need to consider the card's sephiroth and world, as we want only positive effects from our magic. If, for example, we remove the planet and sign from the Five of Cups, we get an energy that represents the will of water, emotional strength, and setting boundaries. This signature is much more useful than the feelings of confusion, loss, and sorrow.

In the following chart, you will notice that the signs are listed as cardinal, fixed, or mutable. In astrology, the cardinal signs represent the first energetic burst of an element. Aries, Cancer, Libra, and Capricorn are the cardinal signs and are placed at the equinoxes and solstices. Fixed signs are when the element stabilizes. These are Leo, Scorpio, Aquarius, and Taurus. These signs are in the middle of each season and represent the stable force of that season. The mutable signs are Sagittarius, Pisces, Gemini, and Virgo. These signs are at the end of the season and are in the process of changing into the next element. There are three per suite. The planets rotate according to what area of the sky is assigned to the cards; each gets ten degrees. These cards are also called decans, meaning "ten." In the chart below, you can see that the wands have all the fire signs, going from Aries, which is cardinal, to Leo, which is fixed, to Sagittarius, which is the mutable sign. The other suits follow the same pattern.

Card	Element/World	Sephiroth	Planet	Sign
Ace of Wands	Fire/Atziluth	Kether	–	–
Two of Wands	Fire/Atziluth	Chokmah	Mars	Aries
Three of Wands	Fire/Atziluth	Binah	Sun	Aries

Card	Element/World	Sephiroth	Planet	Sign
Four of Wands	Fire/Atziluth	Chesed	Venus	Aries
Five of Wands	Fire/Atziluth	Geburah	Saturn	Leo
Six of Wands	Fire/Atziluth	Tipareth	Jupiter	Leo
Seven of Wands	Fire/Atziluth	Netzach	Mars	Leo
Eight of Wands	Fire/Atziluth	Hod	Mercury	Sagittarius
Nine of Wands	Fire/Atziluth	Yesod	Moon	Sagittarius
Ten of Wands	Fire/Atziluth	Malkuth	Saturn	Sagittarius
Ace of Cups	Water/Briah	Kether	–	–
Two of Cups	Water/Briah	Chokmah	Venus	Cancer
Three of Cups	Water/Briah	Binah	Mercury	Cancer
Four of Cups	Water/Briah	Chesed	Moon	Cancer
Five of Cups	Water/Briah	Geburah	Mars	Scorpio
Six of Cups	Water/Briah	Tipareth	Sun	Scorpio
Seven of Cups	Water/Briah	Netzach	Venus	Scorpio
Eight of Cups	Water/Briah	Hod	Saturn	Pisces
Nine of Cups	Water/Briah	Yesod	Jupiter	Pisces
Ten of Cups	Water/Briah	Malkuth	Mars	Pisces
Ace of Swords	Air/Yetzirah	Kether	–	–
Two of Swords	Air/Yetzirah	Chokmah	Moon	Libra
Three of Swords	Air/Yetzirah	Binah	Saturn	Libra
Four of Swords	Air/Yetzirah	Chesed	Jupiter	Libra
Five of Swords	Air/Yetzirah	Geburah	Venus	Aquarius

Card	Element/World	Sephiroth	Planet	Sign
Six of Swords	Air/Yetzirah	Tipareth	Mercury	Aquarius
Seven of Swords	Air/Yetzirah	Netzach	Moon	Aquarius
Eight of Swords	Air/Yetzirah	Hod	Jupiter	Gemini
Nine of Swords	Air/Yetzirah	Yesod	Mars	Gemini
Ten of Swords	Air/Yetzirah	Malkuth	Sun	Gemini
Ace of Pentacles	Earth/Assiah	Kether	–	–
Two of Pentacles	Earth/Assiah	Chokmah	Jupiter	Capricorn
Three of Pentacles	Earth/Assiah	Binah	Mars	Capricorn
Four of Pentacles	Earth/Assiah	Chesed	Sun	Capricorn
Five of Pentacles	Earth/Assiah	Geburah	Mercury	Taurus
Six of Pentacles	Earth/Assiah	Tipareth	Moon	Taurus
Seven of Pentacles	Earth/Assiah	Netzach	Saturn	Taurus
Eight of Pentacles	Earth/Assiah	Hod	Sun	Virgo
Nine of Pentacles	Earth/Assiah	Yesod	Venus	Virgo
Ten of Pentacles	Earth/Assiah	Malkuth	Mercury	Virgo

The Court Cards

In the tarot there are four court cards per suit, and they are traditionally used to signify personality types or people in a divination spread. With there being four suits, this gives us sixteen total court cards. In each suit, there is a king, queen, knight, and page. Some decks change the names of the positions, but there will always be four people in each suit in a standard seventy-eight-card deck. For example, in the Thoth deck, the king is called a knight. The knight then becomes a page, and the page becomes a princess. The queen stays the same since the whole process revolves around her. This has to do with Crowley's interpretation of the cards in a Qabalistic sense. Basically he felt that the king was too static a figure and should be active like a knight. In Crowley's view, the queen activated the knight, and together they produced the page. The page then married the princess, and they became the new queen and knight. Lon Milo explains it all very well in his book *Interpreting the Thoth Tarot*. We are only mentioning this here in case you find yourself using a deck with renamed court cards; the energy of the cards is the same no matter what you call them.

When we have things in a group of four, they relate to the elements. In this case, kings are fire, queens are water, knights are air, and pages are earth. Remember that the four suits correspond to the four elements: wands are fire, cups are water, swords are air, and pentacles are earth. Thus, we can deduce the meanings of the cards by knowing that they are an element within an element. For instance, the Knight (air) of Wands (fire) is the airy part of fire. This card represents thoughts of inspiration or leadership.

All court cards except the pages have a zodiacal flavoring, just like all small cards have a planet and sign except aces. That flavor gives them unfavorable attributes, which is useful in divination but not so much in causing positive change.

We will use the court cards to describe elemental forces when we practice the Elemental Octagram (chapter 23), using them as a powerful source of spiritual energy. For now, just consider the following grid of meanings for the court cards. As an exercise, come up with your own meanings for each of the cards in the grid.

	Kings (Fire)	Queens (Water)	Knights (Air)	Pages (Earth)
Wands (Fire)	Fire of Fire · Gnosis	Water of Fire · Intuition	Air of Fire · Leadership	Earth of Fire · Ambition
Cups (Water)	Fire of Water · Oneness with All	Water of Water · Psychic Abilities	Air of Water · Enthusiasm	Earth of Water · Manifestation of Desires
Swords (Air)	Fire of Air · Invention	Water of Air · Artistic Skill	Air of Air · Science	Earth of Air · Discipline
Pentacles (Earth)	Fire of Earth · Abundance	Water of Earth · Fertility	Air of Earth · Planning	Earth of Earth · Healing

P•R•A•C•T•I•C•E
A STUDY OF TAROT

It's time to do some tarot study. This practice may seem like a big task at first, but we're confident you will love the results. You will want to purchase a new journal to keep all your tarot notes in. You can also use index cards; we have used those as well, and they can become your own set of tarot cards.

Things You Need

A quiet space

A new journal just for tarot or a stack of index cards

Your favorite writing utensil

A ruler

Directions

On the first page of the new journal, draw a Tree of Life diagram and label the paths with the major arcana cards and planets, signs, and elements. Next, skip a few pages and start titling each page with one of the major arcana cards. So, title a page "The Fool," skip a page, and title the next page "The Magician," and so on. Then label a section of pages for the minor arcana cards and finally the court cards. Once you have all your headers written out, go back and make notes under each title of all the information we have just presented, as well as any notes you think are important.

We will return to these cards in later chapters, so having this journal will make it easy to look up any correspondences you might be interested in later. You can also add notes to each card from your favorite tarot books. Erich has a journal like this, and it is an invaluable resource. He only wishes he had allowed a bit more space for each card. If you want to do this with index cards, then you will have a tarot deck you've made yourself. What really matters here are the meanings on each card, not so much the art. If you know how the deck is constructed, you don't need the images.

Feel free to be as creative as you'd like. Use colored pens and pencils, markers, or watercolors to create your own artwork. Paste in images and drawings. Make this your tarot scrapbook if you want.

• • • • • • •

The tarot is a tool that helps us to understand the Hermetic Qabalah. By using the structure of the deck, we can design rituals and create ritual meaning. A standard tarot deck has seventy-eight cards. This includes twenty-two major arcana cards, which represent major life initiations or stages on the Hero's Journey, and forty minor arcana cards that represent day-to-day events. Finally, there are sixteen court cards that can represent people or elemental energies. We can use all of these cards to form a language of ritual meaning, allowing us to express exactly what energies we want to work with in a given ritual.

— CHAPTER 10 —
Breathing and Meditation

To succeed in your Hermeticism journey, as well as in life, you will also need good breathing and meditation practices. Being aware and conscious of your breath and your mental processes is important for your health and for working with energy. You will find that energy follows your intent and your breath. All of the ritual work in this book—and pretty much all ritual work in general—involves trance states that we move in and out of throughout our normal day. A meditative practice will make you more aware and in control of your current state of awareness and any trance that comes up doing these practices.

Breathing

In chapter 2, we began the Qabalistic Cross ritual with a foundational breathing technique called belly breathing, or diaphragmatic breathing. This method of breathing promotes a calm state of awareness. Belly breathing can interrupt the fight-or-flight response or feelings of panic and is often taught as an emotional regulation technique. Strive to make this your normal way of breathing, as it is very good for your health and mood.

It is such a good practice that we want to go through it again here. To belly breathe, put the center of one hand on your belly button and the other hand on your chest. Slowly take a gentle, almost imperceptible breath in through your nose, and guide the breath down into the belly. The hand on your chest will sink slightly and the hand on your belly will rise with the inhalation. Although air is not actually filling the belly, it seems that way. Use your imagination and feel the air go all the way down to press against your seat. Spend a few breaths doing this, noticing the areas of tension. Then breathe into the belly and feel an expansion that moves outward, around the sides of your waist and lower back. This ball of air that you are directing into your belly will not seem to expand in all directions, and that is okay. Just maintain a sense of gentle relaxation and awareness of the fullness of the sensation. After inhaling in this way, simply allow the body to exhale on its own. Inhale with intention, then release.

There are additional breathing techniques that are helpful during ritual.

Four-Fold Breath

One such technique is the four-fold breath. The goal of the four-fold breath is to regulate the breathing so the mind becomes regulated. If you are new to the practice, do it routinely for a while—maybe for a few weeks or until you can do it for at least twenty minutes. You will want to feel like you have mastered it.

To perform four-fold breathing, sit comfortably with your back straight. Simply breathe and count to four internally. Breathe in to the count of four, hold to the count of four, exhale to the count of four, and sit with your lungs empty to the count of four. If a four count is too difficult, find a pattern that works. Perhaps two, four, two, four will work best for you. You don't want to strain yourself or hyperventilate; the goal is to have a very conscious control of the breath. Do this for a few minutes. Work your way up to twenty minutes if you can.

One Through Ten Breath

The first thing to do when starting a meditation practice is carve out a space and time. Find a location where you can sit comfortably for awhile. If you have a temple, that is an ideal location. In front of an altar you are working with is an excellent idea. Another good choice is somewhere you can gaze at the sky. Once you have found a spot that you can use regularly as part of your discipline, find a time. Pick a time during the day where you typically have a habit that you would like to replace. For example, if you like to use your phone while you drink your tea in the morning, try meditating and drinking your beverage instead. Morning is a great time for meditation. The most important elements here are undisturbed space and time. These allow you to develop consistency. They are needed for all magical practices but especially meditation.

Once you've chosen a space and selected a time, allow yourself to settle into your seat. This is a basic practice that many encounter early when they learn to meditate, but it will carry you through a lifetime. The one through ten breath provides a great method for centering yourself and facilitating the clear objectivity of mind that we are striving for. This is an outcome of meditation and not the process, technique, or skill that you apply. If you sit and focus on a one through ten breath, you will develop mental clarity and a relationship with the contents of your mind.

It is highly recommended that you set an alarm for twenty minutes so you don't have to keep track of the time. This allows you to let go more fully into the meditation. Spend a few moments allowing the mind to wander and notice the things it goes to. You may journal these as bullet points. Look for patterns and important revelations. Allow your conscious mind to discharge for a few minutes.

When you are ready, turn the attention to the breath and begin counting, using the belly breath. Count one on the inhale, count two on the exhale, count three on the inhale, count four on the exhale, and so on until you reach ten. Then begin counting at one again. When you acquire enough focus, have one count per inhalation and exhalation. Breathe in, then breathe out. Count one, breathe in, then breathe out. Count two and do the same. Do so until ten. Just let the length of the breath be natural and allow the pattern of breathing to find its own rhythm. Like training wheels on a bicycle, these counts provide an anchor for the mind and create centeredness as your mind and your breath come into conscious harmony. You may also continue the breath count to twenty-one or one hundred if you would like to extend your focus.

Alannah has found this practice useful again and again. She still uses this technique. It is difficult to maintain any kind of disciplined practice over a long period of time, and meditation has helped her cultivate that skill, which is so important in spirituality. Use this one to ten count whenever you want to restore your focus on your practice and at the start of every practice, and see what kind of results you get. When you can maintain focus on the breath all the way to ten for at least one round, you will have the centeredness necessary to begin your daily practice, a ritual, or any other spiritual activity.

Pore Breathing

Pore breathing is deep belly breathing while imagining that we are breathing in energy through every pore of our being. The purpose of this exercise is to begin to feel energy flowing through your body.

Visualizations are important. However, it is more important to really feel the flow of energy through your body. When we begin to use elemental and other energies to create sacred geometry, which will magnify an experience exponentially, we want the feeling of flowing energy to very naturally arise within our bodies. By doing these exercises, we can experience this sensation and instantly recall it for more advanced ritual work.

Pore breathing is one of those exercises Erich thought he invented only to find out that Franz Bardon wrote about it in his book *Initiation to Hermetics*.[40] Our approach is a modified version of Bardon's method.

E•X•E•R•C•I•S•E
BASIC PORE BREATHING

To begin pore breathing, we first want to practice visualization and create the sensation of breathing through our skin, through every pore of our being. You can sit or stand for this practice. It doesn't matter as long as you are in a comfortable position and have no discomfort or distractions.

First, perform the Qabalistic Cross (chapter 2) to connect, center, and ground.

Then visualize yourself surrounded by the vast energies of the universe, the natural life force. While belly breathing, visualize the life force as white light flowing inward when you breathe in. Visualize it traveling in through your nose and every pore of your being. The energy flows inward, filling your body with vitality and life. See this life force flowing inward from the universe, from nature, from all the life in the universe.

Now imagine your body is like a balloon filled with this life force. When you exhale, visualize old and stale energy leaving your body through every pore as spent life force. This exhale is taking stagnation and exhausted energy with it, sending it back to the universe to become recharged. You can see it as tiny sparks of life energy. It flows from all life into you during inhale, healing and recharging your body and spirit. The sparks become darkened when they give their life force to you and flow away as you breathe out, taking old, spent, and stagnant energy with them. The dimmed sparks flow outward and are recharged by the unity of being; the spent energy is food for other life just as the bright sparks renew you.

While you are breathing in the life force, scan your body. Are there any places it is not going? Are your feet filling with life force? Are your hands? Scan your entire body

40. Bardon, *Initiation into Hermetics*, 101.

and see if any part of you is not filled with life force. If there are gaps, gently try to direct the life force to those places. Be gentle. That part of you could be injured or could have been affected by a trauma you have experienced. Softly send the healing life force to that area, and see if it fills. If not, let it be for now. Practice this for no more than twenty-one breaths to start with.

When you are satisfied the life force is filling your balloon body, to the best of your ability, try directing the life force to your head and mind to clear your thoughts. See how it feels. Can you feel the life force clearing and expanding your mind? Next, try to direct the life force to your heart center. Can you feel the energy expanding your emotional center, clearing and enlivening your emotions? Finally, see if you can direct the life force to your belly, the cauldron of life force between your ribs and pelvis. Can you feel this area fill with vitality and strength? Sit with this for a while, and just observe the sensations without judgment. When you are ready to be done, finish with one final exhale and perform the Qabalistic Cross to reground yourself.

Eventually, you will want to develop the ability to breathe life force in everyday life. You want to feel the natural flow of life force from the universe, through your being, and back to the universe again. During your normal day, just recall the sensation of pore breathing for a few moments. Eventually it will become your natural way of breathing. This becomes an informal practice.

Meditation

If you have a meditation practice, great! This will be a review that will allow us to define some terms that we will be using. If not, then this will be an introduction to a basic and approachable practice you can use to gain the benefits of meditation. There seems to be a general impression that meditation is difficult or that it involves spacing out, or dissociation.

Meditation skills will allow you to experience the nature of your mind, which is far vaster than we commonly realize. Thoughts are something that we have, not what we are. This practice will cultivate focused attention and a clear, open awareness that will enable you to be more fully in the present. The practice develops strong, stable attention, and it cultivates spiritual awakening. You will need this skill to commune with the forces of the universe.

When Erich first started his practice, he searched for books that would teach him how to control or really observe his mind, and it was hard to find a good one. One of the very first methods he found was the four-fold breath, which was explained at the beginning of this chapter. Once you have become comfortable in that, mindful meditation is the next place to go. Watching your breath can help you to see the activity of your mind and how it behaves. Mindfulness meditation is then watching your mind to observe but not judge its activity. This ability is going to be essential in ritual practice so you can receive the wisdom of the angels. It will also help you in everyday life, as you will gain better control over your own cognitions and behavior.

E•X•E•R•C•I•S•E
MINDFULNESS MEDITATION

In this practice, you will learn to remove the observation of the breath and sit in nonjudgmental awareness.

To start, sit comfortably so you can be alert and aware of your body and surroundings. Observe your thoughts without being sucked into them and without judging them. Try not to relive the past, control the present, or predict the future. Instead, just be present and watch your thoughts without judgments as to whether they are good or bad.

If you find yourself judging any thoughts or being sucked into their current, then observe that. Each time you find yourself being pulled into thoughts of what you must do, what someone said to you, and so on, notice that and go back into nonjudgmental awareness. It is quite difficult. You will be pulled into your wandering mind, but that's fine. In fact, it's expected. The more you do this practice, the better you will get at it.

When you spend some time simply in nonjudgmental awareness, you will see that you are not your thoughts—thoughts are just things that happen. Your thoughts arise, dance around, and then fade away. Most of the mental word play we have is simply a narration of our lives. You might find the thought "Wow, this is hard!" come up for instance. In time, you will see your patterns of thought, where you get stuck, and what comes up over and over. You may start to see your own social programming and recursive thoughts that continually pop up. You will also be able to act on your thoughts and feelings rather than react to them. As always, start slow. Work up to twenty minutes as a goal, though many people meditate for much longer, and it's okay if you do too.

The ability to watch your thoughts will become very useful when scrying (chapter 13). In order to receive the wisdom of the universe, you will need some ability in this area.

P•R•A•C•T•I•C•E
DEDICATION OF MERIT

In Buddhist ritual, called sadhana, there is a constant moral directional force that flows through all the teachings and culminates at the end of every ritual practice. It is called merit. Merit is said to accumulate with time, focus, and activities that carry a beneficial intent for the well-being of others. Just as we do magic to improve our life, fulfill our purpose, and connect to the Holy Guardian Angel, we can choose to do magic for the benefit of others as well. Although this moral force of merit is not a part of all magic, it is a part of ours. We have chosen to incorporate this beautiful gesture of loving-kindness and direct the benefit of our work outward unconditionally toward others.

We at the Temple of Limitless Light like to use a dedication of merit at the end of all of our ritual workings. We feel that this embodies our intent for our magic: to attain an enlightened state of knowledge, wisdom, and a life that is free of difficulties and to then send that intention out for others to benefit. We want to use our magic to create positive benefits for self, community, and world. And thus, we incorporate this prayer called a dedication of merit.

There are a few versions of the dedication, and this specific one is used by Alannah in her daily practice. She was given this prayer by her Lamas, and it is an orally transmitted tradition. Here is a common Vajrayana version of this prayer in English and Tibetan for you to see and speak with the original words.

Tibetan

Jang chub sem chog rin po cheMa kye pa nam kye gyur chig
Kye wa nam pa may wa yang
Gong nay gong du pel war shog

English

By this virtue may I quickly
Attain the state of Guru Buddha, and then
Lead every being without exception
To that very state

Tibetan

Gewa diyi nyurdu dag
Lama sanggye drupgyur nay
Drowa chigkyang malu pa
Kyekyi sala go par shog

English

May the precious bodhicitta
That has not yet arisen, arise and grow,
And may that which has already arisen not diminish,
But increase more and more.

If you want to incorporate this into your own magical practice, you can learn more about it through a good teacher. In Modern Hermeticism, we often talk about learning the original intent of a ritual as it is presented. Once you have a solid understanding of the intent of this ritual and the cultural issues around those who may use it, you can create one using your own language. But you can also use this version:

By the merit of the works we have performed here today, may all beings without exception attain omniscience, be free of needless suffering, and may loving-kindness magnify infinitely throughout all realms of existence.

Things You Need

Quiet space
The Dedication of Merit Prayer in English or Tibetan

Directions

At the end of a ritual or practice. Take a moment to recite a dedication of merit, such as:

By the merit of the works, we have performed here today, may all beings without exception attain omniscience, be free of needless suffering, and may loving-kindness magnify infinitely throughout all realms of existence.

• • • • • • •

Meditation will begin the process of giving you awareness and then control over your own mind. The benefits for emotional regulation and personal awareness are so great, it is almost like a superpower. By using simple breathing practices and mindfulness meditations, you will gain the ability to observe yourself and begin to understand the utter vastness that is you. A dedication of merit said at the end of a ritual or working will align your intent with the most benevolent outcome for all living beings.

— CHAPTER 11 —
sigils

In this chapter, you will learn how to create your own sigils to represent ideas or spiritual forces you want to manifest. This is a very ancient art, and it's quite useful. You can represent an entire idea with a simple design. This design, or sigil, then attracts the energy of that idea into your microcosm to manifest; it is a sort of archetypical image you create for achieving some goal. Once you learn how to make and use sigils, you will be able to use them as talismans, good luck charms, and a shorthand method for contacting spiritual forces at will.

Sigils

A sigil is a magical design that is the signature or symbol of a spirit or an idea or concept, such as prosperity. The tradition of sigil use goes back to ancient Egypt, where the priests used hieroglyphs for magical or religious writings and a simpler alphabet for everyday documents, such as letters or legal proceedings. These hieroglyphic symbols were drawn rather than written and were interpreted rather than read like ordinary writing. In time the ability to interpret the hieroglyphs was lost (and later regained), but the ancient Greeks and other people still recognized the power of these symbols and used them in their magic.[41] The hieroglyphs became talismans of great power and inspired

41. Gordon, "*Charaktêres* Between Antiquity and Renaissance"; Skemer, *Binding Words*.

people to create their own; eventually they became the sigils found in magic books of the Renaissance such as the famous *Sworn Book of Honorius*.

Think of a sigil as an antenna for the spiritual force you want to contact. The sigil is typically placed on an altar or drawn on a tool in something that can be wiped off later. For example, someone might draw a sigil on a magic mirror using soap. Sigils can also be drawn on paper and used as talismans to bring that spiritual force with you. Say you create a healing ritual and invoke an angel that is good at healing sickness. You can charge the sigil while scrying the angel by drawing an invoking spiral over it and then keep the paper sigil in your pocket as a type of informal ritual that will continually draw that healing energy to you. One can also create a book of sigils and charge them by doing ritual work with the book. We have several of these, and the book you are holding now is modeled after Erich's own *Liber Spiritus*.

Creating a Sigil

The process of creating a sigil for an idea or spiritual being starts with a grid of letters or numbers. The name of the spiritual being or concept is spelled out in this grid. The first letter is usually marked with a circle, and the end of the name or word is marked with a flat line. Often, repeating letters or vowel sounds are removed. There are several standard grids in popular use, including the planetary kameas, which are introduced in Henry Cornelius Agrippa's *Three Books of Occult Philosophy*. There is one grid for each planet, so depending on what you want to manifest, you would draw your design on a particular grid (e.g., if you want money, draw your design on the kamea for Mercury). There is also a popular grid of the twenty-two Hebrew letters called the Golden Dawn Rose Wheel. The Rose Wheel can be found in many of the books on the Golden Dawn written by Israel Regardie and Chic Cicero and Sandra Tabatha Cicero. We have used both the Rose Wheel and Agrippa's grids, and they are just fine. However, when Erich started working with the Enochian angels in earnest, he needed a way to create sigils to represent the angelic powers. To ask the angels for the inspiration for a sigil method, he created a working that took several days and invoked some of the archangels that were contacted by John Dee. From Raphael, Michael, Gabriel, and Uriel, he requested a method of making sigils to represent the Enochian forces. What he received took a while to unpack and understand since he is not the scryer that Edward Kelley was. What follows is the basics of the method Erich received.

The design of Erich's grid is a triangle made of three smaller diamond-shaped grids. This works perfectly as there are twenty-one Enochian letters, meaning there are three groups of seven letters. Once Erich had pulled the grid out of his subconscious, he was able to place the letters in the grid by giving them more meaning, relating them to their Hebrew equivalents by the sounds of the letters. This grid, called the Trigon, gives us (and now you) a unique method of creating sigils in Enochian and also English to represent the Enochian angels and any concept you wish to manifest.

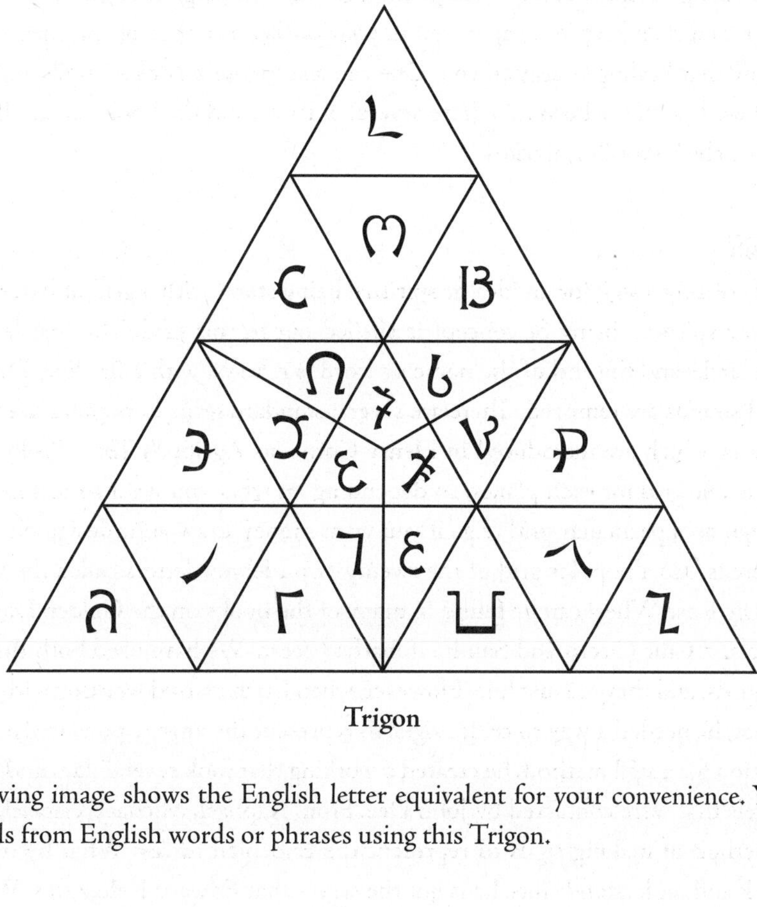

Trigon

The following image shows the English letter equivalent for your convenience. You can create your own sigils from English words or phrases using this Trigon.

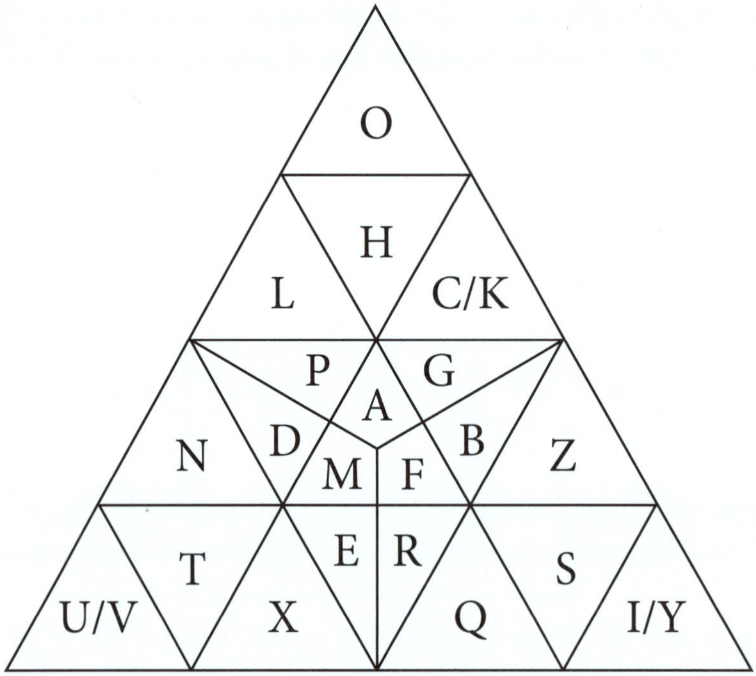

English Trigon

The method of creating a sigil using this grid is simple, and it generates some very beautiful designs. First, decide on a word that you would like to transform into a symbol. You can also use a phrase, but keep it simple. Two or three words will do. Place a sheet of paper over the grid, and mark the first letter in the first word with a small circle. Then draw a line to the next letter and the next until you are finished. Mark the end with a cross to indicate the end of the word. If there are repeating letters, such as *oo* in *look*, for instance, draw a spiral. If a letter repeats after another letter, such as *aba* in *abacus*, draw a line from *a* to *b* and then an arch back to *a* so it looks like a *D* shape.

If this sounds confusing, don't worry. We have an exercise that will walk you through making one of our favorite sigils. It is the sigil for air of water, or the Knight of Cups.

P•R•A•C•T•I•C•E
HOW TO MAKE A SIGIL

The following practice shows you how to create a sigil for an angel's name or any concept. In this example, we're drawing the sigil for the Knight of Cups. This tarot card has a beautiful sigil that we believe expresses the effervescence and joy of the sentient energy. The airy part of water, the Knight of Cups, shows joy, enthusiasm, and forgiveness for others. Its name is OBGOTA AAABKO.

You Will Need

The Trigon image (English)

Some tracing paper

A ruler

A drawing tool, such as a pencil; you can start with something that can erase, then color it in ink

Directions

We start the design of this sigil by placing a small circle over the first letter of the first name, *O*. Normally, we would mark this on tracing paper placed over the Trigon. To illustrate this, we grayed the Trigon to create some contrast. Then we use the ruler to help us draw a line to the second letter, *B*. Now, if we were to connect to the next letter, *G*, we would have to trace over the line we drew from the *O*, which means this new line would not show. In this case, we draw an arch to the G, and now we can see the line. See step 1.

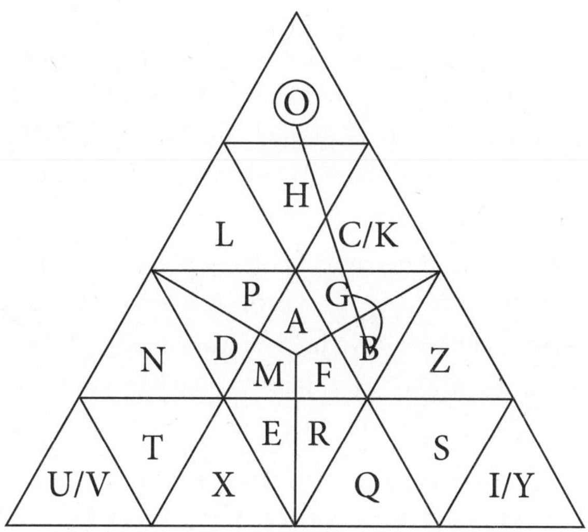

Step 1

Since the next letter is O, we draw another arch to the letter O. See step 2.

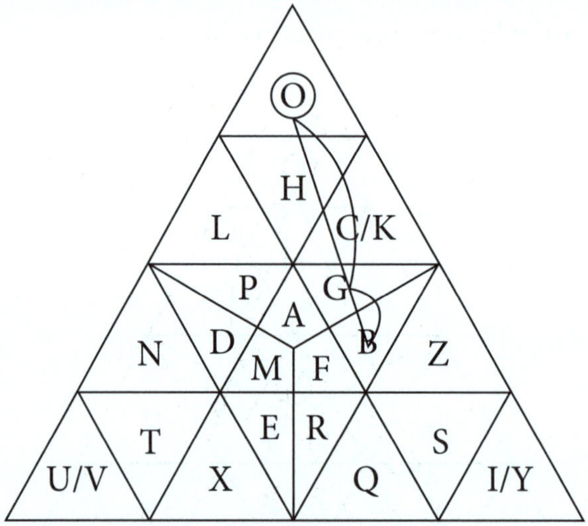

Step 2

We then complete the first name by tracing a line to *T* and *A*, and finish with a little cross mark to denote the end of the design. See step 3.

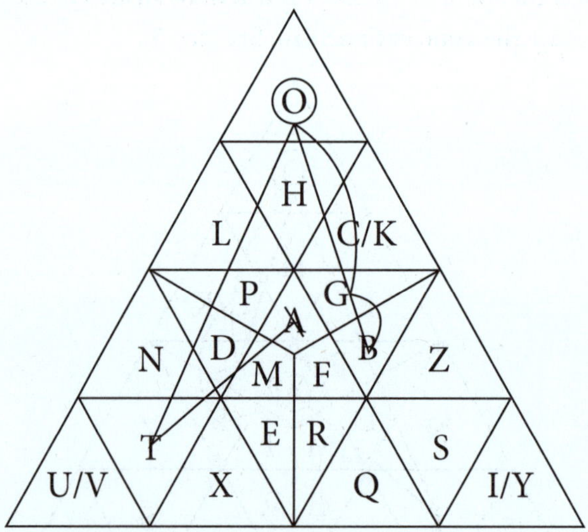

Step 3

Now we need to add the second set of letters. Since the second name begins with *A*, we need to draw a circle there to denote the start of the design. Then we have two more *A*s. We can indicate this by drawing a spiral. See step 4.

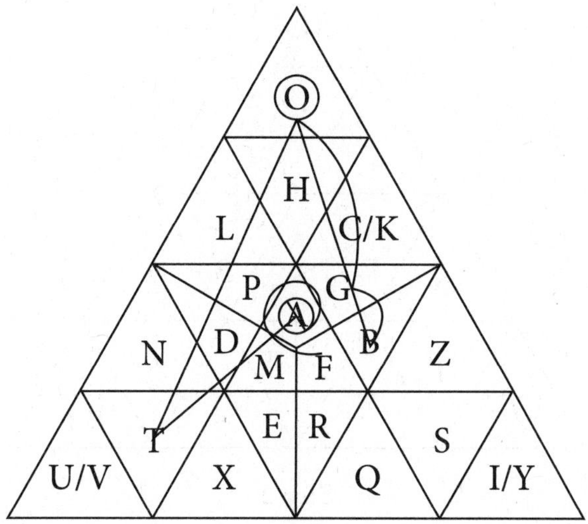

Step 4

We then connect the spiral to the letter *B* and draw an arch to the letter group *C, K*, as those two letters are the same in Enochian. See step 5.

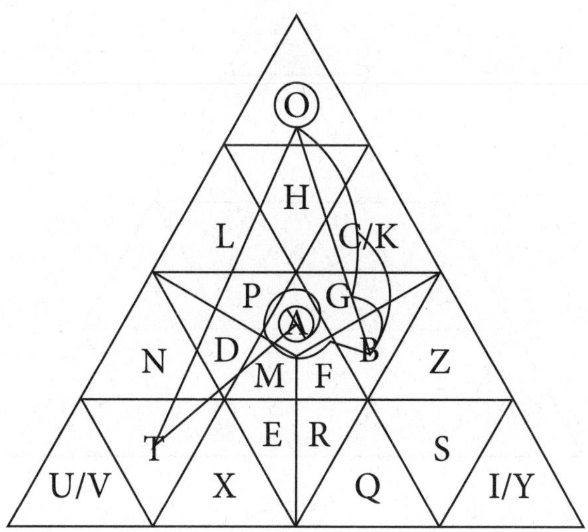

Step 5

Finally, draw an arch to the last letter, O, and add a little cross to indicate the end of the design. See step 6.

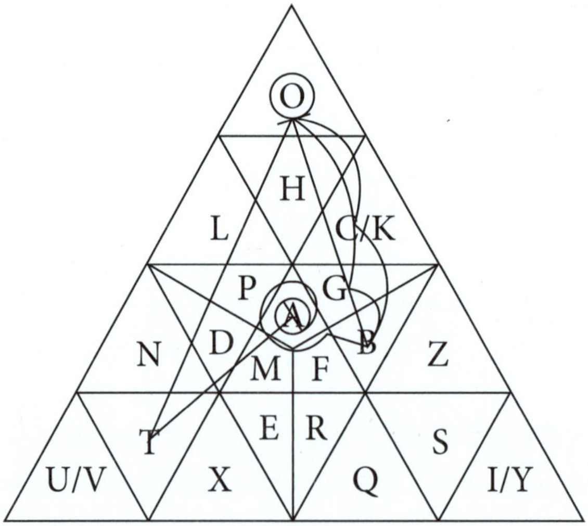

Step 6

The final sigil would look like this.

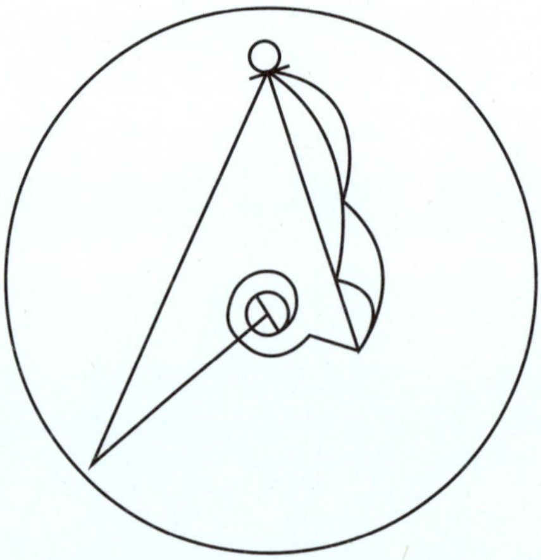

Finished Air of Water Sigil

• • • • • • •

Sigil creation is a way to represent your goals or spiritual forces with a single symbol. This concentrates and simplifies the expression to your goal or spiritual force with a creative design that you can use as a talisman or reminder of what you are trying to manifest or connect with. You can use this method with Enochian words or names, or you can simply spell out the name of something you want to manifest in your life, such as prosperity or a new job. Then you can charge the image using ritual work in this book. Feel free to be creative with this method. Use color if you wish; inks made from plants and herbs that are related to your goals are excellent options.

— CHAPTER 12 —
pentagrams and spirals

When working with elemental forces, the symbols we use are mainly pentagrams drawn with different starting points. The pentagram is chosen because it can be drawn in the air with the hand or another implement in one motion, and it can represent all four elements and two of spirit.

The pentagram is a symbol of power in American culture. Consider the star police wear over their hearts and the white star displayed on military vehicles; it is not a coincidence that this symbol was chosen. We are sure you can think of other examples where the five-pointed star is used. The shape of the star has long been imprinted on our collective consciousness as a symbol of power and protection. Consider this pentagram with the elements marked on it. This pentagram was shown in the chapter on Enochiana (chapter 7). This pattern is the standard way of laying the elements on a pentagram shape.

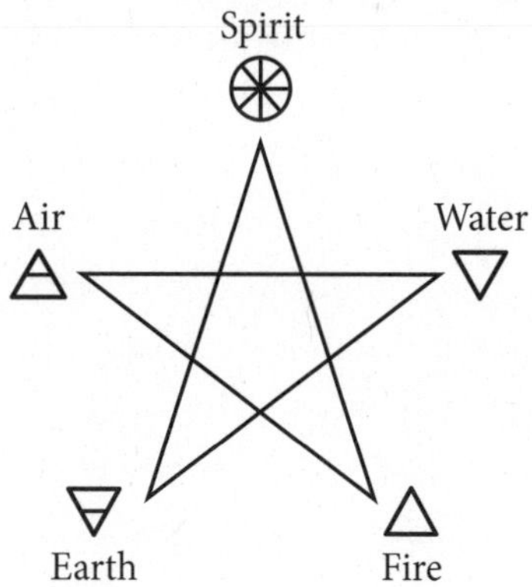

Pentagram with Elements

The drawing of the pentagrams is new to most of our students, but people who practice Wicca or forms of ceremonial magic are quite familiar with the practice. The intent is to "tune" an area to have a particular energy; we will be using this technique often.

In the illustrations of the pentagrams, you can see the wheel of spirit at the top point. Spirit is the fifth elemental energy and acts as both a glue holding the elements together and a grease separating the elements so they retain their individuality. It is also the life force animating the elements.

Invoking and Banishing Pentagrams

When we call something to us, we are invoking that something. So, if we invoke water, we are calling water energy to our area or to the forefront of our consciousness. Likewise, if a ritual is designed to invoke a spirit, that ritual calls, or invites, that spirit to pay us a visit and communicate. Banishing is a little more complicated. It's not just pushing something away. Instead, it's more like cleansing that thing. When we banish earth energy, we clean the earthy energy in our area, and since earth energy contains all four elements and two of spirit, those get cleaned up too. If you were to banish a spirit, then you would cleanse the area of that spiritual energy, or at least its negative aspects. Generally, we invoke, or call, by drawing the pentagram toward each element. We banish by drawing the pentagram away from an element.

For example, one would invoke earth energy by starting at spirit and going toward earth; from there, drawing the rest of the star should be obvious. To banish earth, one would start in the lower left corner and go up to spirit.

Likewise, to invoke fire, start at spirit and draw toward the lower right side.

Air and water are very easy. For water, start at air on the upper left point and draw toward water on the upper right point, then continue until you have a complete star. Air is the opposite. Start at the upper right point and draw across to air, then just follow the natural progression until you have a complete star.

The force of spirit is special, though, and it requires more explanation. If you look at the diagram of the elements on the pentagram, you will see that the element of spirit is symbolized by a circle with eight spokes. If you use your imagination and visualize that there is a person in the pentagram, their head would be the top point, their two hands in the side points, and their feet would be in the bottom two points. Between the bottom two points would be the person's genitals, the place that spirit is manifested into the material world through birth or impregnation. To invoke spirit active, we will connect the two active elements of fire and air across this point. For spirit receptive, we connect the two receptive elements, earth and water, across this point.

While we can draw banishing pentagrams for all the elements, we have only ever used banishing earth. That is because the element earth is considered by most practitioners to contain all the other elements, so by banishing earth energy, we clean and straighten out all the other elements at once. We are sure there are circumstances where someone may want to use the banishing form of other elements. For example, someone may want to banish fire to create calm. In that situation, we would rather invoke water. If we want to disperse the energies of a pentagram we have drawn, we use a banishing spiral. Once you are familiar with the elements and ritual design, you can create your own methods.

Spirals

When we draw pentagrams or other shapes in the air, we infuse them with qualities by imagining color and light and through the way we draw them. To really activate these forms, we need to then imbue them with energy using an invoking spiral.

In the original rituals invented by the Hermetic Order of the Golden Dawn, the pentagram forms were activated by a gesture called the Sign of Horus the Enterer. This sign is made by putting one's palms together and projecting your arms forward like your hands are a spear. Some magical phrase is then said to activate the pentagram.

The invoking spiral is a gesture that imitates the more traditional witches' spiral dance. The spiral dance is a ritual action that generates great power when done in a sacred context. Participants dance from the outer rim of a circle to the center going clockwise, or deosil, while in an ecstatic trance.

In our tradition, we use spiral forms to activate and deactivate signs we draw in the air. The invoking spiral is drawn starting at the groin. You then draw a spiral over the sign you made previously, moving clockwise to the top of your head, around to your navel, up to your forehead, down to your solar plexus, and up to your neck before finishing in your heart. Imagine that you are concentrating energy in the center of the sign you just drew.

You can also draw invoking spirals over talismans or crystals to imbue them with power. We sometimes vibrate a name or a word of power while we make the sign, which is a very powerful practice. If this feels like too many things at once, just say the word and then draw the spiral. We will be using invoking spirals *a lot*, so practice it a bit. Draw the spiral outward to inward like you are gathering energy and concentrating it in the center.

To practice, try drawing spirals over a crystal or to bring healing energy to a plant.

When you are finished with a ritual or a practice or you want to disperse some energy, use the same movement in reverse. Start at your heart and move outward three times counterclockwise. Imagine that you are dispersing whatever sign or energy you want to go away. We liken it to scrubbing away the mark of the sign or clearing cobwebs.

P•R•A•C•T•I•C•E
DRAWING PENTAGRAMS IN THE AIR

The following practice will get you started drawing symbols—in this case pentagrams—in the air. Note that if you do only the four listed invoking practices, you should be able to sense some difference between them. If you can't feel anything or they all seem the same, then practice a bit more. Try visualizing the pentagrams as being made of the element or blue flame. Play around with this to find what works for you, and you should get some effect.

Things You Need

Quiet space

Your journal

A writing utensil; you can also use colored pens or pencils

A ruler

Your favorite pointy thing for drawing pentagrams in the air or your finger

Preparation

In your journal, trace or draw a large pentagram shape. Make it as big as you can on the page, and use a ruler to draw straight lines if needed. Then label the locations for fire, water, air, earth, and spirit. If you like, use colored pens or pencils to color the symbols. Use red for fire, blue for water, yellow for air, and green or brown for earth. You will want a nice image you can use for the study along with another page or two for additional notes as you do this exercise. You may have feelings or images come up, and you will want to note those down.

Directions for Elemental Pentagrams

Before doing one or all of the following, perform the Qabalistic Cross (chapter 2). Then follow the appropriate directions.

Banishing Earth

This is the pentagram we create the most as part of our daily practice. While the other forms of the pentagram call energy, this one *cleanses* energy, so it should feel a bit different. We will do it first to get the space clean and ready. The other pentagrams invoke, or call, energy, and we generally clean up the area before calling anything in. This is a standard practice. It is like cleaning the kitchen before making a meal.

Open your journal to the pentagram drawing you made and point at the earth symbol. This time we draw *away* from the symbol, toward the spirit wheel at the top of the star, then down to fire, up and to the left to air, across to water, back down to earth, and finally up to spirit again. This is the pattern for banishing earth.

Next, draw the banishing earth pentagram in the air before you. Slowly and carefully draw the star shape in the air. Follow your chosen tool or pointer finger with your eyes while keeping your head still as possible. What comes up for you as you do this? Often, thoughts will shake loose and flutter across one's awareness. Just watch them go by. Then empower the pentagram with an invoking spiral. We are often asked why we use an invoking spiral on a banishing pentagram. What we are doing is empowering, cleansing, and purifying the pentagram, but that doesn't sound as cool. Basically, you are pouring bleach in the mop water. Draw the invoking spiral carefully, just as you did in the initial practice, breathing energy into it as you draw it over the pentagram in the air. You don't really need to banish this one unless you feel the need; it will tend to cleanse the space of any negative influences. You will learn a daily practice using the banishing earth pentagram in chapter 15.

Invoking Earth

When it comes to the element of earth, we need to do both the invoking and the banishing forms; both are very useful. In your journal, point at the spirit wheel at the top of your drawing, then trace an imaginary line down to the earth symbol, up to water, across to air, down to fire, back up to spirit, and down to earth again.

Now draw the invoking earth pentagram in the air before you, using your imagination and moving your finger or your favorite pointy thing. Slowly and intentionally draw the star in the air before you. Take your time and draw it with care. When you finish the shape, empower it as before with an invoking spiral. Sit with your empowered pentagram and see what comes up. When ready, disperse it as before, with the banishing spiral.

Invoking Fire

Now we will invoke fire. Again, look at the image in your journal and point at the spirit wheel at the top of the pentagram. This time, trace down to fire, up to air, across to water, down to earth, back up to spirit, and back down to fire.

Now draw the invoking fire pentagram in the air in front of you. Slowly trace the shape. When you are finished, draw the invoking spiral carefully over the shape while slowly exhaling into the drawn shape, imagining it filling with energy. Once you are done, sit with the shape for a minute. Try to see the shape in the air if you can, or just feel or know it is there. Then, with feelings of gratitude, disperse the shape with a banishing spiral. Point at the center and make three turns counterclockwise from the center out, imagining that you are breaking the lines of force like cobwebs, scattering the energy.

Invoking Water

Now it is the time for water. Look at the image in your journal and point to the air symbol. Slowly and with intention, draw an imaginary line across to water, then down to earth, up to spirit, down to fire, back up to the left side to air, and back across to water.

Next, draw the water invoking pentagram in the air before you. Slowly draw it, and as with the others, try to hold your head still and follow your hand with your eyes. Then over the pentagram, draw the invoking spiral as before, going outside to inside clockwise three times. Exhale slowly, filling the pentagram with energy. Sit with this and feel the energy, or just see what comes up for you. When ready, disperse the pentagram with the banishing spiral. Start at the center and move counterclockwise outward three times. Feel the energy being dispersed.

Invoking Air

Finally, we will invoke air. Point at the water symbol in your journal and draw an imaginary line to air, then down to fire, up to spirit, down to earth, and back up to water. Complete the image by returning to air.

Next, draw the invoking air pentagram in the air in front of you. Just as before, draw the shape slowly and with intention. Don't rush. Hold your head still and follow your hand with your eyes. When you are finished, empower the pentagram with an invoking spiral. Breathe out slowly, and imagine the star filling with energy and shining or burning brightly. After you empower the pentagram, sit with it and note any feelings or insights that come up. Then disperse the pentagram as before with the banishing spiral. Feel the lines of forces breaking and dissolving.

Directions for Spirit Pentagrams

Spirit pentagrams are special. As mentioned earlier in this chapter, you draw the pentagram for spirit active by connecting the active elements, fire and air, and the pentagram for spirit receptive by connecting the receptive elements, earth and water. In ritual these can be used to empower other pentagrams to give them a boost, and they then can be used to create an axis mundi in the center of the space, a connection between above and below. In the Greater Ritual of the Pentagram (chapter 20), you will use the spirit pentagrams to supercharge another pentagram. During a temple consecration (chapter 17), you will use them to connect above and below, to act as a connection between above and below and also as a supercharger as the active and receptive change places like an alternating current.

Spirit Active

Let's start with spirit active. Open your journal to the pentagram drawing you made, and starting with fire, trace up to air, then to water, down to earth, up to spirit, down to fire, and back up to air. This is the pattern for spirit active.

Next, trace the same pattern in the air in front of you. Just as before, take it slowly and intentionally. Draw the shape and notice anything that comes up. Empower the shape with an invoking spiral, and see if anything changes for you. If not, that's okay. Sit with this for a time, noticing any feelings or thoughts, then banish as before with a banishing spiral, clearing away the lines of force.

Spirit Receptive

Finally, we will finish these exercises with spirit receptive. On the pentagram you drew in your journal, trace an imaginary line starting at earth. Move up and to the right to water, then across to air, down to fire, up to spirit, down to earth, and back up to water. This is the pattern for spirit receptive.

As before, draw the shape in the air before you. Draw it slowly and mindfully. Be aware of anything that comes up as you do so. Then empower the pentagram with an invoking spiral. Breathe into the star shape as you draw the spiral. Sit with this for a while and note anything that comes up in your journal. When you are done, banish it with the banishing spiral.

• • • • • • •

Drawing pentagrams will enable you to tune a space to have a very specific energy signature. The spirals will enable you to further empower the pentagram or to banish them away once your ritual is finished. We don't want to carelessly leave our magic up once we are finished with a practice or ritual. Memorizing the various invoking and banishing pentagrams will make your practice much more effective.

— CHAPTER 13 —
The Art of Scrying

Scrying is how you communicate with the spiritual forces of the universe. It is the act of sitting mindfully and communing with a spiritual force you have called or invoked to ask for its wisdom or some other favor. The communication happens entirely in your mind. While the experience is somewhat like daydreaming, it is much more focused. When authentic, scrying has a feeling of clarity to it that is not felt in ordinary dissociation.

The images you see of wizards with crystal balls and black mirrors are the fantasy versions of this very real practice. Scrying is similar to the practice of channeling, but the difference is that when scrying, you choose the spiritual intelligence you wish to communicate with and then perform a ritual to tune into that flow of spiritual intelligence and energy. Very often we see people perform a ritual from a book, and then nothing seems to happen. No spirit appears, and they wonder what to do. The usual advice is to continue as if the spirit was there, but the problem is that they were never instructed on how to properly communicate with the spirit after all that ritual work.

There are several ways to scry, and for all of them, you will need the sigil, or signature, of the spirit you want to contact. We provide the approved sigil for all of the spiritual forces we work with in this book, and you can find the method for producing the symbols in chapter 11. You can find the sigils of other spirits in various books, but the ones you make yourself will be the best.

Let's start with what we have found to be the simplest and most effective method of scrying and then discuss the more exotic methods.

Trance States

The purpose of ritual work and invocations is often to induce a specific sort of light trance that attunes to the spiritual force you are wanting to contact. A trance state is defined as an altered state of consciousness where you are neither asleep nor completely awake. You can be in a trance and not know it, and you probably often are. We go in and out of various states of consciousness all day, but creating a focused state of trance at will is a skill you will acquire doing this type of spiritual work.

To begin, first create a sigil for your target spirit. Then view the sigil. You can either look at it in this book or draw it out. Then perform a ritual from this book, such as the Greater Ritual of the Pentagram (chapter 20), and just sit as you would for meditation and watch what comes up. If nothing comes up immediately, then look around in your mind to see if a daydream is happening. If you can't find the daydream, then start daydreaming about the entity you want to contact or the subject you need answers to. You can also repeat the final invocation or chant the name of the spirit you are reaching out to.

It is important to be interactive. Too much emphasis is often placed on being neutral and waiting for a message, as if we could be objective about this very subjective experience. Expecting the spirit to do all the work in communicating is setting too high an expectation. You often need to reach out with your own imagination to make contact and begin the process of communication. This is the Hermetic principle of Imagination as an Organ of Perception.

When you get an image, you may need to interact with it to get the vision going. For instance, if you see a bicycle, hop on it and ride it; if you see a cup of liquid, then drink it. You can't be hurt by anything that happens in a vision, so be willing to take risks. While we accept in movies that if you die in the Matrix, you die in real life, this is just for dramatic fun. In visions, you can have all sorts of adventures with no harmful effects or even fear. Erich has had visions where he stood on high places or saw monsters and such, and it is never even scary.

Some visions stay dreamy and indistinct. Some entities are really not that visual, and you get more of a body sensation. For instance, a water spirit might be very visual, but an earth spirit may manifest as more of a body sensation or vibration. Sometimes when Erich is interacting with a vision, there is a very noticeable shift from the indistinct, dreamy quality to a movie-like clarity. When this shift occurs, that is when the real vision happens, and it is very often quite profound. These movie-like visions often involve all his senses. Erich can hear, see, taste, smell, and feel the environment.

When you first make contact with an entity, ask a series of questions to make sure you have the right spirit and to gain further insight into the spirit's nature. Ask the spirit, "What is your name?" Then, "What is your nature?" and "What wisdom do you teach?" The first time you encounter a spiritual force, simply ask for its wisdom and get to know it. The forces in this book are not the type of spiritual forces that you can boss around and demand things from. You can only get away with being bossy if you work with the chthonic forces, but then you have to deal with all the nonsense that comes along with them. The spiritual forces in this book are angelic, so you can work with them to get their wisdom and their patronage. Once you've done that, ask for the changes you want in your life. We are forging working relationships with the spiritual forces of the universe; this is a power *with* relationship rather than a power *over* relationship.

While we would not expect a technicolor, amazing experience on the first try, it can happen and is okay. You can always end a session at any time if you ever feel uncomfortable. To end a session, just open your eyes, thank the spirit, and do the Qabalistic Cross.

You will want to journal while you are scrying or immediately after. Some people like to use a recording device and dictate the experience. Write down whatever feelings come to you as well as any images and words. Journal writing is very important, and it can be messy and misspelled. Impeccable grammar and spelling are not necessary when journal writing. Scribbled keywords, quick doodles, and so on can all be helpful in later recalling the experience. Visions are like dreams and difficult to recall later. It is best to make some notes right away to act as an anchor for your memory.

Other Methods of Scrying

We have experimented with many methods of scrying, including some that you might find useful such as the focus method, a black mirror scrying, and the operator method. These all have their use, and you may find them more effective than the trance method we like. Consider these three popular methods and experiment with each to find the practice that is most effective for you.

Focus Method Scrying

The focus method involves using something to rest your eyes on while you allow yourself to go into a trance state. A crystal ball, flickering candle flame, and bowl of water with some ink added are all examples of a focus you can use. The method is quite simple and can be very effective for some people. First, find something you think is a good magical receptor. It is usually best if it is something shiny or reflective, such as a crystal ball or a pool of water. When you are ready to scry, just rest your gaze on the object and allow your vision to relax. The images will still form in your mind as before, or at least we have never seen them appear in a crystal or the focus itself. Some people like this, as it gives them a target to focus on.

Black Mirror Scrying

There is also a method developed by the great Carroll Poke Runyon using a black mirror. In his book *The Book of Solomon's Magick*, Runyon describes a method where you use a black mirror and low light, just two candles held beside your face on either side.[42] When you look at your dark reflection in the mirror, your brain struggles to interpret the image. The ritual work you are doing tunes you to the frequency of a particular energetic intelligence that can create very spectacular visions in the glass.

You can experiment with this method using the children's game that helped to inspire it. The game is called Bloody Mary. Light a candle, take it with you into a darkened bathroom, and close the door. The only light in the room should come from the candle. Look at your reflection in the bathroom mirror and notice how it becomes distorted as your brain tries to interpret the image. If you're really brave, say, "Bloody Mary" three times and see if anything happens.

While we don't often use this method ourselves, we have experimented with it and thought it was worth mentioning. You can find a black mirror online or in your local crystal shop; they are often made of obsidian stone and are quite beautiful. Erich's cost him fifty bucks. Optionally, you can find a piece of flat glass and color one side black; spray paint works well for this. A painted piece of glass makes an excellent black mirror. Often people mark the sigil of the spirit to be scried on the mirror with soap or some other material that can be wiped off later.

Operator Method of Scrying

In some traditions, there is a person dedicated to the act of scrying (that person enters into the trance), and other people, who remain in the waking world, ask that person questions. In the Temple of Limitless Light, we have experimented with this method, but we don't prefer it. In our temple, we have always preferred to allow all of the members of our group to have their own personal vision. We have a time after the working to share our experiences, except of course those that we find to be too personal. Most of the work we do, we do as a group. We often divide up parts of the rituals so everyone can be involved at their own level of comfort and skill.

42. Runyon, *The Book of Solomon's Magick*, 32.

License to Depart

Once you are finished with your vision work and anyone else participating is done as well, it is important to wind things down and retrace your steps. Offer thanks to the spirits you have invoked and give the license to depart, as it is traditionally called.

For our work, a license to depart would look something like this: "We thank you, spirit, (Name), for your wisdom and aid in our spiritual searching. Leave if you must. Stay if you can." That is all that will be needed for the spirits in this book.

Dispel any magic circles you may have cast and perhaps say a dedication of merit. You may not realize how deeply into the trance you have become during the working, so winding things down and bringing yourself back to normal consciousness is just as important as any other part of the ritual.

Remember that a ritual, whether it includes scrying or not, is a journey out of the normal world of our culture and normality and into the underworld of our sub- and superconsciousness to gain a boon or insight that we need to carry back into our so-called normal lives. By having a process of return, we can bring our insights back and reenter a grounded nontrance state of mind. This process of return gives the ritual process closure. Concluding with a short journal writing or sharing time afterward helps to cement any insights gained by the whole adventure.

P•R•A•C•T•I•C•E
AN EXPERIMENT WITH SCRYING

In this experiment, you are going to try to scry an angelic force in order to get some ideas about what the force is before reading about it in this book. No cheating. This force is a good angel, and you'll like this one. Note that the listing for this angel is on page 262. Check your results after the experiment.

Things You Need

Quiet space

Your journal and a writing utensil

A ruler

Your favorite instrument for drawing the pentagrams in the air or your finger

Directions

In your journal, draw or trace this Water of Water sigil.

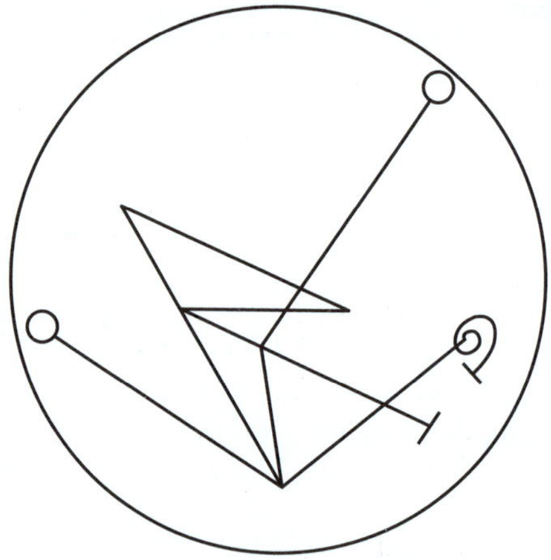

Water of Water Sigil

Find a quite space and perform the Qabalistic Cross (chapter 2), then the Mindfulness Meditation (chapter 10).

Next, view the sigil you drew in your journal. Just look at it and be mindful of anything that comes up in your consciousness. If the symbol does not bring anything up, that's okay.

Vibrate the name of the angel a few times, and again, see if you get any images or feelings. The name is NELAPR OMEBB (Nel-ah-Par Oh-meb-beh).

If you do get some images, go into them, whatever they are, and explore the images and feelings without judgment.

If you do not get anything, then continue to gaze at the image, and remember a time when you were having fun near water. It could be a time at a pool, by the sea, anything water related. Go into that memory while you are looking at the sigil and vibrate the name again. Go into your memory and see if anything changes. Is there anything new? If so, explore what you find. If not, put this aside for now and come back to the exercise at a later time.

You can also try this same experiment with a black mirror or other focus and see if you like the other methods of scrying.

Close with the Qabalistic Cross and a dedication of merit.

• • • • • • •

To gain access to the wisdom of the angelic forces of the universe, we need a method to tune our consciousness to theirs. Ritual will create the circumstance for this to happen, but we need to learn the skills to focus our consciousness into a deliberate trace and look within for the visions and dreams that come. This is called scrying, and while there are many methods, they all involve looking within and interacting with the dream that will be happening within you as a result of the ritual work you have done. You use your active imagination as a screen to view and communicate with the spirit world.

— CHAPTER 14 —
The Art of the Eidolon

In this style of magic, one of the main goals is to contact the various angelic beings that make up the circuitry of our reality to gain their wisdom and awaken the divinity within us. The realization that your mind and the mind of the Creator are the same is the gnosis that we ultimately seek. The technique to create contact with any spiritual force is to first create an energy field that matches the energy signature of the angel or spiritual being we would like to commune with and then invite the angel in to communicate. We call this energy image an eidolon. *Merriam-Webster Dictionary* defines the word *eidolon* as "an idealized person or thing" and also "a ghost or phantasm." Our word *idol* comes from this Greek word.[43] So, in this context, the eidolon is an energy image of our chosen angel or cosmic force that we would like to make contact with. This is a very old style of magic that has its renaissance today. People also call this type of energy invocation an operant field or resonant field. It is the same idea. Once we tune the space to the right energy signature using techniques such drawing elemental pentagrams, we read an invocation that calls the exact spiritual force to us that we are targeting.

To put it another way, let's say you want to contact the goddess Aphrodite. To this end, you research the goddess and find out what she likes according to mythology. You then decorate a space

---

43. *Merriam-Webster Dictionary*, "eidolon," accessed December 31, 2024, https://www.merriam-webster.com/dictionary/eidolon.

with her favorite colors and plants, images of animals she holds as sacred, and perfumes and foods that she would find pleasing. Once this is all assembled, you read a devotional or invocation. She is tempted to come visit you since you have prepared a space with all of her favorite things. We are doing the same thing just with energy rather than stuff. While having objects sacred to your god/goddess is a great idea, a magician can work with dozens or even hundreds of angels. Having objects for so many spiritual forces is just not practical; using energy and the sigils is much more efficient. Creating an energy field or eidolon is also a very reliable approach, as you get exactly the sort of experience or angelic contact that you would expect from the field you create. If we draw pentagrams invoking water, we can expect a field of energy that is more emotional in nature, and only an angel that has that watery nature is *able* to appear in that space. For example, something of a fiery nature would not manifest in a watery energy. Old grimoires and books of magic are full of tests the magician must use to make sure they have called the correct spiritual force; with this style of invocation, we don't need to be as concerned with this.

Elemental Meditations and Pore Breathing with the Elements

The following practices will enable you to feel elemental, and you will gain the ability to call up and use these forces to create eidolons and other effects, such as healing and clearing or banishing the elements. In the more advanced rituals, you will be drawing invoking pentagrams of various elements. For now, you will use basic pore breathing and meditation. Recalling the feeling of these exercises will enable you to pull up the elemental energies and empower the pentagrams with real elemental force in later rituals.

Once you have experienced all six meditations and can really feel these energies flow through your body, you will be empowered to use these energies in ritual. When you draw a pentagram of fire, for example, remember how fire pore breathing felt. Pull up that sensation, and feel the fire energy flow through you. With any of the energies, remember how it felt, sense it within you, and release the power while you exhale. The energy will flow through you and be replaced by more power flowing into you. This technique is how you move energy in ritual, but if you have a hard time feeling these energies, then use your imagination and imagine it flowing.

You will need a quiet space for all of the following practices. If at any time during these practices you start to feel overwhelmed or you just need to quit because someone is at the door or whatever, just imagine the energies leaving your body via your breath and do an informal Qabalistic Cross. That should be enough to ground you out.

P•R•A•C•T•I•C•E
FIRE MEDITATION

In this exercise, we will breathe in elemental fire energy. This begins as in the basic pore breathing exercise (chapter 10), but now we will visualize a universe of elemental fire and breathe this energy in through every fiber of our being. This is very invigorating, but more importantly, this practice will give an innate deep feeling and connection to the energies of elemental fire. Later, we can wield this energy in ritual.

Directions

First, perform the Qabalistic Cross (chapter 2) to connect, center, and ground. Sit or stand in a comfortable position with no distractions.

Perform basic pore breathing, then imagine yourself surrounded by fire. The entire universe is filled with a fiery element. Begin to breathe in this energy, both through your nostrils and through every pore of your body. Imagine the fire energy purifying your entire being.

As you exhale, imagine all the impurities in your body exiting as black smoke. Do this for a number of breaths—no more than twenty-one. All the while, focus on the feeling of fire energy in your body. What comes up for you? Can you feel the intense activity, inspiration, and desire for new knowledge and expansion? Can you feel the heat, hear the crackle of the flames, and smell the smoke? When you are ready, move to the next stage.

Invoking Fire Pentagram

If this becomes too much, imagine the fire fading, and exhale all of the fire energy from your body.

When you are full of fire energy and feel it strongly, draw the invoking pentagram of fire and fill it with fiery energy using the invoking spiral. Do this while vibrating the Enochian secret holy name for fire: OIP TEAA PDOCE (Oh-Ee-Pay Tey-ah-ah Pay-Day-Oh-See).

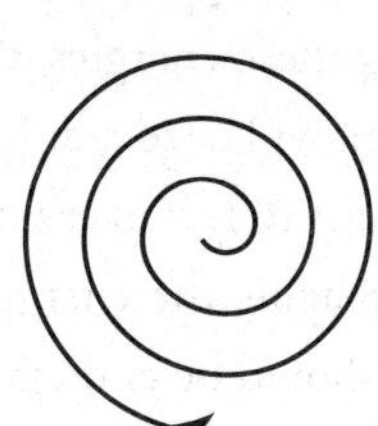

Invoking Spiral

If you are ready to be done, draw a banishing spiral over the pentagram, starting at the center and going counterclockwise three times outward, dispersing the symbol. Then exhale all the fire energy from your body as it winds down and perform the Qabalistic Cross to ground and center.

If you decided to continue, imagine the universe of fire contracting to a single point. This single flame contains all the fire energy. Stare into the flame and observe the colors, the vitality. Realize that in all the universe fire is the same; it is one force. When you are ready to be done, draw the banishing spiral over the pentagram counterclockwise inward to outward three times, and breathe out the fire energy until you feel energized but not uncomfortable. Finally, end with the Qabalistic Cross to reground yourself.

P•R•A•C•T•I•C•E
WATER MEDITATION

In this practice, we will pore breathe the energies of elemental water. Water contains the element of air, otherwise the fish and plants would not be able to thrive in the oceans. We will thrive emotionally and physically by processing the elemental water through our whole being. Later, you will be able to recall the physical sensations of this practice to call up elemental water energy for more complex practices.

Directions

Begin by performing the Qabalistic Cross to connect, center, and ground. Sit or stand in a comfortable position with no distractions.

Perform basic pore breathing as before to connect with the energies of nature. Then imagine yourself surrounded by water. The entire universe is filled with a watery energy. Begin to breathe in this energy, both through your nostrils and through every pore of your being.

Imagine the water energy purifying your entire being. As you exhale, imagine all the impurities in your body exiting as black ink flowing away from you. Do this for a number of breaths—no more than twenty-one, and all the while, focus on the feeling of water energy in your body. What comes up for you? Can you feel the calmness, how the energy embraces you, and the gentle pressure and weight of the water energy? Can you feel the coolness and wetness, hear the flow of the waves, and perhaps taste the salt of the ocean? When you are ready, move to the next step. If you want to be done, imagine the water fading, and exhale all of the water energy from your body. Then perform the Qabalistic Cross again to ground.

When you are full of water energy and feel it strongly, draw the invoking pentagram of water and fill it with watery energy using the invoking spiral while vibrating the

Enochian secret holy name for water: MPH ARSL GAIOL (Em-Pay Ar-Ss-El Gah-Ee-Ol). What comes up for you now? Can you sense a feeling of vastness, of peace?

Invoking Water Pentagram

Sit with the elemental water energies and see what comes up for you. Try to really feel the flow of the elemental water in and out of your being. When you are ready, proceed to the next step. If you are ready to be done, draw a banishing spiral over the pentagram, starting at the center and going counterclockwise three times outward, dispersing the symbol, and exhale all the water energy from your body as it winds down. Then perform the Qabalistic Cross.

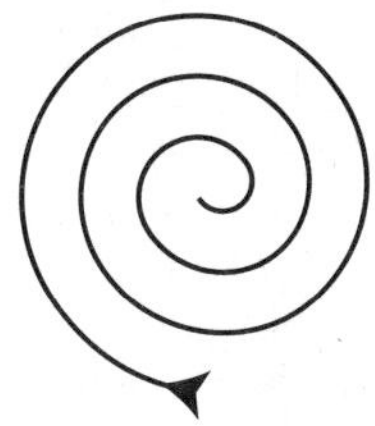

Invoking Spiral

If you wish to continue the practice, visualize all the people you love. Build up the feeling of love within you. Even visualizing pets is fine for this, as our love for our critters tends to be uncomplicated. When you can feel the sensation of love in your body, drop the visualization and simply hold the feeling. Maintain it and abide in this feeling of unattached love. This is the pure energy of Chesed, which we use when drawing symbols, and the highest form of water energy.

When you have experienced the secret of water enough, draw a banishing spiral over the pentagram, starting at the center and going counterclockwise three times outward, dispersing the symbol. Exhale all the water energy from your body as it winds down. Then perform the Qabalistic Cross to re-center and ground.

P•R•A•C•T•I•C•E
AIR MEDITATION

The air pore breathing is both exhilarating and somewhat difficult, as we spend so much of our time caught up in our thoughts that it can be hard to step back and really feel this energy. With this exercise we breathe in the clear, crisp air energy through every atom of our being.

Directions

Begin by performing the Qabalistic Cross to connect, center, and ground. Sit or stand, but be in a comfortable position with no discomfort or distractions.

Perform basic pore breathing to connect with the flow of energy in the universe. Then imagine yourself surrounded by air, that the whole universe is filled with airy energy. It is windy and blowing. Begin to breathe in this energy, both through your nostrils and through every pore of your body. Imagine the air energy purifying your entire being.

As you exhale, imagine all the impurities in your body exiting as gray smoke flowing away from you. Do this for a number of breaths—no more than twenty-one. All the while, focus on the feeling in your body of air energy. What comes up for you? Can you feel the activity, restlessness, and a desire to move and take action? Can you feel the dryness and coolness? What scents can you detect? Do you smell flowers or food? When you are ready, move to the next step, or if you want to be done, imagine the air fading and exhale all of the air energy from your body.

When you are full of air energy and feel it strongly, draw the invoking pentagram of air and fill it with airy energy using the invoking spiral while vibrating the Enochian secret holy name: ORO IBAH AOZPH (Oh-Roh IBah A-oh-Zod-Peh). What comes up for you now? Can you feel clarity, choices, and infinite possibilities? If you are ready to be done, draw a banishing spiral over the pentagram. Start at the center and go counterclockwise three times outward, dispersing the symbol, and exhale all the air energy from your body as it winds down. Then perform the Qabalistic Cross.

Invoking Air Pentagram

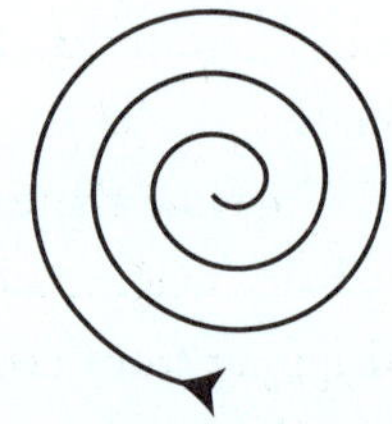

Invoking Spiral

If you wish to continue, visualize a form materializing in front of you. The form is a duplicate of you in as much detail as you can imagine. When you have the form stabilized, transfer your awareness to this form, and view yourself. What do you see?

In your energy form, you can travel to any place you have ever been. First, walk through your home, then imagine you are at your most favorite place you have ever been. This process is known as etheric travel. When we project our minds to physical places, we are seeing the energy form that is very close to manifestation.

When you are ready, return to your body and draw a banishing spiral over the pentagram, starting at the center and going counterclockwise three times outward, dispersing the symbol, and exhale all the air energy from your body as it winds down. Then perform the Qabalistic Cross to re-center and ground.

P•R•A•C•T•I•C•E
EARTH MEDITATION

Earth pore breathing will ground and center you. The earthy energies are very healing and nourishing for our bodies and our nerves. Earth energies contain all of the other elemental energies and also the vitalizing energies of spirit. By breathing in the energies of elemental earth, you will be able to feel the flow of life energies around and through your body, giving you vitality, health, and a grounded connection to nature and the earth.

Directions

Begin by performing the Qabalistic Cross to connect, center, and ground. Sit or stand in a comfortable position with no distractions. Perform basic pore breathing to connect with the flow of energy in the universe.

Imagine yourself surrounded by earth; the whole universe is filled with earthy energy, not just solid rock but the myriad forms of crystal and precious metals and stones. Imagine you are passing through an area filled with the wonders found beneath the ground: living creatures, roots, worms, bugs, and the vast spiderweb-like network of fungi. Begin to breathe in this energy, both through your nostrils and through every pore of your body.

Invoking Earth Pentagram

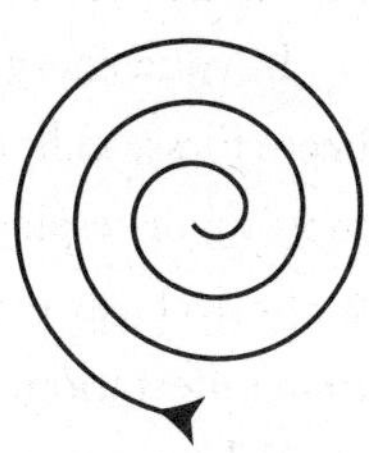

Invoking Spiral

Imagine the earth energy purifying your entire being. As you exhale, imagine all the impurities in your body exiting as black oil, dripping from every pore of your body. Do this for a number of breaths—no more than twenty-one. All the while, focus on the feeling of earth energy in your body. What comes up for you? Can you feel the richness and heaviness? Can you sense the ancientness? Can you feel the cool dryness? What textures can you feel—rough, smooth? Does the energy sparkle? Can you feel a low vibration? When you are ready, move to the next stage, or if you want to be done, imagine the earth fading and exhale all of the earth energy from your body.

When you are full of earth energy and feel it strongly, draw the invoking pentagram of earth and fill it with earthy energy using the invoking spiral while vibrating the Enochian secret holy name: MOR DIAL HCTGA (Mo-Are Dee-al Hec-teh-Gah). This is the Enochian name for Earth of Spirit. What comes up for you now? Can you sense a feeling of connection to the life force, to all living beings?

If you are ready to be done, draw a banishing spiral over the pentagram, starting at the center and going counterclockwise three times outward, dispersing the symbol, and exhale all the earth energy from your body as it winds down. Then perform the Qabalistic Cross.

If you wish to continue, reach out with all of your being and connect with all of the life around you. Feel your connection to the life in the room, then the area around your location. Sense your connection to the trees, grass, people, and animals, bugs, and birds. Reach out to your social network and feel the connections you have with both your friends and those you know but aren't close to. See the complex connections you have with all living beings and feel compassion and nonjudgmental awareness. When you are ready, close as before with the banishing spiral, wind down, and ground with the Qabalistic Cross.

P • R • A • C • T • I • C • E
SPIRIT MEDITATIONS

Spirit active and spirit passive are very special in the way that they enable the other elements to interact and maintain their uniqueness. We will mainly use them to empower elements and to create the central column, or axis mundi, in our rituals. In practice, these two forces act as an alternating current, rapidly cycling back and forth to empower the outer elements of creation.

Spirit Active Meditation

This begins as the basic pore breathing exercise, but now we will visualize a universe of spirit active energies and breathe this energy in through every fiber of our being. This energy is the essence of light; it has penetrating and enlivening qualities. Feeling this force will enable you to connect to the higher planes and empower rituals with great force.

First, perform the Qabalistic Cross to connect, center, and ground. Sit or stand in a comfortable position with no distractions. Engage in basic pore breathing to connect with the flow of energy in the universe.

Invoking Spirit Active Pentagram

Imagine being in a ball of pure, brilliant light. The entire universe is filled with a light so bright it can only be called brilliance, as it is beyond color. Begin to breathe in the brilliance through every fiber of your being. As you exhale, visualize all your spiritual blockages being released with the outflow of active spirit energy.

When you are ready, draw the pentagram of spirit active as shown, and charge it with an invoking spiral while vibrating EHNB (Eh-Heh-Nu-Beh). This is the Enochian Tetragrammaton, spirit of spirit.

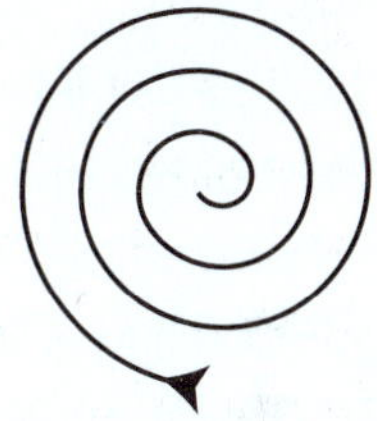

Invoking Spiral

Next make the opening of the portal gesture, which is similar to opening a set of heavy curtains. Extend your hands together forward, and imagine you are grasping two heavy curtains. Then move your hands to the side as if you are revealing what is behind the curtains.

Sit for a time with what is revealed to you. Feel in your body the sensation of balanced active spirit energy. When you are finished, use the banishing spiral to disperse the pentagram and slowly return to normal consciousness. Finish with the Qabalistic Cross.

Spirit Receptive Meditation

The energies of spirit receptive are very unique and rarely discussed in any depth, though the topic is very important to our exploration of magic and eidolons. Spirit energy has both an active invigorating aspect and a quieter aspect that is receptive in nature. Experiencing spirit receptive energies provides an understanding and the ability to use this force to empower other elemental energies and to connect with the essence of the source of form, stability, and calmness.

To begin, first perform the Qabalistic Cross to connect, center, and ground. Sit or stand in a comfortable position with no distractions. Perform basic pore breathing to connect with the flow of energy in the universe.

Sit as you would for meditation. Imagine the universe filled with light, except this time the light is dark—like a blacklight. It is deep and dark, but you can still somehow see. Begin to breathe in this dark light through every fiber of your being, feel the calming embrace of this receptive energy.

As you exhale the dark light, feel that all your aggressive and angry emotions calm and flow out of every pore of your body.

When you are ready, reach out and trace the pentagram of spirit receptive. Fill it with energy by using an invoking spiral while vibrating BNHE (Beh-Nu-Heh-Eh), the reverse of EHNB, representing the energy flowing inward rather than outward.

Invoking Spirit Passive Pentagram

Then make the closing of the portal gesture. This time, you are closing the curtains. Reach outward with both hands as if to grab open curtains, then bring your hands together but to your heart. Imagine you are closing the curtains on a bright day. The light in the room becomes muted and relaxed, but you can still see.

Sit with the cool dark for a time, and see what comes up for you. When you are finished, use the banishing spiral to disperse the pentagram and slowly return to normal consciousness. Finish with the Qabalistic Cross.

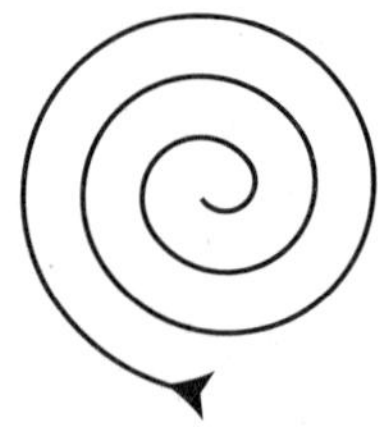

Invoking Spiral

• • • • • • •

The eidolons tune the space around you to enable very specific spirits to come forward so you can create a spiritual experience. Every action in a ritual should have symbolic meaning. From how you move to what you speak, every part of your being should be involved meaningfully and mindfully for the rite to be fully effective. Acrobats, martial artists, and actors all move with great intention, and you can tell if you watch them carefully. Treat ritual like a Tai Chi practitioner treats their practice, with much awareness and focus. When you read or say words of power, say them with great intent and attention. Be the words when you speak them. Ritual is in the reenactment of myth. A good ritual reenacts the mythic content of our collective unconscious thus tapping into an unlimited source of power. These movements, vibration of words, and visualizations are the techniques that will bring those myths to life and give them power. You are the hero. These are your tools to complete your heroic journey.

PART THREE
Rituals and Rites

— CHAPTER 15 —
The Lesser Ritual of the Pentagram

One of the most important practices in the Hermetic tradition is the Lesser Ritual of the Pentagram (LRP). This simple ritual contains all of the fundamental skills used in the most advanced rituals, and fundamentals are not the most important thing—they are literally the *only* thing. The word *lesser* here refers to this ritual being a daily practice and for any situation that requires a simple sacred space, such as tarot reading, for instance. We could call it the "Everyday Purification Ritual of the Elements," but that does not have the same gravitas. So, we are stuck with the term *lesser*, even if it is a bit confusing.

As a daily practice, it also puts order and cleanliness to your entire microcosm. We often compare this practice to cleaning the kitchen. If you go into the kitchen to make a great meal and the kitchen is a mess with dirty dishes, cluttered counters, and things out of place, what is the first thing you do? Do you cook? Or do you clean the whole thing up? Only with a clean and orderly kitchen can you really prepare a fine meal. Performing this ritual is much like doing the same.

By beginning your day with this rite, you clean up your microcosm and get it ready for you to express your True Will. You can use this to begin a meditative practice, to bless a house, or in any situation where you need to clean the psychic atmosphere. The rite is very short. In fact, you can complete it in five minutes, and it is easy to memorize. While very short and easy to perform, it encompasses all the basic skills needed to perform advanced ritual magic. But for now, as you begin to learn this magical system, simply start your day with this practice and see what comes up.

Consider making this a daily practice; each morning perform this rite. You should also do the Liber Resh and mediate when you can. A daily practice is necessary to make any real spiritual progress.

History

The LRP was originally developed by the Golden Dawn in the 1890s. According to Chic Cicero and Sandra Tabatha Cicero, who are the chief adepts of the Hermetic Order of the Golden Dawn as re-established by Israel Regardie:

> The Lesser Ritual of the Pentagram (or LRP) is a ceremonial magic ritual devised and used by the original order of the Golden Dawn that has become a mainstay in modern occultism. This ritual is considered by many to be a basic preliminary to any other magical work, so much that it was the only ritual, besides initiation rituals, taught to members of the Golden Dawn before they advanced to the Inner Order.[44]

The process to advance to the inner order could take years—if the initiate was able to complete the process at all.

There are many versions of this simple ritual. The version taught to Limitless Light students contains some small modifications we have added over the years and is more in keeping with the style of magic taught to Erich by Frater Barrabbas.

Also note there are typically two forms of the LRP: invoking and banishing. The banishing form is normally learned first. *Banishing* is another confusing term. Here the word has a meaning closer to "cleaning or purification" rather than "removing or excluding," which most people think. The object is really to clean and order our microcosm rather than to exclude anything.

The Watchtowers

In this ritual, we introduce the concept of the four watchtowers. These are originally from a vision by Edward Kelley as told to John Dee.[45] The watchtowers are spiritual stations at the four cardinal points. They are usually guarded by an angel, but the guardian can be another spirit in other traditions. This is a hugely influential concept that is used in not only ceremonial magic but Wicca as well. The most standard attributions for the directions and the ones used in this book are air to the

---

44. Cicero and Cicero, *The Essential Golden Dawn*, 147–49.

45. Turner, *Elizabethan Magic*, 24.

east, fire to the south, water to the west, and earth to the north. There are other patterns, but this is the one most commonly used by ceremonial magicians.

When performing rites that are intended to affect the microcosm, you will move deosil, or clockwise, following the course of the sun through the day. The sun rises in the east when we wake and our minds become active, so the east is air. At noon, the sun is at its hottest and is generally in the south, so south is fire. The sun sets in the west. This is when we start to relax and get ready for bed and the atmosphere cools off, so the west is water. At night, the sun is on the other side of the world, so the north is earth. Now, this is from a perspective in the northern latitudes; we are not sure if people in the southern latitudes change out north and south. We suppose they could.

LRP Stages

The LRP is our kata, or set series of actions, for learning the skills of the magical practice. The ritual practices the skills of movement, drawing devices in the air, visualization, and vibrating divine names. Let's look at the stages of the Lesser Banishing Ritual of the Pentagram (LBRP).

Introit

Most rituals will have a simple statement or prayer to start the rite, called an introit. This acts as the departure stage of the Hero's Journey and give us a starting point. For the LRP, you will use the Qabalistic Cross as the introit.

Setting the Four Watchtowers

When setting the four watchtowers, we do the main ritual work. This stage includes drawing the pentagrams and vibrating divine names, which cleanses and purifies the elements within our lives and mind. While drawing pentagrams, you should hold your head straight and follow your hand with your eyes. The eye movements activate stored memories and release energy. Pay attention to what comes up when drawing these shapes. Take time to journal and consider it.

We are banishing the earth element because earth contains all of the other elements within it; this was mentioned in the earlier chapter on the elements. We are cleaning out the airy part of earth in the east, which is our thoughts and monkey mind. We clean the fiery part of earth in the south; this is our passions and desires. The watery part of earth in the west corresponds to our feelings and emotions. In the north, we clean and order the earthy part of earth, our physical and social environments. Using the earth element acts like a big broom that sweeps all the dirt and dust from these areas of our lives, leaving us clean and empowered.

Ideally, you will also want to visualize the pentagrams and the circle connecting them as being made of blue flame-like energy, similar to the appearance of burning alcohol. The blue is for the sephiroth Chesed, which is called "mercy" or more literally "loving-kindness." Perform the actions and mentally know the forms are there, burning with light and power throughout the rite.

Visualization is a skill that comes in time. No need to rush it.

As you move through the ritual, be mindful of where your body is. As you walk or turn, be in your feet. As you move your hands to draw the shapes, be mindful of how you are moving your hands. After each pentagram, stop for a second and be mindfully in your body.

The Sign of Silence

The Sign of Silence also comes from the Golden Dawn practice and is the complement of the penetrating Sign of Horus the Enterer. To perform the Sign of Silence, simply put your left forefinger or two fingers to your lips as if to shush someone who is talking too loudly. This sign is very protective in nature. It is also known as the Sign of the Harpocrates. Harpocrates was the child form of the god Horus and was the god of secrecy and protection.

When performing the LRP, make this sign after you send out energy to protect yourself from any of the energy reverberating back. You can use this sign whenever you feel attacked or unsafe. It is a very powerful and important technique to know.

Invocation of the Archangels

The invocation of the archangels calls on spiritual allies for this journey. During the invocation of the archangels, call the archangels to come and bless and protect you. You can visualize them in any way that makes sense to you.

Then you will say, "For around me flame the pentagrams and within me shines the six-rayed star." This statement reaffirms the presence of the pentagrams you made. This reaffirmation is an important step you will see in ritual design. Sometimes a reaffirmation of a previous ritual step is called the analysis of the keyword. This action unifies and cements the previous ritual actions.

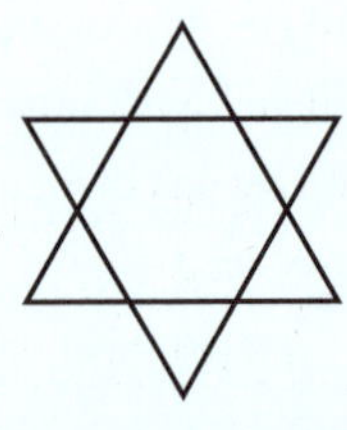

Hexagram

The shining six-rayed star is also known as the hexagram. It is visualized in the color gold. It represents the macrocosm flooding into the cleared and sanctified space. The macrocosm is the larger universe of all space and time. Once your local microcosm is cleared of day-to-day static, your connection with your greater purpose can be made apparent.

The four archangels of the tetramorph are the beings that revealed the Enochian system to John Dee, which we will be using. They have quite complex personalities and will appear uniquely to each practitioner. To some, they appear as classic Renaissance paintings, but to others, they will appear in a fully modern form, wearing blue jeans and polo shirts, or as pillars of light. The four archangels are Raphael, Michael, Gabriel, and Uriel.

The mythology that surrounds the four archangels of the tetramorph is complex and sometimes contradictory. These beings fulfill many roles, and according to legend, they have free will like humankind. Such complex and mysterious beings within a monotheistic tradition has always fascinated us. The four archangels are much larger and older than the Judeo-Christian tradition that we are familiar with. Having worked angelic and Enochian magic for decades, we have come to the conclusion that the beings we call angels represent the fundamental synergistic or building-up energies of the cosmos. The Big Four, as we like to call them, are special and stand apart from all the other forces we have ever encountered. They are very friendly and helpful, though, and we have learned to trust them.

Raphael means "God has healed" and is a great healer. Raphael is also the embodiment of the east, the intellect, and the element of air, as well as all airy things, such as music, which is complex vibrations in the air.

Michael means "one who is like God" and is probably the most popular of the four. Michael is a great healer of disease and the embodiment of the south and the element of fire. Michael is also a powerful protector.

Gabriel means "strength of God." Gabriel embodies the west and the element of water, which is the realm of emotions and creativity. Gabriel is often the angelic messenger in biblical stories, coming to announce the birth of Jesus, for instance.

Uriel means "light of God." Here is the embodiment of the north and the element of earth. Uriel is also said to guard the entrance to the Garden of Eden, or paradise by another name.

These four powerful archetypes show up in religion and in the practice as both the guardians and the guides on the path. They reveal only what you are ready for within the magical circle. They will veil with obscurity any practice you are not ready for or any knowledge that would be too disruptive at your current level of spiritual attainment. They are also allies you can call on when you have need.

When you are in the center of your cleansed and empowered world at this stage, it is okay to proclaim your will and state what you want to manifest. This is particularly good if you are doing this as a daily practice first thing in the morning or after your coffee. You might say something to express what your True Will is for the day. For example, "It is my will that I approach all with loving-kindness, do well at my job, and stop smoking. So mote it be."

Closing

When you finish this simple rite, you are standing on the earth with the four elements cleansed and empowered, the archangels guarding the four directions, and your whole universe ordered and empowered. You may wish to state what your will is along with what you want to accomplish this day if you are using this as a daily practice. Then close the rite with a second Qabalistic Cross; you may perform the final Qabalistic Cross in an informal way if you wish.

R•I•T•U•A•L
LESSER BANISHING RITUAL OF THE PENTAGRAM

The LRP creates an energy field, one that is cleansed and purified. Each direction has an associated element that is cleansed and purified by this short ritual. This enables the four archangels of the tetramorph to manifest. Or, really, it reveals them as if they are already there.

Here is the full ritual.

Things You Need

A private space

Room to move around is ideal, but you can sit and do all the work in your mind, in spirit form

Something pointy to draw the lines of force or your finger

Directions

Introit

Ground yourself and center into your breath. Perform the Qabalistic Cross.

Setting the Four Watchtowers

While facing east, draw the banishing pentagram of earth. Start at your left hip, at earth. Trace a line of blue flame up to the top of your head, down to your right hip, up to your left shoulder, across to your right shoulder, and then down to your left hip again. Finally, repeat the first action by tracing up to your forehead again. This ensures you have completed the shape.

Banishing Earth Pentagram

Invoking Spiral

Inhale and draw an invoking spiral over the pentagram to activate it. Once your hand is in the center, powerfully vibrate the Hebrew god name *YHVH* (Yeh-ho-wah). *Yod Heh Vav Heh* are the four letters of the Tetragrammaton.

Make the Sign of Silence by putting your left forefinger or two fingers to your lips.

Keep your arm outstretched and turn ninety degrees to the south. Draw another banishing pentagram of earth. Then draw an invoking spiral over the pentagram to activate it. Once your hand is in the center, powerfully vibrate the Hebrew god name *ADNI* (Ah-do-nhai). *Adonai* is Hebrew for "lord."

Make the Sign of Silence again. Keep your right arm outstretched and turn ninety degrees to the west. Draw another banishing pentagram of earth. Draw an invoking spiral over the pentagram to activate it. Once your hand is in the center, powerfully vibrate the Hebrew god name *EHIH* (Eh-heh-yeh). *Eheieh* is Hebrew for "I am."

Make the Sign of Silence. Keep your right arm outstretched and turn ninety degrees to the north. Draw another earth pentagram, and then draw an invoking spiral over the pentagram to activate it. Once your hand is in the center, powerfully vibrate the Hebrew god name *AGLA* (Ah-gwh-lah). *AGLA* is a Hebrew acronym for "Thou Art Mighty Forever, O Lord." In Hebrew, it is "Adonai Gibor Le Olam Amen."

Make the Sign of Silence. Keep your right arm outstretched and turn ninety degrees back to the east, completing the circle that connects the centers of each pentagram.

Invocation of the Archangels

Still facing east, stretch out your arms to the side and vibrate the names of the angels. While visualizing the archangels in the form that suits you best, say or vibrate:

Before me Raphael,
Behind me Gabriel,
On my right hand Michael,
On my left hand Uriel,
For about me flames the pentagrams,
And within me shines the six-rayed star.

Be mindfully present in your sanctified space. Sense in your body how it feels to be in a space you sanctified and purified. Can you see or feel the banishing pentagrams you placed in the four directions? Can you see or feel the presence of the archangels? Have a moment of mindfulness and presence.

State your will. You may, if you wish, say a dedication of merit or express what you are feeling at this moment. When we do our daily practice, we state what our will is for the day and the things that are most important to us at the moment and over the long term, then we say a dedication of merit. Since you are standing in a magical model of your universe that is ordered and cleansed, now is a good time to impress your will upon your microcosm and focus on what you wish to manifest.

Closing

To close and finish the rite, repeat the Qabalistic Cross. You may do an informal version if it feels appropriate.

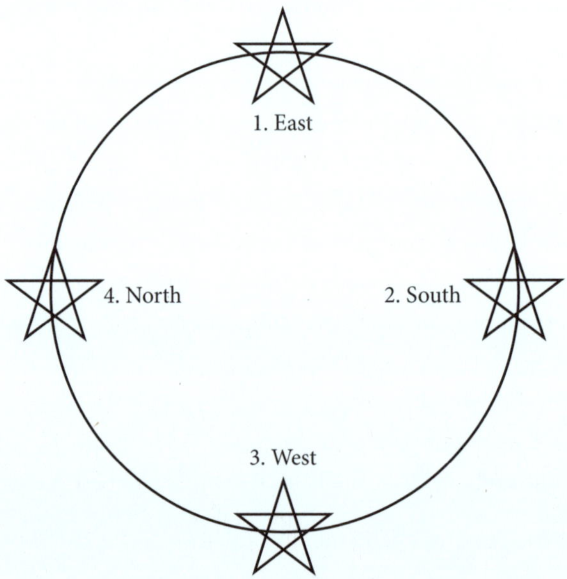

Lesser Banishing Ritual of the Pentagram Final Form

• • • • • • •

This daily practice will, over a relatively short time, create a sense of calm and order in your life. Ordering the elements of your world and inviting in the forces of the macrocosm will put you in a place of power and calm in your life. Sometimes it takes weeks, sometimes only days, but you will feel the difference this daily practice makes. This is now your magical form to develop all the skills you need to realize the divine within you and make reality mutable. We suggest that you copy this ritual into your journal. Copying something in your own hand makes it much easier to remember.

— CHAPTER 16 —
The Middle Pillar

This rite was originally developed by the Golden Dawn and published by Israel Regardie in his book *The Middle Pillar*. Israel Regardie was a writer and occultist, among other things, and published a great deal of the Golden Dawn material that is popular today. *The Middle Pillar* was originally published in 1938 and contained Regardie's thoughts on psychology and magic as well as the Qabalistic Cross, Lesser Ritual of the Pentagram (LRP), and the Middle Pillar rituals. These basic rituals trained us to become magicians. The Middle Pillar taught us to call up and move very large amounts of spiritual energy.

This simple rite develops the middle pillar of the Tree of Life within your aura. While the Qabalistic Cross also develops the Tree of Life within your personal energy field, the Qabalistic Cross is about connection and balance. The Middle Pillar is about generating powerful magical energies and moving them around in your aura. By visualizing the sephiroth in a column of light and vibrating the god names, you bring into your awareness a powerful sensation of energy that really has to be felt to be believed. This will enable you to handle and direct ever more powerful fields of energy. It's like lifting weights. You build your strength and endurance so that you can later manage even more spiritual energy. You can work with this exercise at your own pace.

The Middle Pillar can be added to your daily practice, and it can be performed after the LRP and before the final Qabalistic Cross. You may also want to just do it a few times a week; that is fine as well. After you are familiar with the more advanced rituals in this book, you might want to work

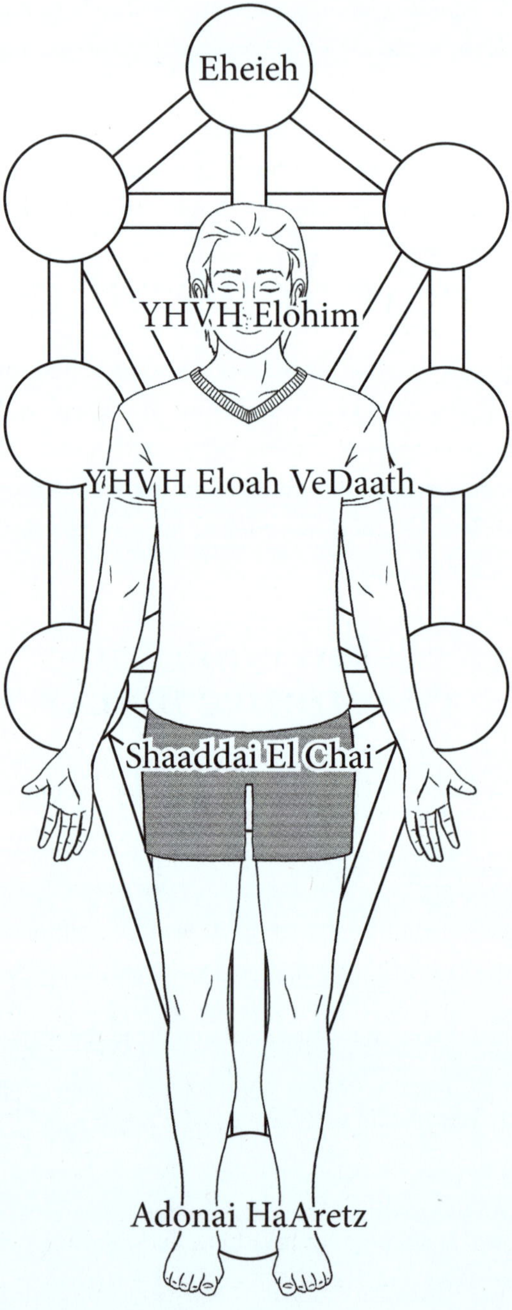

Middle Pillar

in the Middle Pillar at the beginning of an exercise or ritual to help you get a boost before you go any further. Once you have some success with this ritual, you can use your intuition on how best to apply it.

We start at the top, at Kether, and bring the power down to Daath (the hidden Sephiroth), then to the heart at Tipareth, then to Yesod, and finally ground the power in Malkuth. Opening this central channel of the Tree can develop tremendous spiritual power that remains balanced since it is traveling down the pillar of balance.

In Daath, we vibrate YHVH Elohim, which is the god name for Binah. Daath does not have its own god name, as it really isn't part of the Tree. The four letters *YHVH* represent the power of the creator manifested through the four elements. *Elohim* is a very interesting word; it is the plural of the name Eloah, meaning "gods." It is also the god name of the sephiroth Binah, the great mother. So, perhaps the great mother manifests the universe through the fourfold elements and the archetypes of the gods and goddesses. The sephiroth Daath is not shown on the Tree, as each person must manifest it for themselves. The meaning of Daath is a spiritual state where all is one, a level of enlightenment where there is no other.

R•I•T•U•A•L THE MIDDLE PILLAR

This exercise aligns and empowers the individual in a way that is similar to the Qabalistic Cross; however, it generates far more spiritual power, an order of magnitude more. You can add this exercise before any ritual you perform. Just don't do it before you go to bed, otherwise you will be up all night.

Things You Need

A quiet space

Room to move around is ideal, but you can sit and do all the work in your mind, in spirit form

Something pointy to draw the lines of force or your finger

Directions

Begin by grounding and centering your breathing. Perform the Qabalistic Cross (chapter 2). Perform the Lesser Banishing Ritual of the Pentagram (chapter 15).

Then visualize and vibrate the names as follows. We recommend vibrating each name once at first, working your way up to five repetitions per name. If you feel dizzy or overwhelmed, back off the count until you feel comfortable. It is important to keep the practice at a level you feel comfortable with but also challenged to the degree you want to be challenged.

To start, vibrate *Kether*. Visualize a ball of brilliant energy above your head, place your consciousness there, and vibrate the god name *Eheieh* (Eh-he-yeh), meaning "I am" or "I will be."

Vibrate *Daath*. Visualize a ball of purple or blacklight-type energy at your throat and place your consciousness within it. Vibrate the god name *YHVH Elohim* (Ye-ho-wah Elo-him). Traditionally, it is pronounced *Yod Heh Vav Heh, Elo-him*. Try it both ways, and use what works best for you.

Vibrate *Tipareth*. At your heart, visualize a ball of solar energy like the sun. Place your awareness within it and vibrate *YHVH Eloah VeDaath* (Ye-ho-wah El-Oh-Ah Ve-Daath). It's meaning is "the Creator made manifest through absolute unity and diversity." Tipareth is the home of your Higher Self and the balance point of the Tree—one light through ten vessels.

Vibrate *Yesod*. Visualize a ball of yellow energy and place your consciousness at your genitals. Vibrate the name *Shaddai El Chai* (Shad-Di El Hi), meaning "the gracious living god" or "god of life." This is referring to the life-giving powers of our genitalia.

Vibrate *Malkuth*. At or beneath your feet, visualize a ball of green or earthy energy and place your mind there. Vibrate *Adonai HaAretz* (Ah-do-nhai Ha-Are-Etz), meaning "lord of the earth."

Hold the energy as long as you feel comfortable. When you are ready to be finished, perform the Qabalistic Cross again. If you feel too charged, breathe out slowly, imagining the energy flowing out with your breath until you reach a level of energetic charge you feel comfortable with.

Alternative Practice

If this ritual seems too complex, use a simpler method such as visualizing a ball of light at the appropriate location and vibrating the names. Start simple and add in layers of visualization. Do not get caught up in doing the exercise exactly *right* at first. Do what you can, and in time, it gets easier and easier.

You can also write the names and locations on a sheet of paper and tape it to the wall to read from if you wish. Erich does it all the time to help him learn a practice. Draw a picture in your journal, fill in the names and locations on a stick figure, and color in the spheres.

The following chart summarizes the god names and the locations and colors for the Middle Pillar practice.

Middle Pillar Names and Locations

Location	God Name	Color of Sephira
Above Head	Eheieh	Brilliance
Throat	YHVH Elohim	Black Light
Heart	YHVH Eloah Ve-Daath	Yellow
Genitals	Shaddai El Chai	Purple
Feet	Adonai HaAretz	Citrine/Russet/Olive/Black

Once you can vibrate the names with ease and can feel the flow of spiritual power, then you can add in circulating energy. Visualize the energy flowing up your back, over your head, and down your front. Do this several times and then reverse the flow. Experiment with this visualization until you can move the force anywhere in your sphere of awareness. You can also have it go up your sides and wrap around you like a blanket.

Always perform the Qabalistic Cross when you are finished to ground and balance the energies.

• • • • • • •

The Middle Pillar, Qabalistic Cross, and the LRP are the three basic practices that will train you to become a magician. The Middle Pillar itself is the best ritual we know of to raise your energy level quickly and controllably. This will enable you to raise and *feel* energy quite reliably so you can train yourself to control even higher levels of energy. You can use the Middle Pillar as a daily practice and before any ritual work you may be doing where you feel you need a boost.

— CHAPTER 17 —
Temple Consecration

The Lesser Ritual of the Pentagram (LRP) is wonderful as a daily practice, and it can also create sacred space for simple, more informal practices, such as meditation or divination. However, it does not create the type of sacred space needed for the complex rites of our practice. Up until now, the rituals and practices have been to help you master the basics and build a daily practice that will ready you for the more advanced work.

Like the Hero's Journey, we need a departure stage, where we leave behind the mundane world and journey to the space beyond what our normal social condition expects and allows. That is where sacred space comes in and the consecration of the temple.

To contain the more advanced magical practices we need a powerful container. A temple consecration is a departure state that will serve as the context for the sacred geometry and rituals that follow. Further rituals will be performed in the sacred space of the temple consecration and will build to ever higher levels of spiritual ecstasy and revelation.

The Journey

When we perform a temple consecration, whatever place we are in becomes a sacred temple and more. There is a feeling of vastness, as if the small room or grove is transformed into a vast temple capable of traversing space and time. While some traditions employ magic circles drawn on the floor to protect the practitioner from contact with spiritual forces, our circle is immersive. We want to directly experience the divine light without and within our own being, so we call the spiritual entities into the circle. Our spiritual allies will protect and guide us on the journey.

Some lodges, such as the Golden Dawn, have temple openings where each opening is based on an element from their initiatory grades. These rituals are called Opening by Watchtower and are quite beautiful. In the Temple of Limitless Light, we only have one pattern, but there are many versions based on different mythologies. Any mythology you consider sacred can serve as the inspiration for a temple consecration, but it should follow the general template outlined in this chapter. Within our tradition, we have several temple consecrations, including one based on Enochian mythology, one rooted in Egyptian mythology, and one based on the Grail Cycle. The Grail Cycle is a group of myths centered around the knights of Camelot seeking the Grail in order to heal the land and their king.

Tools Needed

This is always a tricky subject. As we discussed in chapter 8, tools are great, but a lack of tools should not prevent you from doing the work. Ideally, you want a private space for the work, a cup of clean water, and a dish of salt; sea salt is nice. A dagger is normally used to bless the water and the salt. A sword is normally used to separate the mundane from the sacred. To draw the pentagrams, use a wand or a crystal. Incense is nice to have as well.

If any of these things are unavailable or impractical, then think of a substitution. A nice crystal point can be used in place of any of the pointy things listed above. Sometimes in group workings, we use a crystal point that is passed from person to person as we each perform a part in the overall ritual. Of course, you can always substitute your imagination for any object that you lack or find impractical.

It is very helpful to have an altar as a focus of your intent and a place to put tools, books that you will be reading from, incense, cups and water, and so on. It is great to have at least one central altar. We have the luxury of maintaining an altar for each element, meaning there's one in each cardinal direction, as well as a center altar to place special items on. Our eastern altar is larger and holds most of the tools. If you lack temple furniture, then the floor works, too; that is how we started.

Candles are nice if your space can accommodate them. We place two small oil lamps on each altar. Always consider safety and practicality when organizing your working space.

Ritual Flow

Our temple consecration rite is called the Temple of Limitless Light. You should eventually make your own temple consecration in your own words, but your ritual should still follow this template.

Introit

Begin with a short guided meditation to bring you and your audience from the everyday world to the brink of sacred space. In our ritual, we use a vision Erich had long ago while doing ritual work. Erich was brought before an obsidian mirror, and in the polished surface, he could see himself darkly. This is a common vision of our shadow, or dweller on the threshold, with all the parts of ourselves we hold back and try to ignore, both positive and negative. This is a very common theme in mythology. The obvious resolution is to step into the reflection and accept ourselves in total. Once we are made whole, we can be truly powerful people.

Any sacred story can be an inspiration for this rite. Are we going to Asgard across the rainbow bridge or perhaps to the Isle of Avalon? Once you decide on your theme, the rest of the ritual will write itself. Ritual is acting out mythology, especially personal mythology.

Sacred Marriage

During the sacred marriage stage, we create the holy water that we will use to sanctify the area. The combining of the salt and water is the first act of uniting the polarities and transcending the apparent duality of our universe. Some words are said as the water is blessed, representing the spirit passive, and words are said as the salt is blessed, representing the spirit active.

The salt and water are combined, representing the uniting and transcending of duality. It is the creation of a holy elixir that is then sprinkled around the space to sanctify the area. Of course, now you have holy water that you can use for any other purpose you can think of. This could be cleansing crystals, blessing an ancestor altar—whatever you wish and deem appropriate. You can store your holy water in the cup you made it in, allowing it to slowly evaporate, or in some container you use just for that purpose. You did this in chapter 8 when you consecrated your tools.

Sanctifying the Space

Next, you want to next sanctify the area you are using. This is traditionally done with the four elements. The holy water we made during the sacred marriage stage is a combination of the earth element and the water element. Sprinkling the water around the area purifies the earth and water elements.

Incense is usually burning, which represents the elements of fire and air. Taking the incense around the circle and blowing the smoke with your breath will purify the air with fire. If you can't or don't want to use incense, then just imagine you are blowing incense smoke around the space.

As far as the choice of incense is concerned, we leave that up to you. Erich favors frankincense for its cleansing and traditional use, but the two of us use many types and grow some of our own. If you like, research what traditionally is used in different types of ceremonies and explore that. Crowley's book *777* is the perfect place to begin your research.

Separating the Space

Traditionally a ring of fire is drawn around the sacred space to represent a wall of protection and a separation of sacred space from mundane space. Personally, Erich sees this action as defining the rim of the cauldron of transformation, which is how he sees the magic circle. All can be true at the same time.

The traditional tool of choice to separate the mundane from the sacred is a sword. You can also use a dagger, a crystal, or your finger. The idea is to walk or point to the periphery of the space and draw a separating line. Normally, you say something impressive while you are separating the space.

Setting the Four Watchtowers

Setting the four watchtowers is the "meat" of the ritual; it is where we call our spiritual guardians to witness, guide, and empower our sacred space. It is similar to the LRP, except that you are *invoking* rather than *banishing*. Remember that the four elemental watchtowers are like lighthouses to call our spiritual allies to assist us, and they act as anchor points to any additional work we might do within the sacred space.

The invocation needs to be short and contain a brief description of the guardian being called as well as what you are asking them to do. We used the traditional archangels of the tetramorph, which are used in many rituals, including the LRP. By this point, you should be familiar with them. They are fantastic allies for any work. You can, of course, replace them with other allies that you work with.

In the following rite, there is a fifth node and sixth node for the directions above and below. Spirit active is above and spirit passive is below, and we unite the two to create the axis mundi, or center of the world. Spirit active and spirit passive act like an alternating current to enliven the entire circuit of elemental energies.

Final Blessing

Having created our sacred temple space, some final words are a nice way to give a sense of completion to this stage of the work. At the very least, confirm and ground what you just accomplished by saying, "The sacred temple has been opened." You would not say a dedication of merit at this point. You only say that when you are completely finished with your working.

R • I • T • U • A • L
TEMPLE CONSECRATION FROM THE TEMPLE OF LIMITLESS LIGHT

This temple consecration ritual is a version of the one used by our Limitless Light temple. You can take this example and modify it as you see fit for your practice. Note that performing the Lesser Banishing Ritual of the Pentagram (LBRP) is not necessary, as the temple consecration contains the effects created by the LBRP.

If multiple people are performing this ritual, then the roles should be clearly defined before you begin. You can easily divide up the stages between multiple people if you have a group to do the working.

Things You Need

Space for the ritual

A bell or chime; if you don't have one simply knock on the table or floor

Optional: An altar in the center and altars at the four cardinal points

Optional: A wand, crystal point, or something else pointy for drawing shapes

A cup or chalice with water

A dish with salt

Optional: Incense

Optional: A sword for separating the space

Preparation

Begin by performing belly breathing and the Qabalistic Cross. When everyone feels ready, all participants should face east. Ring the bell four times and read the introit.

Directions

Introit

Recite the following meditation:

We stand in a garden of our own creation. The foliage is luxuriant and in full bloom. The fruit trees hang heavy with the harvest of our own effort and diligence. For a moment we pause at the fountain to refresh ourselves and enjoy the gentle aromatic breeze. Then we stand and start down the path that leads beyond the wall to the wilderness.

The forest beyond the wall is ancient and huge; we hear the calls of birds, beasts, and insects. The path leads to an ancient place in the heart of the wilderness, to a megalithic circle of polished stone wherein is found the obsidian gateway. There, we are confronted with a dark reflection of ourselves within the cold stone.

With courage, we banish all doubt and fear, and with acceptance, we claim our power. Thus, whole and empowered, we pass through our reflection and into the beyond.

Sacred Marriage

Place the cup or chalice of water on the dish with salt. Stand before the altar and use a pointy tool (or your finger) to draw an invoking pentagram of spirit receptive. Set it with an invoking spiral.

Invoking Spirit
Passive Pentagram

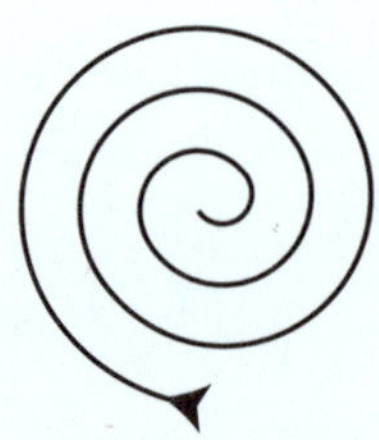

Invoking Spiral

Slowly exhale and direct the power down into the chalice. This charges the water contained therein. Then say:

Most pure substance, you are the first, without limits and without form. You are the basis for all that is.

Lift the chalice of water off the dish and set it nearby, thus exposing the salt that is sitting in the middle of the dish.

Then take up the pointy tool and draw an invoking pentagram of spirit active. Set it with an invoking spiral.

Invoking Spirit Active Pentagram

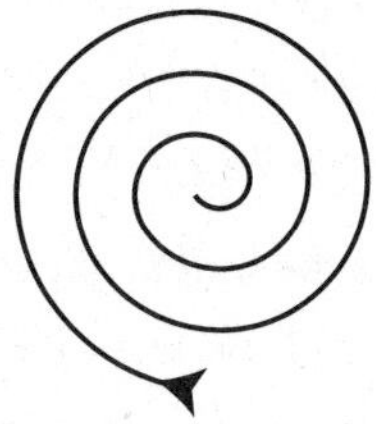

Invoking Spiral

Slowly exhale and direct the power down onto the dish, thus charging the salt contained therein. Then say:

Most perfect fractal, you are the second. You are found within all things but have no substance of your own. You are the pattern of all creation.

Then take the dish and carefully pour some of the salt into the chalice. Set down the dish and place the chalice back upon it. Then take the pointy tool up for a final time and draw an invoking spiral.

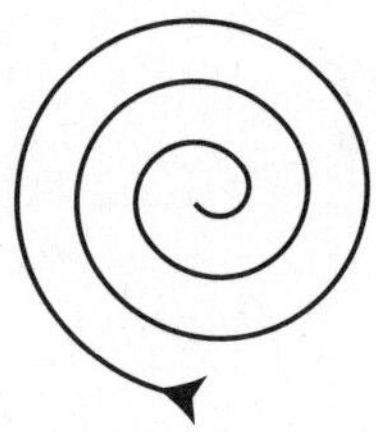

Invoking Spiral

Lower the pointy tool into the chalice, slowly exhale, and stir the mixture three times. Finally, kneel before the resultant sacrament, lean over it, and blow your breath over the surface of the water. Then say:

> *Motion is the child of time and space. All things move and all things change. This holy elixir embodies the forces of Creation that it may sanctify this sacred temple.*

Lift up the chalice and say:

Let there be light!

Sanctifying the Space

Take the holy water and walk deosil (clockwise) around the temple, sprinkling the temple and any other participants. Next, walk the incense around the space so all participants are briefly enveloped. When the circuit is finished, proclaim:

The temple has been purified.

Separating the Space

Take a sword or other tool you have been using and draw a ring of white light around the periphery of the circle. Say:

> *Circle of light, this is the cauldron of transformation wherein all wonders are possible. Let the great works accomplished here reverberate throughout heaven and earth. As it is below so shall it be above. As it is within so shall it be without.*

Setting the Four Watchtowers

Face east and draw the invoking pentagram of air.

Invoking Air Pentagram

Vibrate *YHVH* (Yeh-ho-wah). Then draw the invoking spiral.

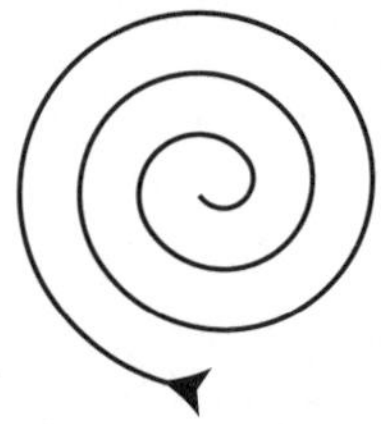

Invoking Spiral

Say:

> *I invoke thee Raphael, regal archangel of healing. Grant us clarity that we may understand the voice of the Higher Self.*

Turn and face south. Draw the invoking pentagram of fire.

Invoking Fire Pentagram

Vibrate *ADNI* (Ah-do-nhai). Then draw the invoking spiral.

Invoking Spiral

Say:

> *I invoke thee Michael, armored archangel of protection. Grant us your insight that we may evolve to reach the most sublime aspects of our Higher Selves.*

Turn and face west. Draw the invoking pentagram of water.

Invoking Water Pentagram

Vibrate *EHIH* (Eh-heh-yeh). Then draw the invoking spiral.

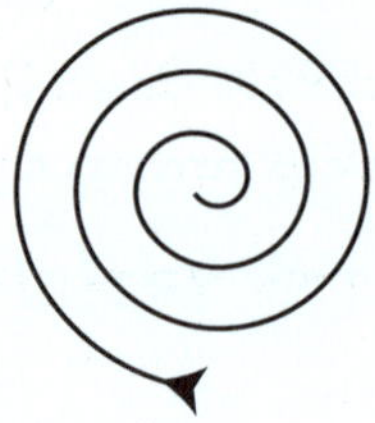

Invoking Spiral

Say:

> *I invoke thee Gabriel, the archangel of the chalice and silver crescent. Grant us your compassion and help us to be patient in our connection to others as we evolve along the path.*

Turn and face north. Draw the invoking pentagram of earth.

Invoking Earth Pentagram

Vibrate *AGLA* (Ah-gw-lah). Then draw the invoking spiral.

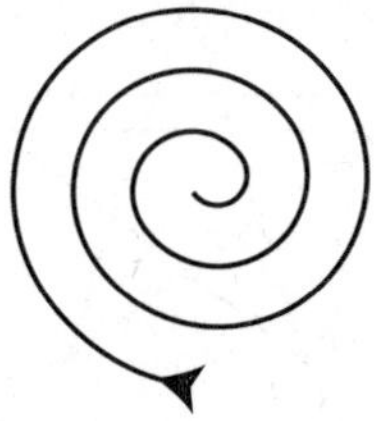

Invoking Spiral

Say:

> *I invoke thee Uriel, archangel of abundance. Help us to thrive in this material world that we may have the resources to pursue our spiritual path.*

Turn and face center. Draw the invoking pentagram of spirit active to the ultrapoint, a space above the center.

Invoking Spirit Active Pentagram

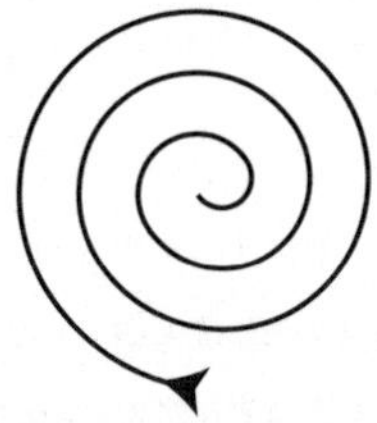

Invoking Spiral

Draw the invoking pentagram of spirit receptive to the infrapoint, a space below the center.

Invoking Spirit Passive Pentagram

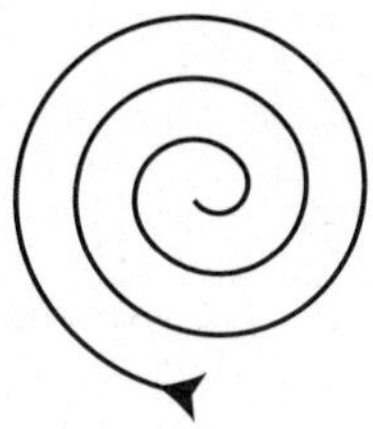

Invoking Spiral

Connect the two spirit pentagrams with an invoking spiral while vibrating *Ararita*. The spiral should start very wide to encompass both pentagrams. In the mezzo point, a space in the very center, an axis mundi, or navel of the world connecting the heavens and earth, is created. Say:

I invoke the power of my holy guardian angel. With the assistance of the archangels of the tetramorph we can obtain the knowledge and conversation of our holy guardian angel and thus achieve our life's potential. The temple structure is now complete!

Final Blessing

Next say:

We have traveled to the regions beyond to create a place of power, a place that once was dark and is now filled with light. The forces of the universe have come to sanctify this sacred space and witness the great works that shall herein follow. By the names of God, through the ministries of the archangels, shall our will thus be made manifest.

Continuing Practice

Within this sacred space other rituals are performed, such as the Rose Ankh Vortex (chapter 18) or the Elemental Octagram (chapter 23). The rest of the rituals in this book will require a temple opening to be effective. When you have completed any additional rites, dismiss each pentagram with a banishing spiral in reverse order (going north, west, south, and east) while giving feelings of thanks and farewells to each of the archangels, gods, or other ally spirits you have invited in. You can then say a dedication of merit if you wish.

• • • • • • •

Practice this ritual until you feel you can comfortably perform it with confidence before moving on to other more complex rituals, such as the Rose Ankh in the following chapter and the rituals in later chapters. You do not need to fully memorize the rite; just be able to perform it, reading from the book, with confidence. Practice creating sacred space and just being mindful in the space. Meditate and really try to appreciate the sacred space you have created, then close.

— CHAPTER 18 —
The Rose Ankh Vortex

The Rose Ankh Vortex rite is intended to contain, heal, and ground. It can also offer a powerful protection against magical attack and all forms of negative energy. It is used to contain and amplify invocations of angels and archetypal beings, such as gods and goddesses.

This ritual was originally presented in Frater Barrabbas's book *Mastering the Art of Ritual Magick* and again in a slightly altered form in *Spirit Conjuring for Witches*. It was presented as a template with the intention that the reader would create their own version after studying and understanding the original. We have done just that. Erich himself struggled for years to find the inspiration to rewrite this ritual, and he only found it when he invoked the angelic presence Hcoma. She gave him permission to express this aspect of himself and cleared the blockages he had. She let him hear his own words.

We will mainly use the Rose Ankh to contain and enhance the eidolon fields of energy we will work with. Combined with a temple consecration, it creates the perfect womb that will allow us to commune with angelic forces, gods, and other archetypes. The chapter on godforms (chapter 19) has two example invocations you can use with this rite.

We have found the Rose Ankh to have many useful purposes. It can also be cast as an extremely powerful banishing and protecting ritual. If invoked with the goddess's dark aspect, the energy spirals downward, forming a psychic black hole capable of capturing any energy and transforming the energy into a beneficent form.

It is important to understand that the Rose Ankh requires a temple consecration to be performed first in the area that the Rose Ankh will be performed. The temple consecration creates the sacred space and context for the Rose Ankh. The Rose Ankh is performed to the angels between the watchtowers. If the watchtowers are not there, then the Rose Ankh will fizzle out. Nothing bad will happen; it's just that the ritual won't be nearly as strong.

The Archetypes

The design of this ritual requires five feminine archetypes to represent the cycles of feminine experience. The number five is chosen because the ritual design employs four angels united to a central point that represents the great feminine spirit herself. The geometry created by this rite is shaped like an inverted pyramid, pointing downward.

In order to rework the ritual, we first examined the archetypes and came up with working definitions. We believe each archetype has its own wisdom and insight to offer. Likewise, each of these archetypes has its own ability to nurture. Briefly, we'll review the construction of the Rose Ankh Vortex and its archetypes.

Maiden Archetype

The maiden represents independence and originality; she is uncorrupted and authentic. She answers to nobody. Her nurturing powers are directed inward, as she is developing her vision of what could be: an idealized view of a world of possibilities. A nonconformist, the maiden does not follow the crowd. Bohemian in style and thought, her wisdom is that of the outsider. She is able to render judgment and advice without bias or preconceived notions.

The maiden archetype we chose is Neith (Nayeth). Neith is a very old goddess from the ancient Egyptian pantheon who was considered to be eternally virgin and able to create parthenogenetically. She was considered to be self-created at the dawn of time. She was very wise, and even the gods came to her to settle disputes because of her impartiality. Her major festival was the Feast of Lights, where multitudes of colored lights were lit in her honor. Like many Egyptian goddesses, she has many aspects. As a war goddess, she was called on to bless weapons. As the goddess of weaving and other domestic arts, she was said to be the creator of mummy wrappings and to weave the world into existence each morning.[46] She is usually shown as a woman wearing the red crown of lower Egypt and holding the Was scepter, showing she has power over the forces of chaos. The Was

46. Bolton, *Lady of Arrows*; Pinch, *Egyptian Mythology*.

scepter is a thin staff with a small fork at the bottom and a Set-like head at the top. Another one of her symbols includes arrows crossed over a shield.

Other maiden goddesses could include the Greek goddesses Persephone and Hestia.

Amazon Archetype

The Amazon encounters the world directly. She fights for justice and takes her rightful place in the world without asking for permission. She has the focus the maiden lacks. She now knows what she wants and pursues it without hesitation. She is liberated sexually, and she is free to pursue all of life's pleasures as she sees fit. She is in control of her body.

The Amazon's wisdom comes from self-understanding and self-mastery. Her nurturing aspect is that she breaks up old patterns and others' projected expectations. This can be a harsh lesson in boundaries, but it is necessary for the growth of individuals and society as a whole, as it expands opportunities for expression.

The goddess Bast from the ancient Egyptian pantheon is the Amazon archetype that has both the protectress aspect of Sekhmet and a hedonistic aspect as well. Bast is the warrior daughter and protector of Ra and was quite dangerous to anyone who had been abusive to others. In her more hedonistic form, Bast was the goddess of sunrise, music, dance, and pleasure as well as family, fertility, birth, and perfume and other luxuries. She was one of the most worshiped deities in ancient Egypt. Her festivals were very popular and included music, dancing, and drinking to excess. She is often represented as a woman with a cat's head holding a sistrum, a type of rattle used to create music.[47]

Other examples of the Amazon archetype include the Greek goddesses Athena and Artemis and perhaps the Norse goddess Freyja.

Mother Archetype

Giver of life, the mother archetype nurtures her creations with immense powers of unconditional love, devotion, and caring. The mother's children are the visions of the maiden actualized with the power acquired by the Amazon. These creations can be a family, a business, books, research, gardens, art, and all things creative. The ultimate expression of the mother archetype is civilization itself and culture. Her unique wisdom is in knowing when to nurture and when to remove

---

47. Pinch, *Egyptian Mythology*, 115–17; Budge, *The Gods of the Egyptians*, 444.

the training wheels. She understands how to guide her creations from childhood to strength and independence.

The mother archetype we chose is the Egyptian goddess Mut, whose name literally means "mother" in ancient Egyptian. She is the world mother, having given birth to the gods, and she was the queen of the goddesses. At her festival, her statue is placed on a bark and sailed around Isheru (the crescent moon–shaped lake at her temple at Karnak). She is depicted as a regal woman wearing a headdress that combines a vulture and a rearing cobra. Vultures were considered to be good mothers with protective powers. The cobra, or uraeus, was the supreme symbol of power and authority in ancient Egypt. She is also shown holding the Was scepter.[48]

Other examples of the mother archetype include the Mesopotamian goddess Ninmah, the Norse goddess Frigg, and perhaps the Greek Gaia and Hera.

Crone Archetype

The crone is the source of wisdom and experience, having seen the world and witnessed its rhythms. The crone understands cycles and the importance of death and renewal. She is very capable of reinventing herself, having been through the circle of life, and she is now free once again to define herself as she sees fit. Her particular wisdom, though, is not just the vast experience she has gained but also the ability to solve problems that seem impossible. She knows secrets that hold the way to both worldly and spiritual transformation. Her vast life experience has also given her great compassion and understanding; wherever you are, she has been there and will help you with insight so you can figure it out for yourself.

We will use Egyptian goddess Nephthys as our crone archetype. A complex goddess, Nephthys is one of the original five gods of ancient Egypt. She was a member of the Ennead of Heliopolis, a tribunal of nine deities of immense power. She is also called the excellent goddess or useful goddess, as she represented divine assistance and protective guardianship on a multitude of levels.[49] As a funerary goddess, who represented the normal transitioning of life and death, she is shown as a hawk or as a woman with wings outstretched for protection.

Nephthys is nearly always depicted crowned by the hieroglyphics for her name. This is made of a combination of the sign for a sacred temple enclosure (*hwt*) and the sign for neb, or lady. She may also be seen on top of the funeral boat, accompanying and assisting the dead in several stages of the afterlife. Because of this, she was given the title Friend of the Dead. As goddess of mourning, she

48. Pinch, *Egyptian Mythology*, 168–69; Budge, *The Gods of the Egyptians*, 28.

49. Pinch, *Egyptian Mythology*, 171–72; Budge, *The Gods of the Egyptians*, 260–64.

comforts the relatives of the dead. She is believed to be the personification of the idea of darkness and everything it entails and covers. Nephthys is also the sister of Isis and her complement. As Isis represents the experience of birth, Nephthys represents the experience of death.

Other crone archetypes include the Norse Hel and the Welsh Cerridwen; the Greek goddess Hekate is also a possibility.

Unifying Archetype

In this ritual, the four great goddess archetypes are invoked to the four angles between the four watchtowers and then united to the infrapoint. The infrapoint is a point in space below the center of the sacred space. A vortex then forms, flowing upward from this point or downward into it depending on the intent of the ritual.

The unifying archetype we will work with is the Egyptian goddess Isis. Her main aspect was that of a great magician whose power transcended that of all other deities. Several narratives tell of her magical prowess, which was far stronger than the powers of Osiris and Ra. She was frequently invoked on behalf of the sick, and with the goddesses Nephthys, Neith, and Selket, she protected the dead. Isis became associated with various other goddesses, including Bast, Nut, and Hathor, and thus her nature and her powers became increasingly diverse. It is impossible to list the attributes of Isis, as she possessed the powers of a water goddess, earth goddess, star goddess, queen of the underworld, and woman. She united in herself one or more of the attributes of all the goddesses of Egypt known to us. Isis was pictured as a woman wearing a long sheath dress with the horns of a cow on her head, with the solar disk between them. She is also depicted nursing a young Horus (Harpocrates).[50]

Other unifying goddess archetypes include the famous Venus of Willendorf, one of the oldest representations of the female form, discovered in the village Willendorf in Austria. It is estimated to have been made in Paleolithic times, between 25,000 and 20,000 BCE. There is a tendency to choose Mother goddesses for the unifying archetype, but what we need is a creator goddess, such as the Sumerian Nammu or the ancient Mesopotamian Tiamat. We have to go way back to find creator goddesses.

---

50. Pinch, *Egyptian Mythology*, 149–52; Budge, *The Gods of the Egyptians*, 186–94, 202.

The Flow of the Rose Ankh

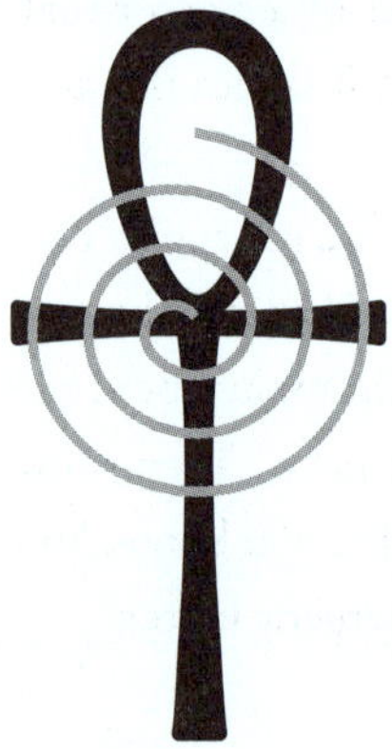
Rose Ankh

Now that we have reviewed the archetypes, let's look at the parts of the ritual. The words of power in this rite were taken from a dictionary of Egyptian language of the Middle Kingdom. The book is called *Egyptian Grammar, Being an Introduction to the Study of Hieroglyphs* by Alan Gardener. It is a wonderful old book Erich rescued from a library sale a long time ago. A local university library has annual sales of books no one is checking out to make room for new stuff; it's often full of treasures.

Introit

The introit, or introduction, is intended to convey a sense of mystery and the sacred feminine.

Setting of the Angels

The Rose Ankh is a combination of the life-giving forces of the ankh and the passion of the rose. It is drawn in the air starting at the bottom, looping over the top, and then the cross bar is drawn first to the left and then to the right, reinforcing the bar. An invoking spiral is then drawn over the center of the ankh.

This device will be drawn to the angles between the watchtowers. It helps to visualize the ankh as implanted in the ground. When you draw the ankh, pull the energy up from the fiery center of the earth so the final symbol is of a glowing, powerful ankh firmly connected to the power of the earth. This ritual fits into the diamond shape created by the consecration rite, stacking and enhancing the sacred space. The fifth point is below the floor, like an inverted pyramid.

Keyword Analysis

You did a keyword analysis in the Lesser Banishing Ritual of the Pentagram at the end. This method is commonly used to join together a series of ritual actions into one expression. In the Rose Ankh and many other rituals, we first repeat the invoking word used on the watchtowers, then each letter is used to form a new word that summarizes the ritual actions. Our new word based on the sacred words used to invoke the watchtowers, or watch-angles in this case, is *usasat*, ancient Egyptian for "sanctuary." Next, you fuse the whole structure together with a ritual gesture called the Assumption Sign.

The Assumption Sign

The Assumption Sign is a gesture that allows the magician to assume the power of a given ritual, becoming its mediator, and it also serves to fuse the ritual actions together. This finalizes the keyword analysis.

To perform the Assumption Sign, stand, reach down to your feet, and visualize the infrapoint that is below the space. Using your imagination, grab the infrapoint with your hands. Then slowly raise your arms while imagining you are still holding the infrapoint, pulling it up to the ultrapoint above the space. Once the infra- and ultrapoints are united, pull them both down into your heart. Then bring your hands down across your chest, with your arms crossed and your hands on your collar bones. You are taking the ritual and its energies into your being and becoming one with the energetic vortex.

Walking the Spiral

Walking the spiral raises energy to fill and activate the spiral, to get it spinning. The chant used during this action was given to Erich during an invocation of the spirit Hcoma. We move counterclockwise, as we are grounding energy. This spiral dance is the real point of the ritual; the previous steps create a container of sacred geometry to hold the vortex.

R•I•T•U•A•L
EGYPTIAN ROSE ANKH VORTEX

The following is the full Rose Ankh Vortex ritual. Note that you will need to perform a temple consecration first, and you will need to gather those tools and supplies as well as what is listed here.

Things You Need

A bell or chime; if you don't have one simply knock on the table or floor
Something pointy to draw the rose ankhs

Preparation

Begin by performing a temple consecration (chapter 17). This gives the Rose Ankh Vortex a context to form within. The temple consecration creates the watchtowers to the four directions, and then the rose ankh fits within this by occupying the angles between the directions.

When the temple is raised, ring the bell once.

Directions

Introit

All face east. Recite the following:

The valley spirit never dies.
It is the woman, the primal mother.
Her gateway is the root of heaven and earth.
It is like a veil barely seen.
Use it; it will never fail.

Setting of the Angles

Move to face the northwest angle. Draw a rose ankh and vibrate the word *uaabti* (one who is pure). Say:

I call thee Neith, pure one who stands at the dawn of time weaving the world into being. Wearer of the red crown of lower Egypt, you hold the Was scepter of power over chaos. Your judgment is respected even among the gods, for you see the truth of how our world could be—perfect and ideal. Hail and welcome, Neith!

Draw a circle of blue flame to the southwest angle. Draw a rose ankh and vibrate the word *saah* (to be born free). Say:

I call thee Bast, cat-headed goddess of justice and pleasure. You drink deep of life's pleasures and command respect from all. You are the imperative of true desire, and all follow you in pursuit of their True Will. Hail and welcome, Bast!

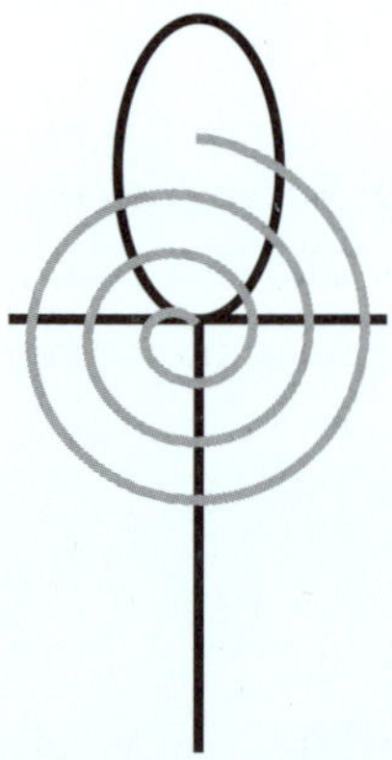

Rose Ankh Simple

Draw a circle of blue flame to the southeast angle. Draw a rose ankh and vibrate the word *aanmer* (to love). Say:

I call unto thee Mut, primal mother of the gods. Regal goddess, wearer of the vulture crown, whose soft wings protect and nurture all, your selfless love is what teaches us to be human. Hail and welcome, Mut!

Draw a circle of blue flame to the northeast angle. Draw a rose ankh and vibrate the word *shesa* (wisdom). Say:

> *I call upon thee Nephthys, excellent goddess whose outstretched wings offer comfort and assistance to all. From you we learn not to fear the darkness and the transformation it contains. Hail and welcome, Nephthys!*

Draw a circle of blue flame back to the northwest angle and face the center of the circle. Draw a rose ankh to the infrapoint below the center of the circle and vibrate the word *tchet* (eternity). Say:

> *Great goddess Isis, I call to you. Isis, who is crowned with the sun, the moon at her feet, Isis, the greatest of all magicians, you are all goddesses and all women. You are the eternal spirit of womanhood, the sustainer of peace, of life, and giver of civilization. Hail and welcome, Isis!*

Unite the four angles to the infrapoint and to each other, creating an inverted pyramid shape, using a blue flame as before.

Keyword Analysis

Direct energy into each of the five nodes. Perform the Assumption Sign by standing, raising your arms, reaching down to your feet, and slowly raising your arms until they are above your head in a V shape. Then bring your hands down to your chest with your arms crossed and your hands on your collar bones. While doing so, vibrate: *"Uaabti, saah, aanmer, shesa, tchet, USASAT. I* (we) *seek sanctuary in the embrace of the goddess."*

Walking the Spiral

Starting at the edge of the sacred space, walk a spiral path widdershins (counterclockwise), making three revolutions before reaching the center. The following invocation can be intoned while walking the path, or you can intone any favorite goddess chant you like.

She is the unity of all.
She is the light on the path.
In her all things move.
In her all things live.
She is love and all things respond to her.

Rituals within the Vortex

Within this vortex more rituals are performed. Ideally you would invoke a deity, an angel, or other being to gain their wisdom or even ask for help with your life. Invoked archetypes can even be asked to empower other rituals you are performing. You can also take on a godform, which is described in the next chapter. The Rose Ankh Vortex will enhance any contact you create with an angel or an archetype especially.

When you are finished with this rite, send feelings of gratitude and thanks to the archetypes and disperse the rose ankhs with a banishing spiral in reverse order. Chapter 19, "Godforms," has examples of a ritual that you would perform within the Rose Ankh Vortex.

• • • • • • •

The Rose Ankh Vortex is an unusual and highly useful ritual that is not often mentioned. The ritual can generate a powerful vortex of healing and concealing energies that will both enhance any invocation of an archetype and act to conceal you from negative energies. We would recommend performing it and then just enjoying the energies the first time. Once you understand the ritual flow, proceed to the next ritual and invoke one of the godforms into a Rose Ankh Vortex.

— CHAPTER 19 —
godforms

We have said that our real nature is divine, and we have a spiritual guide, or Holy Guardian Angel, to lead us in our spiritual journey. We need a way to shift our awareness to this divine state, to wake up a bit so we can commune and work with the forces of the universe. Our nous is the same as the Creator's nous; we just need to come into our awareness of what is truly real.

In many spiritual traditions, a practitioner or a priest must first gain the spiritual authority before performing a spiritual task or ritual. In Solomonic traditions, the magician takes on the mantle of the Christian or Jewish God to command the forces of the universe by praying—lots of praying. In Buddhist traditions, a primary archetype (or *yidam*) is employed as a representation of certain divine qualities the practitioner wishes to exemplify. This is very similar to the method we will use.

What we want to do at the beginning of a ritual is activate a magical self, a self that is divine in nature and is used at least primarily in spiritual practices. We call this a godform. We choose a representation of the Divine that we can feel close to, and rather than overcoming the personality, we merge with it to enhance our identity. Thus, empowered by the archetype, we will then have much greater magical force to use in ritual since we are then connected to the collective unconscious and its limitless reservoir of power.

In the chapter on archetypes, we mentioned that Jung considered all gods and goddess of mythology to be representations of the Self archetype. Here we are stepping directly into this and assuming the godform intentionally.

Accessing a Godform

To gain access to a godform, it is necessary to first do a formal practice of invoking and contacting the archetype. This formal practice will give us the experience of being that godform, with all of its powers and abilities, and it gives us an opportunity to ask the archetype to be a part of our spiritual practice.

The formal process is actually very simple and straightforward, but it can be difficult if you are not used to working with divine archetypes. For many of us, modernity teaches us that imagination is dangerous and not to be trusted. If you can hold in your mind that you are doing a practice that is designed to awaken the divinity within you by connecting with the divinity of tradition, you can quiet the inner warnings of cultural taboo.

As Lon Milo DuQuette reminds us, it's okay to pray;[51] it's fine to feel reverence for these archetypes that represent our highest ideals. You are not worshiping a false idol. Rather, you are seeing the infinite in a single expression that you can comprehend. Since you are the Creator dreaming a life as a human, it's okay to dream you are Zeus or Ganesha for a bit. And yes, it is a lot of fun.

First, think of a divine being you can feel real reverence and respect for. Better yet, find one you can love intensely. This is a very important part of your spiritual journey. Choosing a vision of the Divine that you can feel real awe and love for is important, as all spiritual growth and even mundane growth is powered by the emotion of love. Anything you love to do, you will eventually do well.

By forming a loving connection with some vision of the Divine, you set up a sort of feedback loop where the love you send is returned at a higher frequency. This love loop is important, as it forms the basis of all our spiritual practices. As Aleister Crowley famously said, "Love is the law, love under will."[52] Our will must be directed by our capacity for feeling love.

First feel love specifically and then generally. Find the divinity within and you are on your way to meeting your Holy Guardian Angel. If you can see divinity within another person, then you will fall in love; find the divinity with all creation and you are on your way to enlightenment. In Buddhism there is a similar concept. *Bodhicitta* is the Sanskrit word for "awakening mind." It represents

---

51. DuQuette, *Enochian Vision Magick*, 30.

52. Crowley, *The Law Is for All.*

cultivating wisdom and compassion for all sentient beings. Without bodhicitta, we can become lost in a meaningless state of existence.

Your chosen god or other being can be from any pantheon, culture, or time in history. You can change your archetype later, so feel free to experiment. We suggest that it not be a character from modern fiction, a comic book, or an anime. The archetype should be considered sacred in order to have that deep link to the collective unconscious. But it is up to you. Success will be your indication that you are on the right track.

Once you choose your archetype, research them; there is so much information online now this should be easy. Find out what they like, stories about them, what things they rule, and any poetry or invocations that are traditionally used to call or worship them. Get to know them.

The Greek gods are easy if you are just starting to work with archetypes. There is a wealth of information available online to begin your research. For Example, the Orphic Hymns, which are eighty-seven hymns to the Greek gods from the fifth century BCE, can be found online. If you wanted to commune with Jesus, then perhaps read Matthew 5:3–12, the eight beatitudes in Matthew. You need some really inspiring words and to speak them well with emotion. This practice requires that you really feel and emote in order to call forth the archetype.

In the Temple of Limitless Light, we start people out with Ma'at. She is a great goddess to start with because she represents the universal quality of order and balance. We also have a public ritual on the fall equinox where we invoke Ma'at since the sun is moving into Libra. Having Ma'at on your side as you go into spiritual practices that can potentially be unbalancing is a great idea.

Don't worry about mixing the Egyptian gods found in these rituals with a god from another pantheon because within the sacred space, everything is sacred and worthy. If you want to rewrite the Rose Ankh Vortex to fit your favorite pantheon, then please do.

The Flow of Accessing Godforms

Once armed with knowledge, decorate your sacred space with objects and symbols that your archetype likes. While not required, this step helps to create an atmosphere that is conducive to communing with the sacred archetype. The formal practice of a godform rite involves performing a temple consecration and then the Rose Ankh Vortex, reading an invocation that is designed to call the deity, and then assuming the archetype. The rite should mirror the following three-step pattern.

Reverence

The first part of your invocation should be a reverent address of your chosen deity. With as much poetry as you can muster, state the deity's attributes, appearance, and abilities. While the gods know flattery for what it is, they all enjoy it. Read the invocation you are using with real feeling.

Invocation

In the next part, you ask your deity to come and appear and bless the ceremony. At this point, visualize the form of your archetype slowly appearing and then becoming more solid until you see it in your imagination strongly. See it wearing the clothes it should have and breathing—really alive. See the deity above you, radiant with power and light, then project feelings of devotion and love. Sit with this in nonjudgmental awareness and see what comes up for you.

Merge with the Godform

In the final section of the invocation, speak as the deity. Imagine merging with the archetype and becoming empowered by it. This section should read something like, "I am Isis, the greatest of magicians. I did resurrect Osiris; it was I who humbled great Ra…" Imagine the godform floating down and merging with you. Feel its power, its abilities, merging with yours.

Once you have assumed the godform, you can do several things. You may wish to bless some sacrament, such as wine and bread, and consume it. You may wish to sit in awareness and scry your deity. You can also do further rituals empowered by the godform. You can also do all three. It's up to you.

Ending the Godform

When you are done, imagine the deity leaving your body. Give feelings of thanks and farewell and close the temple. This would be a good time to say a dedication of merit.

• • • • • • •

Following are two examples of godform rituals. The first is for the Egyptian goddess Ma'at, a goddess of balance. The second example ritual is for Thoth, the Egyptian god of all knowledge. These are two great allies for you in your quest for liberation. You should perform this ritual until you feel an authentic connection to your chosen deity, then you can use the informal practice to add power to your rituals.

Once you have that authentic connection, you can assume a godform at the start of a ritual practice and carry it through to add power to any rite you perform. Many ritual magicians have several godforms that they use at different points in the ritual flow. For example, you may assume Horus in the creation of sacred space or select some other protector god, goddess, or hero. Perhaps the point of the ritual is healing, so you switch to Isis or Nephthys or some other healing god, goddess, or hero. How you apply this technique is up to you and your own intuition and experience. Start by leaning one well, then expand as you feel comfortable.

R•I•T•U•A•L GODFORM OF MA'AT

This is the first godform that we give to our students. Thoth is given next, after the student feels proficient with Ma'at. You will need to perform two preparatory rituals first: a temple consecration and the Rose Ankh Vortex. Read through the instructions so you are prepared.

Things You Need

Space for the ritual

Directions

To begin, perform a temple consecration to create the sacred space and context for your deity to appear (chapter 17). Then perform the Rose Ankh Vortex to create an energy field that will nurture and empower your archetype (chapter 18).

Next, you only need to read the reverence, invocation, and godform words that follow. Read them with real feeling, like a priest or priestess of the deity, which is what you are for the duration of the ritual.

Reverence

Homage to Ma'at, who is order personified. Without you, Ma'at, the sun and stars could not shine. Without Ma'at, there is no meaning and understanding.

I raise my hands in honor to your name, which is both right and truth. Without Ma'at, I could not recognize the truth and would be lost in confusion.

Ma'at, whose white feather rests upon the scales of the universe. Ma'at, you await in your hall of judgment to weigh the heart of the initiate. Your judgment is fair and understanding.

Ma'at, without you there would be no ethics. You are the foundation of the cosmos and civil society. Ma'at, lady of justice and harmony, to you we sing praises of your grace and our gratitude.

Invocation

I invoke thee, Ma'at. She who is order; she who makes it possible for the sun to shine, the Nile to flood, and humanity to have understanding.

Let my heart be placed upon the scales of truth by Ma'at herself that I may be found worthy. Do not condemn me; do not let my heart be devoured by Ammit. Do not let me die a second death. Let me be reborn in light and glory as the sun god Ra each day.

I invoke thee, Ma'at. You infuse all of creation with order. When we are in tune with you, we will prosper.

Ma'at, you are the cosmic order. You are the model for human behavior. As the stars move in their due course, we all must follow our inner nature. Ma'at, show us the way of truth, of morality, and of cooperation with the universe.

I invoke thee, Ma'at. Your husband is Thoth, god of the moon, writing, and all knowledge.

Without Ma'at, the world would return to the primal chaos from which it came.

Godform

Ma'at, who comes into being with the universe, unborn and eternal, let my heart merge with yours. Let us become as one.

I am Ma'at. It is I who judges the souls of the departed in my dual hall. It is I who goes forth in secret with Ra to unite all the gods in the heavens.

Ma'at, who comes into being with the universe, unborn and eternal, let my heart merge with yours. Let us become as one.

I am Ma'at, and I ask that you do not burn with rage or seek vengeance on those who have wronged you.

Ma'at, who comes into being with the universe, unborn and eternal, let my heart merge with yours. Let us become as one.

I am Ma'at, and I ask that you do not disrespect the sacred, ignore the truth, or pollute the sacred waters, land, and air.

I am Ma'at, and I give you control over your thoughts and actions.

I am Ma'at, and I give you devotion and purpose.

I am Ma'at, and I ask that you seek awareness of truth.

I am Ma'at, and I give you the ability to wield the truth.

I am Ma'at, and I have spoken.

At this point you should sit and be with Ma'at. Feel the fusion of yourself with the goddess and concept of Ma'at. At first, sit in mindful meditation with the goddess. When you are ready to close, release your connection to Ma'at and send her feelings of gratitude. Then shut down the temple and say a dedication of merit.

Once you feel like you have an authentic connection, you can use this goddess form in ritual. You may also want to create a small shrine to Ma'at if you wish to continue working with her.

R•I•T•U•A•L GODFORM OF THOTH

The next godform you will experience is that of Thoth, the god of writing and all knowledge. Thoth, or Tahuti, is also the god of magic; only Isis is a more powerful magician. Once again, you will be performing preliminary rituals before this one.

Things You Need

Space for the ritual

Directions

The ritual is the same as before. First, consecrate the temple, then cast the Rose Ankh. Next, you only need to read the words that follow. Do so with real feeling, as a true priest or priestess of Thoth.

Reverence

Great Thoth, your knowledge spans all space and time. Thoth, who is the scribe of the gods and records all deeds and speech.

Thoth, who has the head of an ibis bird and who holds an ankh in one hand, the staff of power in the other. Giver of writing and of the calendar.

O Thoth, who is as the baboon who greets Ra in the morning as the moon god.

You are the god of equilibrium and the enforcer of Ma'at. You, who brings the universe into balance. Great Thoth, I call to thee in the names of Dajuti and Hermes Trismegistus. You are the master magician and architect of our reality.

Invocation

Inventor and teacher of astronomy, astrology, engineering, botany, geometry, and surveying, thee I invoke.

Reckoner of time, thy name means truth; wearer of the lunar disk, thee I invoke.

Author of the spells in the book of coming forth by day, master magician, thee I invoke.

Thy head is as an emerald, thy nemyss as the night sky, holder of the double wand of power, thee I invoke.

You who pilot the ship of Ra as it sails through the heavens, thee I invoke.

Godform

"I am thy writing palette, O Thoth, and I have brought unto thee thine ink-jar. I am not of those who work iniquity in their secret places; let not evil happen unto me."[53]

53. Budge, *The Book of the Dead*, 562.

The god of wisdom in my heart and in my mouth. I travel upon the heights of Nuit. Behold Thoth is in me, and I am in him. My tongue is a sanctuary for truth.

I am Thoth. It was I who broke the curse of Ra; it was I who won the five sacred days from Khonsu so Nuit could bear her children.

I am Thoth, self-begotten. I am yesterday, today, and the brother of tomorrow. I am the order of time itself.

I am Thoth, my wife is Ma'at, who is order itself, and my daughter is Seshat, goddess of science.

I am Thoth. I am wisdom eternal. I am thrice great, and I am the lord of balance and equilibrium.

At this point you should sit and be with Thoth. Feel the fusion of yourself with the god and concept of Thoth. At first, sit in mindful meditation with the god. When you are ready to close, release your connection to Thoth and send him feelings of gratitude. Then shut down the temple and say a dedication of merit.

Once you feel like you have an authentic connection, you can use this godform in ritual. You may also want to create a small shrine to Thoth if you wish to continue working with him.

• • • • • • •

With some practice, you will be able to assume a godform automatically while in ritual without an invocation, but it is wise to first establish a relationship with the deity by practicing this rite. If you remember the body sensations and how it feels to be in the godform, you will be able to recall the change of consciousness later. This is the informal practice.

Once the formal practice is accomplished and you know the feeling in your body of being at one with your chosen archetype, you can just quickly remember this when you are doing ritual work as a way to enhance your spiritual abilities in all aspects of ritual. You can shorten the invocation and remember the feelings of awe and power that come over you as you invoke the god or goddess. This then can become an informal practice, which you can use as an enhancer for any ritual work. A single paragraph of intoned or mentally recited invocation will be all that is needed to trigger the full effect of the ritual, but from time to time you will want to do the full ritual, such as at a public ceremony marking the equinox or solstice. You can continue to do the formal practice as well.

Once you have done the full ritual a few times, it should be easy to assume the godform of your choice. People who have developed several godforms will sometimes switch during a longer, more complex rite. They may start out as a messenger and guide, like Anubis, then switch to a healing goddess, like Nephthys, if that is the point of the ceremony.

— CHAPTER 20 —
The Greater Ritual of the Pentagram

The Greater Ritual of the Pentagram (GRP) combines all the skills and techniques you have been learning during your adventure with this book to create your first pure eidolon. This ritual is the simplest pure eidolon we can create, yet it is powerful enough to call the elemental kings. We will use the GRP to call forth the elemental kings to gain their wisdom and create positive change in our lives. These will be your first encounters with the forces of the universe that make up the structure of our reality; they are the workers that are very close to creation. This ritual is the best way to begin to experience a much larger reality.

When Erich first started studying the Hermetic art of enlightenment, he quickly latched on to the books by Israel Regardie. He studied Aleister Crowley's books, too, but they were too dense for his young mind to understand and frankly mostly still are. Those books contained such mystery and power to him compared to all else that was available. Everything else seemed too simple or too risky. He still has his old copy of Francis Barrett's *The Magus,* which is full of images of scary things to summon. Why would he want to do that? Erich studied and practiced what he could understand from *The Golden Dawn,* written by Israel Regardie, and Crowley's writings. He was able to understand and practice the Qabalistic Cross, the Lesser Ritual of the Pentagram (LRP), and the Middle Pillar exercise, but when he got to the GRP, he got stuck.

The books Erich found didn't have much for practical explanations of what and how to use the more advanced practices. Those early books were just printings of Golden Dawn internal documents.

You needed initiation and training from a teacher to understand the documents, and it could take years of training and initiations from a lodge for an initiate to rise to the point where they could learn the greater pentagram rituals. Since Erich had no teacher or lodge, he studied other things, including the Qabalah, tarot, and meditation.

Enlightenment of the Eidolon

When Erich met Frater Barrabbas, Frater Barrabbas informed him that the GRP created an eidolon, an energy field that matched the signature or frequency of the spirit you wanted to contact. Then it all finally made sense; Erich understood the how and why of these rituals and how to create his own resonant field rituals. He could then see how the preliminary practices, such as the LRP, created a basic eidolon that was general in nature, and thus it is called lesser. The greater ritual is *tunable* to create eidolons of different energies.

The GRP is the best way to learn how to create an eidolon to make contact with the forces of the universe. So far you have been learning all the skills to put the GRP to work for you. Simple but effective and useful, this ritual allows someone new to this style of spiritual practice to gain experience in working with the forces of the universe with the minimum number of moving parts. Once the technique is understood, it can be expanded upon.

This one ritual can create four different resonant fields, one for each element. One simply changes the pentagrams they draw and the final invocation at the end; most of the ritual stays the same. This creates efficiency, as you don't need four different rituals, one for each element. Combining an element with an element will result in sixteen unique resonant fields and much more power. As we start to combine fields, the resulting power and states of consciousness expand exponentially. For now, though, let's use what we have learned so far and start at the beginning.

The Four Elemental Kingdoms of Malkuth

We imagine the Golden Dawn used the GRP for a number of purposes, but we will use it to open the four elemental kingdoms of Malkuth, the last sephiroth on the Tree of Life. On most diagrams of the Tree of Life (if not all), you will notice that the last sephiroth is divided into four sections, obviously for the four elements.

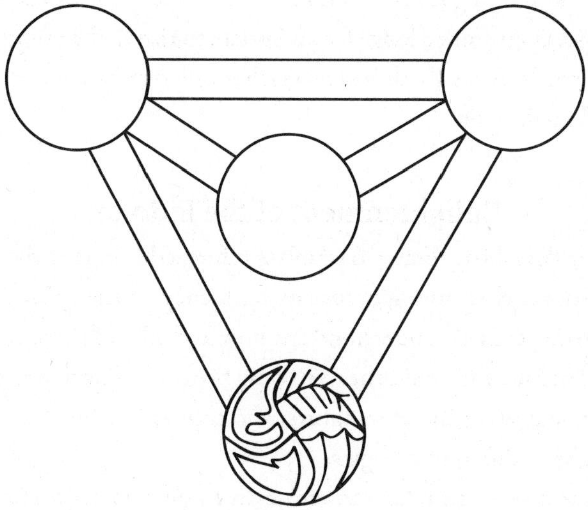

Malkuth

These four kingdoms represent the life force of spirit flowing through the elements in the world around us. By coming to awareness of our world in this way, we can affect positive change in our microcosm.

Paracelsus originated the idea of the elementals representing the life force flowing through the world around us and gave the names of the elementals themselves.

Element Wheel

Fire: Salamanders

Water: Undines

Air: Sylphs

Earth: Gnomes

Originally, he called the earth elementals pygmies, but that word has been abused, so we now call them by the much more friendly term *gnomes*.[54] Who wouldn't want to summon gnomes?

The elementals are the emissaries of the four great archangels that you met when practicing the LRP. We will be invoking the elemental king of each elemental. These are quite powerful spirits but also friendly and helpful. The names of the elemental kings are given to us by Éliphas Lévi in his

54. Paracelsus, *Four Treatises of Theophrastus Von Hohenheim*, 222.

landmark book *Transcendental Magic*. Lévi also gives us the invocations for the elemental kings, which you will be using to invoke and call the kings.[55]

Fire Sigil

Salamanders

Salamanders are the representation of the life force moving through the heat and combustion required by all living things. They also represent the heat energy and light released by the combustion of the other elements. The catabolism of food and light (for plants) gives us the energy and will to act in the world.

The elemental king of the salamanders is Djinn, who is the emissary of archangel Michael in the physical world. While the word *djinn* has become a name for an entire group of beings from Islamic folklore, here we are concerned with the singular entity who is the ruler of the elementals of fire in Malkuth. Djinn is invoked for the healing of disease and vitality. He can teach you to control your own temperature and increase your physical strength and energy. He has abilities associated with the wands suit of the tarot, such as expressing your will to control your own fate in material matters. To us, Djinn appears as a man made of living flame with smoke for hair and a very pleasant smell similar to incense.

Water Sigil

Undines

Undines, the spirits of water (another element needed by all life), are the life spirit animating water. Passing the chemicals of life from creature to creature, keeping all the chemicals of life in solution, and penetrating the cell walls of all living beings, these beings entered our folklore as the mermaids.

The king of the undines is called Nixsa. She is the emissary of archangel Gabriel and is invoked for emotional healing and connection. She also grants clairvoyance and the ability to scry, and she is creative inspiration. She has the powers of the cards from the cups suit of the tarot. Nixsa is a guide to the invisible realities of intuition, emotion, and relationships. She appears to us as a beautiful woman made of water, with an emotional intensity, brooding and full of secret wisdom.

55. Lévi, *Transcendental Magic*.

Air Sigil

Sylphs

Sylphs are the spirits that transfer the life force of the air around us, the spark of life in each molecule of oxygen that almost all living things need to live. Air is the most penetrating element in manifestation, passing through earth and water and feeding fire. Sylphs are said to be lively and fun and very friendly to humans who can communicate with them.

Their king is Paralda, the emissary of archangel Raphael. Paralda is called upon for healing, communication, clarity, and focus. Musical ability and higher learning are also within his ability to bestow. He also gives protection in times of conflict and connects to all things airy, including the suit of swords in the tarot. His true joy is to instruct his magical students in the arts of divination, clairvoyance, and astral projection and the more practical methods of attaining mental clarity, raising alertness and general awareness, and improving memory. He appears to Erich as a young, spritely man wearing the colors of the sunrise surrounded by clouds.

Earth Sigil

Gnomes

Gnomes are the life force responsible for making the earth alive. They make the soil rich and create veins of valuable ore and gemstones and all the riches and resources of the earth. Gnomes are said to be hard workers but dense and stuck in their ways.

Their king is known as Ghob. He appears to Erich as a small humanoid with a largish nose, unkempt hair and beard, dark brownish-red skin, and leather clothing, clutching a satchel. He is the emissary of the archangel Uriel and can help with earthly matters such as finances, stability, vitality, and other things associated with the pentacles suit in the tarot. He is also said to be very good at physical healing and especially at healing bones and joints. He is quite helpful. To us, Ghob appears as a short, muscular humanoid with dark, brownish-red skin, wild hair, and a satchel made of furry animal skin.

The Elemental Kings at a Glance

Name	Element	Emissary of	Powers
Djinn	Fire/Wands	Michael	Will, Vitality, Healing of disease, Protection
Nixsa	Water/Cups	Gabriel	Intuitive knowledge, Emotional healing
Paralda	Air/Swords	Raphael	Learning and memory, Decision-making
Ghob	Earth/Pentacles	Uriel	Wealth, Physical healing, Material stability

Greater Ritual of the Pentagram Design

Now that we've covered the elementals, let's take a look at the flow of the GRP.

Introit

The basic ritual presented in the source material is very skeletal, and our temple needed a version that was more engaging. Since these beings have come into our culture as creatures of the fair folk, we looked for writings and lore that would help make the GRP more interesting. We found our muse in Shakespeare's play *A Midsummer Night's Dream*. While the Bard is not considered sacred within Western culture, his writings are ubiquitous in cinema, theater, and on the small screen. Shakespeare's plays are filled with magic, witches, and even real invocations. John Dee is said to be the inspiration for Prospero in *The Tempest*, and Prospero even has a sylph as a familiar spirit. Shakespeare is absolutely part of the collective unconscious for lots of people, so his work makes a great place to look for verbiage to fill out the ritual. The addition of his verbiage enthralls the imagination of the participants and makes the whole process more engaging and effective. If you are not invested in the process, then it will not change your consciousness as much as if you were enjoying what you were doing.

Creating the Eidolon Field

We create the eidolon by invoking the element we are calling to each of the four directions. What makes the GRP so powerful is the addition of a pentagram of spirit to each direction. First drawing either the pentagram of spirit active or the pentagram of spirit passive (depending on the element) and then fusing with the elemental pentagram generates tremendous power.

For the active elements (air and fire), first draw the pentagram of the spirit active, then the specific invoking pentagram of the active element. For the passive elements (water and earth), first create the invoking pentagram of spirit passive, then the specific invoking pentagram of the passive element. Fuse them, then speak the verbiage listed for the direction. After the invocation to the center, read the individual invocation for the elemental king to be invoked.

Uniting the Center and Opening the Portal

Once you have set the element in each direction, it is time to connect them to the center. You may recognize this pattern presented before as the analysis of the keyword. This creates the field by setting up sacred geometry. In this case it is similar to the Temple Consecration—a double pyramid shape. We create the central axis mundi by invoking the spirit active above and spirit receptive below and drawing lines of force to each point to create the double pyramid.

Next, we need to activate the field. We do this by invoking the opposite forces and uniting and transcending polarity. The obvious choice here is to choose the king and queen of the fay as presented in Shakespeare's play.

At this point, our eidolon is complete, but we need one more step. We need to open a portal into the field to really unite and experience the energy. The simple gateway presented in the ritual opens the entrance into the element and greatly magnifies the feeling of immersion.

Invocation of the Elemental King

Next, we add in an invocation for each of the four kings. Once the resonant field is created, we need to call in the spirit we are wanting to work with. For this, we need a prayer or invocation of some sort.

The first part of the invocation is taken from *Transcendental Magic*; the elemental invocations in that book are really just perfect.[56] For the second part, we had to write the call and charge, and then there's the Imago, or image of the spirit. The Imago helps with the visualization of the spirit, creating an image to focus on. The Imago in the text is based on our own experience with the entity. You may have different imagery. If your imagery is different from what we have but still seems to relate to the invoked spirit, then it is not wrong, and you should consider rewriting the text to match your own experience.

---

56. Lévi, *Transcendental Magic.*

Closing

Having called forth our king, we need to have a way to wind down the process. We thank and dismiss our king and then read the closing. There is a speech in *A Midsummer Night's Dream* that is perfect for a closing. Having read this, we unwind the temple consecration and say a dedication of merit.

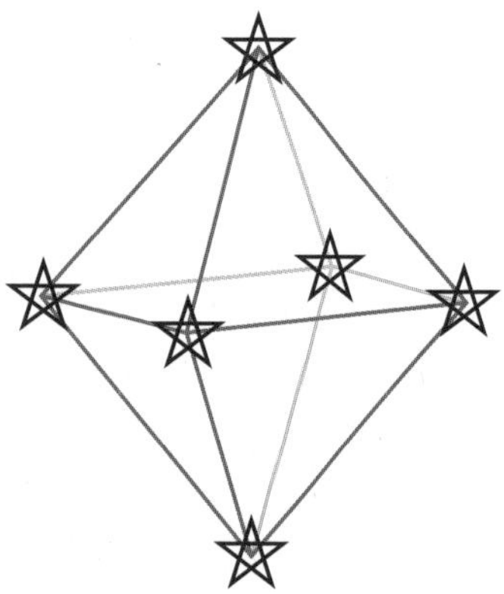

Double Pyramid

The whole process is much simpler than it probably sounds. The GRP takes us about forty-five minutes to an hour. We suggest you perform all four invocations starting with earth, then air, then water, and finally fire. The first time, only ask the spirit for its wisdom and get to know it. Spend some time scrying and sit with the feelings that arise. After you have done all four and feel confident, invoke one of the kings and make a request for whatever you need.

The final shape of the eidolon is a double pyramid, or octahedron. The stars in the image represent the pentagrams drawn, and the lines connect the nodes. This is very similar to the Temple Consecration, and it overlaps the watchtowers and central axis mundi.

R • I • T • U • A • L
GREATER RITUAL OF THE PENTAGRAM

Before trying the Greater Ritual of the Pentagram for the first time, read through the following text and walk yourself through it so you can get a sense of how it flows. You don't need to memorize the ritual, as you can just read it out of the book, but you should be familiar enough to move through it with confidence. Some of the text can be a bit tricky, so read it out loud for practice. Also practice drawing the pentagrams and performing the gestures; you should be an expert on this by now.

Plan out how you will perform this rite. You will need to at least perform a temple consecration. Will you add the Rose Ankh? How about the Middle Pillar or a godform? We would keep it simple at first. But as you can see, you have options in your ritual design, and you can go simple or complex depending on what your needs are. The Rose Ankh is not absolutely required but recommended.

Set a date for your first ritual performance; set it in the near future so you can have it to look forward to. Then be aware of any synchronicities that may manifest *before* the ritual. This is actually pretty common, as time is not as solid for these entities as it is for us.

Things You Need

Space for the ritual

A bell or chime; if you don't have one simply knock on the table or floor

Directions

Perform the Qabalistic Cross (chapter 2). If you would like, perform the Middle Pillar (chapter 16) and assume a godform (chapter 19). The Middle Pillar and godform can dramatically increase the power of the ritual, use your best judgement on whether they are needed. Try without first and add them in later to see how they enhance the ritual effects.

Perform a temple consectration (chapter 17) and then the Rose Ankh Vortex (chapter 18) if you want the additional boost.

Introit

All participants face east. Ring the bell four times or knock four times, then read the following:

Over hill, over dale,
Thorough bush, thorough brier,
Over park, over pale,
Thorough flood, thorough fire,
I do wander everywhere,
Swifter than the moon's sphere;
And I serve the fairy queen,
To dew their orbs upon the green.
The cowslips tall their pensioners be:
In their gold coats spots you see;
Those be rubies, fairy favours,
In those freckles live their savours:
I must go seek some dewdrops here
And hang a pearl in every cowslip's ear.
Farewell, thou lob of spirits; I'll be gone:
Our queen and all our elves come here anon.[57]

57. Shakespeare, *A Midsummer Night's Dream*, act 2, scene 1.

Creating the Eidolon Field

Still facing east, draw the appropriate pentagram of spirit, then the element to be invoked. Fuse them together with an invoking spiral while vibrating, ORO IBAH AOZPI, infusing them with yellow energy.

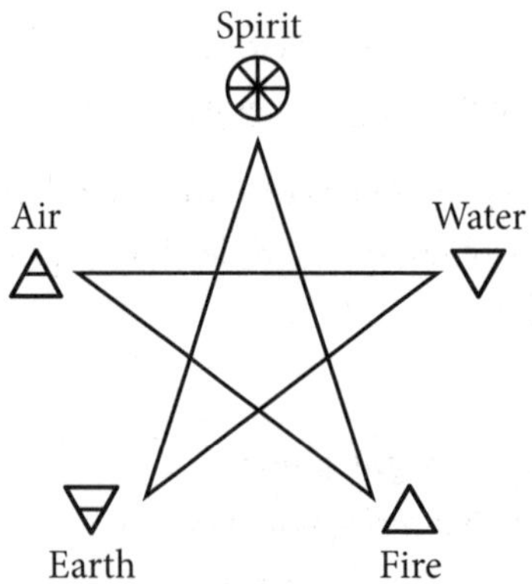

Pentagram with Elements

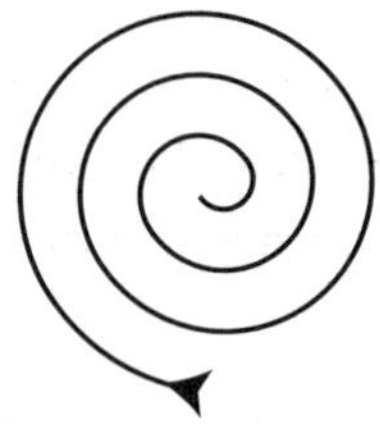

Invoking Spiral

Say:

As when the golden sun salutes the morn,
And, having gilt the ocean with his beams,
Gallops the zodiac in his glistering coach,
And overlooks the highest peering hills.
The heavenly harness'd team Begins his golden progress in the east.[58]

Turn to face south. Draw the appropriate pentagrams of spirit and the element to be invoked, then fuse them together with an invoking spiral while vibrating, OIP TEAA PDOCE, infusing them with red energy.

Say:

O for a Muse of fire, that would ascend
The brightest heaven of invention,
A kingdom for a stage, princes to act
And monarchs to behold the swelling scene![59]

58. Shakespeare, *Titus Andronicus*, act 2, scene 1; Shakespeare, *Henry IV*, Part 1.

59. Shakespeare, *The Life of King Henry the Fifth*, act 1, prologue.

Turn to face west. Draw the appropriate pentagrams of spirit and the element to be invoked, then fuse them together with an invoking spiral while vibrating, MPH ARSL GAIOL, infusing them with blue energy.

Say:

The setting sun, and the music at the close,
As the last taste of sweets, is the sweetest last,
Writ in remembrance more than long things past.[60]

Turn to face north. Draw the appropriate pentagrams of spirit and the element to be invoked, then fuse them together with an invoking spiral while vibrating, MOR DIAL HCTGA, infusing them with green energy.

Say:

On your eyelids crown the god of sleep.
Charming your blood with pleasing heaviness,
Making such difference 'twixt wake and sleep
As is the difference betwixt day and night
The hour before the heavenly-harness'd team
Begins his golden progress in the east.[61]

Uniting the Center and Opening the Portal

Next, center above by drawing the pentagram of spirit active in white light above the center of the space while vibrating: Eh-Heh-Nu-Beh.

Center below by drawing the pentagram of spirit passive in black light to a place below the center of the space while vibrating: Beh-Nu-Heh-Eh.

Draw an invoking spiral in a wide arc, connecting both pentagrams.

60. Shakespeare, *The Life and Death of Richard the Second.*

61. Shakespeare, *Henry IV, Part 1*, act 3, scene 1.

Invoking Spirit Active Pentagram

Invoking Spirit Passive Pentagram

Invoking Spiral

Next, connect the four pentagrams to the spirit pentagrams above and below with lines of force. The result will be a double pyramid shape. Then say:

Of all the kings
Bear him to mind
Eternal ruler of these
Riches, magic, and wine
Of fairies and song
Now praise Oberon

Glorious queen
Her kindness well known
All nature obeys you
Your honor is renown
Now praise Titania

We call Oberon and Titania
Graceful, elegant Lord and Lady
Your kingdom we would enter
Open the way in between
To the world of the Fay

I open the gates between worlds
I open the kingdom of ______ (insert the element to be invoked).

Make the opening the portal gesture. Do this with both hands, miming that you are opening heavy curtains. This opens the gateway to the elemental kingdom.

Invocation of the Elemental King

Read the appropriate invocation from the following section "Invocations of the Elemental Kings." Once the invocation is read, sit in mindful meditation and scry the king you have invoked. Even if nothing seems to have happened, you will have opened a connection to the elemental king. Look in your mind and find the dreaming. You can repeat the king's name as a mantra if needed as well.

Closing

When you have made contact with your king and are satisfied with the result, it is time to close out the ritual. It is generally appropriate to have a closing statement for when the ritual is over. This is said to bring everyone back to normality. Make a ritual gesture of closing the gate, wind down by banishing and thanking the guardians of the watchtowers, and give a dedication of merit.

If we shadows have offended,
Think but this, and all is mended,
That you have but slumber'd here
While these visions did appear.
And this weak and idle theme,
No more yielding but a dream,
Gentles, do not reprehend:
If you pardon, we will mend:
And, as I am an honest Puck,
If we have unearned luck
Now to 'scape the serpent's tongue,
We will make amends ere long;
Else the Puck a liar call;
So, good night unto you all.
Give me your hands, if we be friends,
And Robin shall restore amends.[62]

62. Shakespeare, *A Midsummer Night's Dream,* act 5, scene 1.

Invocations of the Elemental Kings

The following invocations are intended to be used after the appropriate eidolon is created. If you cast the GRP for fire, invoke Djinn, or if you cast it for water, call Nixsa. The first portions of these invocations come from the book *Transcendental Magic: Its Doctrine and Ritual* by Éliphas Lévi.

Invocation of Ghob

This invocation is for Ghob, the king of elemental earth and the manifestation of the archangel Uriel. Read it after you have created an eidolon of elemental earth energy.

> *King invisible, who, taking the earth as a support, didst furrow the abysses to fill them with Thine omnipotence; Thou whose name doth shake the vaults of the world, Thou who causest the seven metals to flow through the veins of the rock, monarch of the seven lights, rewarder of the subterranean toilers, lead us unto the desirable air, and to the realm of splendour.*
>
> *We watch and we work unremittingly, we seek and we hope, by the twelve stones of the Holy City, by the hidden talismans, by the pole of lodestone which passes through the centre of the world! Expand our hearts, detach and elevate our minds, enlarge our entire being! O stability and motion! O day clothed with night! O darkness veiled by light! O master who never keepest back the wages of Thy labourers!*
>
> *O silver whiteness! O golden splendour! O crown of living and melodious diamonds! Thou who wearest the heaven on Thy finger like a sapphire ring, Thou who concealest under the earth, in the stone kingdom, the marvellous seed of stars. Live, reign, be the eternal dispenser of the wealth whereof Thou hast made us the warders!*[63]
>
> *I summon the spirit of Ghob, the emotional ideal earth in Malkuth by the names of IAO, Abrasax, and Protonoia!*
>
> *I call thee to appear, O Ghob, I summon thy ray of blended power with being to come forth and empower this work of magic!*
>
> *I reveal the secret of thy Image, O Ghob! Thou art the emissary of Uriel, you are short in stature but muscular, with dark reddish-brown skin. Your hair and beard are wild and unkempt, you wear rough skins and hold a satchel of the riches of the earth.*

---

63. Lévi, *Transcendental Magic*, 220.

Invocation of Paralda

This invocation is for Paralda, king of elemental air and manifestation of the archangel Raphael. Read it after you have created an eidolon of elemental air energy.

> *Spirit of Life, Spirit of Wisdom, whose breath gives and takes away the form of all living things; Thou before whom the life of every being is a shadow which transforms and a vapour which passes away; Thou who ascendest upon the clouds and dost fly upon the wings of the wind; Thou who breathest out and the limitless immensities are peopled; Thou who breathest in and all which came forth from Thee unto Thee returneth; endless movement in the eternal stability, be Thou blessed for ever! We praise Thee and we bless Thee in the fleeting empire of created light, of shadows, reflections, and images, and we aspire without ceasing towards Thine immutable and imperishable splendour.*
>
> *May the ray of Thine intelligence and the warmth of Thy love descend on us; then what is volatile shall be fixed, the shadow shall become body, the spirit of air shall receive a soul, and the dream be a thought. We shall be swept away no more by the tempest, but shall bridle the winged steeds of the morning, and guide the course of the evening winds, that we may flee into Thy presence. O Spirits of Spirits, O eternal Soul of Souls, O imperishable Breath of Life, O Creative Sigh, O mouth which dost breathe forth and withdraw the life of all beings in the ebb and flow of Thine eternal speech, which is the divine ocean of movement and of truth!*[64]
>
> *I summon the spirit of Paralda, the emotional, ideal air in Malkuth, by the names of IAO, Abrasax, and Protonoia!*
>
> *I call thee to appear, O Paralda! I summon thy ray of blended power with being to come forth and empower this work of magic!*
>
> *I reveal the secret of thy Image, O Paralda! Thou art the emissary of Raphael, and you bring healing and balance and compassion for others.*
>
> *Your eyes are silver, slanted moonbeams, darting and alert, you are slender, wearing the morning rays of the sun as your vestment. You have gossamer wings and your billowing hair is streaked with sunlight and shaded with the gray whiteness of the clouds.*

---

64. Lévi, *Transcendental Magic*, 216–17.

Invocation of Nixsa

Read this invocation after you have created an eidolon of elemental water. It invokes Nixsa, the emissary of the archangel Gabriel.

> *Dread King of the Sea, who hast the keys of the floodgates of heaven, and dost confine the waters of the underworld in the caverns of earth; King of the deluge and the floods of springtime; Thou who dost unseal the sources of rivers and fountains; Thou who dost ordain moisture, which is like the blood of earth, to become the sap of plants: Thee we adore and Thee we invoke!*
>
> *Speak unto us, Thine inconstant and unstable creatures, in the great tumults of the sea, and we shall tremble before Thee; speak unto us also in the murmur of limpid waters, and we shall yearn for Thy love! O Immensity into which flow all the rivers of life, to be continually reborn in Thee! O Ocean of infinite perfections! Height which reflects Thee in the depth, depth which exhales Thee to the height, lead us to immortality by sacrifice, that we may be found worthy one day to offer Thee water, blood, and tears, for the remission of sins!*[65]
>
> *I summon the spirit of Nixsa, the emotional ideal water in Malkuth by the names of IAO, Abrasax, and Protonoia!*
>
> *I call thee to appear, O Nixsa. I summon thy ray of blended power with being to come forth and empower this work of magic!*
>
> *I reveal the secret of thy Image, O Nixsa! Thou art the emissary of Gabriel, you are a swirling, majestic figure of brooding intensity. Your hair is long and flowing, touched with the shine of dampened seaweed, and splashed with tentacles of silver and gray. Your eyes are luminous droplets, quivering in movement.*

Invocation of Djinn

Use this invocation after you have created an eidolon of fire. It will call the elemental king of fire, Djinn, who is the emissary of the archangel Michael.

---

65. Lévi, *Transcendental Magic*, 218–19.

Immortal, eternal, ineffable, and uncreated Father of all things, who art borne upon the ever-rolling chariot of worlds whichever revolve unceasingly; Lord of the ethereal immensities, where the throne of Thy power is exalted, from which height Thy terrible eyes discern all things, and Thy holy and beautiful ears unto all things harken, hear Thou Thy children, whom Thou didst love since before the ages began; for Thy golden, Thy grand, Thine eternal majesty shines above the world and the heaven of stars! Thou art exalted over them, O glittering fire!

There dost thou shine, there dost Thou commune with Thyself by Thine own splendour, and inexhaustible streams of light pour from Thine essence for the nourishment of Thine infinite spirit, which itself doth nourish all things, and forms that inexhaustible treasure of substance ever ready for generation, which adapts it and appropriates the forms Thou hast impressed on it from the beginning! From this spirit the three most holy kings who surround thy Throne and constitute Thy court, derive also their origin.

O universal Father! O sole and only Father of blessed mortals and immortals! In particular Thou hast created powers marvellously like unto Thine eternal thought and Thine adorable essence; Thou hast established them higher than the angels, who proclaim Thy will to the world; finally, Thou hast created us third in rank within our elementary empire! There our unceasing exercise is to praise Thee and adore Thy good pleasure; there we burn continually in our aspiration to possess Thee. O Father! O Mother, must tender of all mothers! O son, flower of sons! O form of all forms, soul, spirit, harmony and number of all things![66]

I summon the spirit of Djinn, the emotional ideal fire in Malkuth by the names of IAO, Abrasax, and Protonoia!

I call thee to appear, O Djinn. I summon thy ray of blended power with being to come forth and empower this work of magic!

I reveal the secret of thy Image, O Djinn! Thou art the emissary of Michael, you are a living flame with eyes like stars that flash and dazzle. Your hair is the smoke of incense, fragrant and pleasing.

---

66. Lévi, *Transcendental Magic*, 219–20.

• • • • • • •

Our recommendation is that you should invoke all four elements at least once to get a good feel for how the process of invocation works. Space them out over a month, doing one a week. This will give you some time to feel the manifestations appear in your life and for any additional insights from the ritual workings to come into your awareness.

In our temple, we invoke the kings on the solstices and equinoxes as the sun is moving into the cardinal element on those days. We do this to welcome in the energies of the new quarter of the year and align ourselves and our intent with them. We included the approximate date of the solstices and equinoxes. The dates change every year, and you don't need to do the ritual on the exact date for it to be effective. Just do the work when you can.

Equinoxes and Solstices of the Year and the King to Invoke

Quarter of the Year	Sun Enters	Cardinal	King	Approximate Date
Spring Equinox	Aries	Fire	Djinn	March 21
Summer Solstice	Cancer	Water	Nixsa	June 20
Fall Equinox	Libra	Air	Paralda	September 22
Winter Solstice	Capricorn	Earth	Ghob	December 21

Very often, these manifestations appear before the ritual work is even performed, as time does not seem to be a limitation for spiritual forces like these. Start with earth, then air, then water, and finally fire. This will help you to build and expand your experience with the elements. This will help you to become familiar with working with elemental beings and all that they can manifest into your life.

Once you have invoked and feel you have an authentic connection with all four elemental kings, you will have their inspiration on how best to apply this ritual in the future. The kings will be great allies for you and your spiritual process moving forward.

— CHAPTER 21 —
The Pyramid of Power

The Pyramid of Power is a ritual of pure practical magic intended to cause immediate and positive change in your material life. By combining a sephiroth and an element, we can activate the power of the forty small cards of the tarot—just the positive meanings. Here we are wielding the energies of creation to rewrite our current situation in life to more suit our needs and goals.

Since you now have experience with the Rose Ankh, most of this will be familiar to you. However, there will be some new skills to master. As the Rose Ankh is a feminine vortex, the Pyramid of Power is a masculine cone of power. They complement each other, and they can be used together to express the Great Rite. The Great Rite is an extremely ancient ritual that symbolically simulates sexual intercourse, drawing power from the union and transcendence of opposites. The creation of holy water in a temple consecration ritual also contains this symbolism.

The Pyramid is one of our favorite rituals, and it is extremely effective. It can be done alone after creating sacred space or after the invocation of an angel or godform. Done alone, it is a powerful agent to impress your will on reality. You can also combine this rite with a godform or an invoked angel or elemental for an additional boost. Empowered by an angel, this rite can be extremely powerful. This ritual is practical magic; it impresses your will upon reality to cause change.

For our group, we sometimes demonstrate this ritual with just a temple consecration or even just the Lesser Banishing Ritual of the Pentagram (LBRP) so students can experience the basic rite alone and feel its effects. In practice, we would normally use this ritual as a culmination of a series of rites to gather, focus, and exteriorize all of the work done in the sacred space to a single expression. By the time we release the energy at the end of the rite, participants often describe feeling a pressure wave leaving the temple space. It can be that powerful. We are sure the effect is subjective; nonetheless, the Pyramid of Power ritual functions as the tip of the spear, gathering all of the energy generated by a series of rituals and releasing it into the physical world to create change.

The Pyramid, the Tarot, and the Qabalah

The following version of the Pyramid of Power ritual is a Qabalistic one. You will combine one of the ten sephiroth with one of the four elements. In chapter 9, "The Tarot," we discussed how the minor arcana are made of a sephiroth in one of the four worlds along with a planet and a sign. For this ritual, we are only using the sephiroth in one of the four worlds. We don't want the influence of the planet and sign, as those can make the resulting energies very difficult, and we only want positive changes in our microcosm.

The Pyramid of Power Ritual Pattern

Before attempting this ritual, it is important to walk through it. You don't need to memorize the ritual at first, but you will need to see how it flows. There are many places where you need to insert your own words, so if you want to just try it out, pick a goal you have, something measurable that you can test the ritual with, such as cutting down on smoking or making three new friends in the next week. Set a goal with a definite time frame, then look through the following chapter and select a power you think expresses that goal best. That power will give you the keywords to put in the ritual for the god name of the sephiroth, the world, and the title of the card. You will need to come up with your own phrase to insert into the Setting of the Angles phase of the rite. Your phrase does not need to be fancy; the angels already know the truth in your heart.

To prepare, you will need to decide on:

- A measurable goal and time frame; keep it simple and short
- A power to invoke, found in the Concourse of Forces, a sephiroth in a world
- Your own phrase of what you want to have happen; again, keep it simple and short

Walk through the ritual a couple times—until you feel confident with the flow.

Introit

As with the other rituals, you want to start with a brief statement that sets the intent of the rite and begins it. For this version of the Pyramid of Power, we chose to use our own personal mythology and refer to the symbol on our ubiquitous dollar bill, the pyramid with an eye, as the capstone. To us, this is at once mystical and associated with material progress. You may want to add your own personal statement of intent as described above to set the goal of the ritual. You may also rewrite this section into your own personal mythology once you get a feel of how this ritual works.

Setting of the Angles

We invoke the element or archetypal world to the angles between the watchtowers. The previously created sacred space provides context for our sacred geometry to attach. In this ritual, you invoke all parts of the element: first the fiery part, then the watery part, then the airy part, and finally the earthy part. This is similar to what you did in the Greater Ritual of the Pentagram (GRP; chapter 20). Using the angles also matches the structure of the Rose Ankh Vortex, as this ritual is its complement, or opposite.

What you will do is carry the base element through all four Qabalistic worlds, from inspiration to perspiration. We imprint our will on the highest plane of Atziluth through the feelings of Briah to the many thoughts of Yetzirah and carry it to manifestation in Assiah. In each world, we ask for the blessings, wisdom, and guidance of the spirit or presence of that world. The invocations used come from personal revelations and work we have done in ritual. Try them and see if they resonate with you as well.

Here we are using the Enochian names for the spirit of each element, invoked over the correct pentagram of the element we are using. Some students like to use the four archangels for the angles instead, and they simply reuse the verbiage from the Temple Consecration (chapter 17). They call Michael for the fiery part of the element, Gabriel for the watery part, Raphael for the airy part, and Uriel for the earthy part of the element.

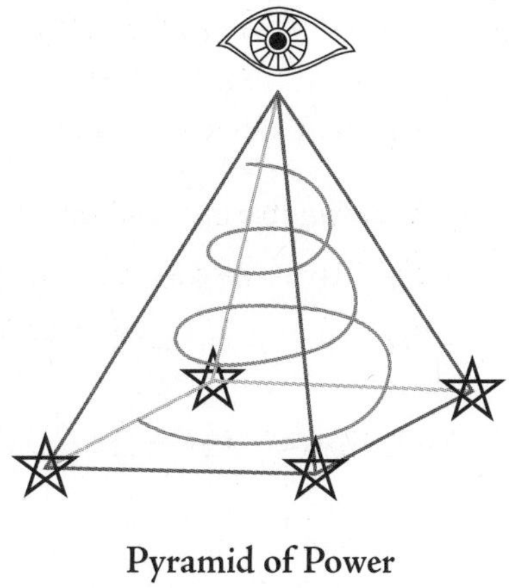
Pyramid of Power

Invoking the element to the angles creates the square base of the pyramid. The angles are drawn together and to a point above the center, the ultrapoint, and the name for spirit of spirit is invoked. This completes the base and empty sacred geometry of the pyramid. Draw the lines of force as you did for the circle in the LBRP, only straight from the corners to the point above the center. This is often done with a ritual sword, if you have one, a wand, or just your hands.

Cone of Power

The Cone of Power generates a vortex of energy and is imprinted with the will or purpose of the participants. This power is then released into the material world to cause some practical effect.

For the Cone of Power, walk clockwise around the center of the sacred space and vibrate as powerfully as you can the power chant included in the ritual instructions. This particular chant is one Erich wrote and developed under the inspiration of his Holy Guardian Angel. In time, you may wish to write your own. After each recitation, use your pore breathing and belly breathing to powerfully inhale the energy generated, with your hands and fingers outstretched. This is called the *cooling breath*. Trace the circuit three times and end at the center of your space. Once at the center, perform the Assumption Sign (page 185) by drawing the power in the infrapoint through the body and up into the ultrapoint, becoming its mediator.

Imprinting the Power

Once you complete the circuit of walking the spiral, you will be supercharged with magical force, crackling with energy. Now imprint it with the god name of the sephiroth you are working with and fuse it with the base element, creating the exact force you want to work with. This is done by first imprinting the force with a god name pair. Here we use Nuit and Hadit, representing the unity of the divine force. You then name the power, vibrating the god name of the sephiroth you are working with.

Next, you fully absorb the power into yourself so you can wield it by chanting Eheieh, the god name of Kether, which means "I am" or "I will be." By now, you should feel like you are about to explode with power, and that is what comes next.

Releasing the Power

First, charge the chosen tarot card with the sigil or stone you placed in the center of the sacred space. Do this by drawing an invoking spiral over it and breathing some of the power you have gathered into the object. Then walk the releasing spiral. Starting in the center, walk the spiral outward and counterclockwise while chanting the release chant, slowly at first and then faster. Make three revolutions, and on the final syllable of ja-i-DA, throw the energy out through the north watchtower and bring your hands together in the loudest clap you can manage. Then make the Sign of Silence (page 154) to prevent any of the force from rebounding back. You will probably want to sit for a while and meditate on what just happened. Then close as you see fit. A dedication of merit would be great here.

R•I•T•U•A•L
THE PYRAMID OF POWER

Depending on the level of power you intend to evoke, you have several options for the Pyramid of Power ritual. You can simply do a LBRP and then this ritual, or you can stack all the rituals in this book to build power. A more advanced working would have a temple consecration, a Rose Ankh, then either a GRP or an Elemental Octagram (chapter 23). The difference in power created by these two patterns is of an order of magnitude. You will have to use your own judgment on how much power you wish to experience, as it will be flowing through you. Remember, however, to start slow.

In this example, you will create the energy of the Nine of Cups. We use the Nine of Cups, known as the Wish Card, as it is a good choice for general manifestation. The manifestation of a new house or home will be the target of this example. Adjust as needed.

Things You Need

Space for the ritual

Something pointy to draw the shapes in the air

Optional: The tarot card representing the force you are employing; place this card on a central altar or in the center of the space

Optional: A sigil to charge as a talisman to place in the center (see chapter 11 for the process)

Introit

Face east. Stand in the center of the circle and say the following introit:

> *By this ritual of most Sacred Geometry, we call the elements together. United they form the Pyramid of Power, and when the Pyramid is crowned with the Open Eye of Spiritual Awareness, it shall become an expression of my one True Will. Then we shall find that all our desires have come to be. Now add your intent. For this example: It is my will that I find the perfect home for our family.*

Setting of the Angles

Face the southeast angle. With the wand or your hand, draw an invoking pentagram of the chosen element. For this example, it is water for the Nine of Cups. If your card was, for instance, the Ten of Pentacles, then the element would be earth. Draw first the pentagram and visualize it as a crimson light. Then draw an invoking spiral around it and visualize it as a bright green light. Then vibrate the name of the spirit of fire, Bitom.

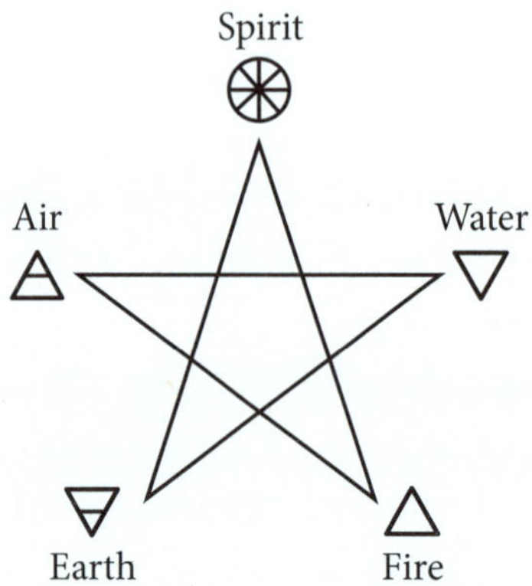

Pentagram with Elements

Invoking Spiral

Say:

Bitom, you are the presence of the archetypal world of Atziluth. You are the spark of insight that inspires us to seek out our True Will. Inspire us to find the perfect home for our family.

Next, turn to face the northeast angle. Draw an invoking pentagram of the chosen base element—in this example, water—and visualize it as a blue light. Then draw an invoking spiral around it and visualize it as a bright orange light. Vibrate the name of the spirit of water, Hcoma.

Say:

Hcoma, you are the presence of the archetypal world of Briah. You are the power of unity, the force of love which holds and moves all things. It is with love in our hearts that we set out to change the world. We will find the perfect home for our family. Love is the law, love under will.

Now, turn to face the northwest angle. Draw an invoking pentagram of the chosen base element. In this example, it is air. Visualize the pentagram as a yellow light. Then draw an invoking spiral around it, visualizing it as a purple light. Vibrate the name of the spirit of air, Exarp.

Say:

> *Exarp, you are the presence of the archetypal world of Yetzirah. In your world, the one becomes the many. You separate cause and effect so we may make choices that will change our world. Guide us with your subtle synchronicities as we seek to find the perfect home for our family.*

Turn to face the southwest angle. Draw an invoking pentagram of the chosen element. In this example, it is earth. With the wand or your hand, draw the pentagram and visualize it as a green light. Then draw an invoking spiral around it and visualize it as a red light. Vibrate the name of the spirit of earth, Nanta.

Say:

> *Nanta, you are the presence of the archetypal world of Assiah. Pure one, in your world, we manifest our will, not only by the efforts of our own hands but with other beings on the path. Your lesson is all things of real value come to us from the people in our lives. Help us find the perfect home for our family.*

Stand in the south, facing the center of the circle, and use the wand or your hand to draw in the infrapoint an invoking pentagram of the chosen element of the ritual (water). Visualize it as darkness. Draw an invoking spiral around it and visualize it with a white light. Then draw an inverted invoking pentagram of spirit active in the ultrapoint and visualize it with a gold light. Finally, draw an invoking spiral around it and visualize it with a silver light. Vibrate the word *EHNB* (Eh-Heh-Nu-Beh) to invoke, representing spirit descending into matter.

Say:

> *The Pyramid of Power is complete only when crowned with the Udjat, thus becoming a complete symbol of the Great Work and a projection of my True Will.*

Setting the Angles

Proceed to draw the four angles together in a square, beginning in the southeast, and going deosil (clockwise) to the southwest, the northwest, the northeast, and completing the circuit in the southeast. Then draw each of the four angles to the center of the circle in the ultrapoint, beginning with the southeast angle, proceeding widdershins (counter-clockwise), and ending in the southeast.

Say:

The pyramid structure is now fully erected.

Cone of Power

Circumambulate the magic circle deosil, beginning in the east. Chant the power chant as you walk a spiral path from the outside of the circle to the center, circumambulating the circle three times. Once in the center, draw the power in the infrapoint through your body, up into the ultrapoint, thus becoming its mediator.

The following is the power chant in Enochian and translated:

GIGIPAH DE YABES UNIGLAG PUGO BIEN

Living Breath of God descend unto my Voice

ADO DE LONUSA LAP ZIR HOATH DE JAIDA.

With your Power for I am a true worshiper of the highest.

Next, perform the Qabalistic Cross (chapter 2) briefly, as an informal practice.

Imprinting the Power

Facing north, say the following preamble:

I summon and call this Spiritual Power, in the names of
Nuit and Hadit and their union within the All.

The magic power is thus imprinted with the authority of the god name pair.

Next, say:

I name you, Ray of Life from my God. You are Shaddai El Chai!

Make an invoking spiral in the center of the circle to the ultrapoint. This statement identifies the magic energy with one of the ten aspects of the deity. In this case, the magic energy is that of the ninth emanation or attribute of the deity (the ninth Sephirah Yesod).

Substitute the god name for the appropriate sephiroth based on the number of the minor arcana card chosen. See the following list for the god names.

1. Eheieh
2. Yah
3. YHVH Elohim
4. Al
5. Elohim Gibor
6. YHVH Eloah VeDaath
7. YHVH Tzabaoth
8. Elohim Tzabaoth
9. Shaddai El Chai
10. Adonai HaAretz

Next, draw an invoking spiral in the center of the circle to the ultrapoint. Imprint the energy with the specific card that's invoked for the rite. Each of the small cards of the tarot has a title. The titles can be found in the following chapter, "The Concourse of Forces for the Pyramid of Power." The title for the Nine of Cups is Lady of Material Happiness.

Say:

I summon and call this glorified light, the qualified power of potent intent.
You are Yesod of Briah, the inspiration of the Lady of Material Happiness.

Make an invoking spiral in the center of the circle to the ultrapoint.

Say:

I summon the inspiration of the Lady of Material Happiness.
I cause you to come. I draw you down.
I absorb you into me. Eheieh! Eheieh!
Eheieh!

This final statement uses the description of the magic power and reinforces it within the mantric chant. This mantric round is repeated in ever faster revolutions until it is reduced to the last word. The three syllables (Eh-he-yah) are chanted ever faster until reaching a climax. The final expression at the end is the "YEH!" (*EHIH* is *Eheieh*, which is Hebrew for "I am.")

Charge the prepared magic sigil, which embodies the purpose of the rite. This is accomplished by first holding it in the incense smoke, placing it upon the altar over the selected tarot card (Nine of Cups), and drawing an invoking spiral upon them with the wand or hand. Then concentrate on the talisman, sigil, or other object to be empowered with the force of this rite and the selected tarot card together.

Releasing the Power

Circumambulate the magic circle widdershins, beginning in the north and in the center. Recite the release chant while tracing a spiral path from the center of the circle to the outside, circumambulating the circle three times.

At each circuit of the circle, the energy becomes more intense, almost resisting your passage. At the end of the circuit, stand in the north and send the power out with a forced exhalation, projecting the power with both arms extended out. A single loud clap with outstretched hands sends the power out as a lightning bolt. Make the Sign of Silence to keep it from reverberating back. The following is the release chant:

AVAVACO DE KAOZIOR DARBS BIEN MOLVI S PUGO

Thunders of Increase obey my voice Surge forth unto

QAA PILD LAP ZIR HAOTH DE IAIDA.

Creation Continually for I am a worshiper of the Highest.

At this point, the power is released and the ritual is complete. You should sit in mindful awareness until you feel the energy is completely released. Shut down the ritual by using banishing spirals to disperse the watchtowers. Also say some words of thanks to the archangels and any other spirits you invoked. Finish by saying a dedication of merit.

• • • • • • •

This is a complex rite at first. The best approach is to walk through the ritual instructions a couple times until you get the gist of the pattern. Basically, it is just this: You say what you are doing, invoke the base element, draw a pyramid with lines of force, fill it with energy, imprint and name the energy, then release it.

We use the power chant listed in the ritual instructions as a general mantra to call in magical power for anything we want to do. If you resonate with it, then you can use it that way as well. If the provided power chant is not to your liking, then feel free to substitute any powerful chant you find more appropriate.

In the simple illustration of the Pyramid of Power, you can see the elemental pentagrams, the sephiroth as the open eye of spiritual awareness above, and the spiral of power. The straight lines represent the outer shape of the pyramid that, in essence, holds the forces together and allows them to work as one.

— CHAPTER 22 —
The Concourse of Forces for the Pyramid of Power

This chapter contains a concise list of effects that can be created by combining an element, or Qabalistic world, with one of the ten sephiroth. When you are planning a ritual, browse through the list and choose the power that best expresses what you want to manifest. Naturally, there are some effects that you will use more than others. It would be easy to write an entire volume on the effects of the Pyramid of Power and all the Qabalistic correspondences. We will try to be clear and comprehensive without going into elaborate detail. You can gain further insights by referring to *Mastering the Art of Ritual Magick* by Frater Barrabbas.

You should read through the listings to get a full understanding of the powers available to you from this one ritual and to get a feeling for the way these powers are created. There is a thinking process that comes up again and again, where we consider one effect as a subset of another, effectively combining and focusing those powers, such as the forceful part of fire rather than the emotional effect of fire. This is important to grasp, as we will be using this thought process a lot.

In the listings, you will find the keys you will need for the Pyramid of Power Ritual (chapter 21). Each one includes the attribute of the deity, the name of the force combination, and a keyword to define the power. We have also included a short description with our notes, the tarot card, and the title. The lord/lady part of a title is based on whether the element is said to be active or receptive. Feel free to create titles that you feel better suit your practice.

World of Atziluth

Atziluth is the archetypal world of fire. These effects can grant inspiration, the initiation of new projects, gnosis, and visions of truth. Invoke fire for guidance in new activities when you are unsure of what to do next.

Kether of Atziluth

Kether of Atziluth is the source of fire: **initiation.** The source of fire energy helps with creating new beginnings and breaking through to new ways of being, new opportunities. It is the great vision of how all things are interconnected. Kether of Atziluth is good to invoke if you feel lost and are in need of inspiration.

Tarot Card: Ace of Wands

Title: Root of the Powers of Fire

Chokmah of Atziluth

Chokmah of Atziluth is the force of fire: **foresight.** Chokmah of Atziluth gives the power of prediction to know what actions are needed to create the most optimal outcomes. If you feel overwhelmed by the choices in life, this will help you to intuit the correct choices.

Tarot Card: Two of Wands

Title: Lord of Dominion

Binah of Atziluth

Binah of Atziluth is the form of fire: **clarity.** Binah of Atziluth gives the power to perceive the truth without emotional content. Using this form will help you see things as they are, without personal bias.

Tarot Card: Three of Wands

Title: Lord of Established Strength

Chesed of Atziluth

Chesed of Atziluth is the love of fire: **guidance**. This form provides the power to be in tune with the divine plan and effortlessly work with others toward a common goal. It will help in understanding your best profession, your purpose in life. It is good for issues at work or in your career.

Tarot Card: Four of Wands

Title: Lord of Perfected Work

Geburah in Atziluth

Geburah in Atziluth is the will of fire: **efficiency**. Geburah in Atziluth gives insight into the best use of our time and energy. Using it will help with setting appropriate boundaries as well as the ability to focus to meet deadlines or accomplish great tasks.

Tarot Card: Five of Wands

Title: Lord of Strife

Tipareth in Atziluth

Tipareth in Atziluth is the harmony of fire: **epiphany**. Tipareth in Atziluth gives insight into the self and the true nature of your innermost identity. This power not only illuminates the inner nature of the self but is also expansive in that it illuminates the connection we all share with one another. Invoked for personal insight, it also brings great confidence and charisma.

Tarot Card: Six of Wands

Title: Lord of Victory

Netzach in Atziluth

Netzach in Atziluth is the emotions of fire: **charisma**. Netzach in Atziluth gives insight and inspiration to the emotions that give personal radiance, which is felt as charisma. This understanding can unite people in a common cause and bring harmony.

Tarot Card: Seven of Wands

Title: Lord of Valor

Hod in Atziluth

Hod in Atziluth is the intellect of fire: **eloquence**. Intuitive understanding of the patterns underlying society and social structures and language is found with Hod in Atziluth. It also helps with the ability to clearly communicate your ideas and to understand others.

Tarot Card: Eight of Wands

Title: Lord of Swiftness

Yesod in Atziluth

Yesod in Atziluth is the dreams of fire: **idealism**. Yesod in Atziluth provides the power to break through negativity, destructive patterns, and inner blockages. This power illuminates the inner blocking beliefs and negative emotions to free us from the limitations imposed upon us by culture or negative experiences.

Tarot Card: Nine of Wands

Title: Lord of Great Strength

Malkuth in Atziluth

Malkuth in Atziluth is the manifestation of fire: **ideas**. The manifestation of fire blows open our creativity, offering new ideas and solutions to problems. For both the scientist and the artist, this power helps with fresh ideas that transcend boundaries and synergize in our minds to create solutions and inspirations without limits.

Tarot Card: Ten of Wands

Title: Lord of Inspiration

World of Briah

Briah is the archetypal world of water. The effects of water are emotional in nature, invoked for healing and clarifying our needs. By working with these energetic effects, we can identify and separate our emotions and gain clarity and strength; it is like exercising our emotional muscles.

Kether of Briah

Kether of Briah is the source of water: **union**. Kether of Briah is invoked to connect and synchronize with the emotional core of the source. This creates emotional harmony and rejuvenation.

Tarot Card: Ace of Cups
Title: Root of the Powers of Water

Chokmah of Briah

Chokmah of Briah is the force of water: **passion.** Chokmah's unrestrained energies exalt the emotions and bring new passions and excitement to life. It is invoked to create both inner happiness and a form of infectious charisma to bring positive people into your life.

Tarot Card: Two of Cups
Title: Lady of Love

Binah of Briah

Binah of Briah is the form of water: **compassion.** Binah's power to give form to anything allows us to feel and connect with others without being lost in their emotional drama. It is invoked so we can connect with the emotional world around us without being controlled by it. It can also be invoked to create deeper emotional connections with clarity in our relationships.

Tarot Card: The Three of Cups
Title: Lady of Abundance

Chesed of Briah

Chesed of Briah is the love of water: **catharsis.** Chesed is the overall power of emotional healing. It is not spiritual bypassing but the fusion of spirit with our emotions, which brings about insight and catharsis, allowing a resolution of the bound up emotions around an issue. It is invoked to heal emotional injuries or to gain understanding on why we have a specific hang-up or neurosis.

Tarot Card: The Four of Cups
Title: Lady of Blended Pleasure

Geburah of Briah

Geburah of Briah is the will of water: **boundaries.** Geburah's power of emotional strength allows complete certainty of our convictions and the ability to set appropriate boundaries. This strength transforms adversity into opportunity and respect. It is invoked when we need to set strong boundaries to clear space for growth and expansion.

Tarot Card: Five of Cups

Title: Lady of Judgement

Tipareth of Briah

Tipareth of Briah is the harmony of water: **mindfulness.** Tipareth brings both harmony and a solar awareness to the emotional world. The effect is a mindfulness that shows us that our emotions arise, exist, and then fade away. Being in the here and now grants serenity and calm in the midst of any storm. It is invoked for creating a mindful centeredness, to ground when emotions are overwhelming.

Tarot Card: Six of Cups

Title: Lady of Pleasure

Netzach of Briah

Netzach of Briah is the emotions of water: **ecstasy.** The exaltation of the emotions within the world of Briah brings the feeling of complete ego destruction, like when an orgasm temporarily dissolves our ego into great bliss. It is invoked to create sensual desire that leads to liberation of the ego or to enhance sexual bliss and connection with a partner. This can also open up new avenues of sexual expression.

Tarot Card: Seven of Cups

Title: Lady of Illusory Success

Hod of Briah

Hod of Briah is the intellect of water: **understanding.** Hod of Briah aids in intellectual grasping of one's own emotions as well as others', assisting the ability to communicate emotional needs clearly without creating conflict. This power can help to reconcile people from different backgrounds. It is invoked to manifest understanding between yourself and others. This power can also help create eloquence of speech and writing.

Tarot Card: Eight of Cups

Title: Lady of Allies

Yesod of Briah

Yesod of Briah is dreams of water: **wishes.** Yesod aids the power of the imagination emerging from the dream realm, which is the foundation of manifestation. It creates opportunities for us to obtain our deepest desires. This is the combination we use the most. Within a group working, each person can focus on making real what they desire most. It also works as a general spell for manifesting pretty much anything.

Tarot Card: Nine of Cups

Title: Lady of Material Happiness

Malkuth of Briah

Malkuth of Briah is the manifestation of emotions: **availability.** Malkuth has the power to manifest emotional situations in our lives. It is invoked to become more emotionally available and authentic, to be vulnerable yet safe in romantic or emotional relationships. This power can create ideal romantic partnerships, as it manifests our true feelings without fear or limitations.

Tarot Card: Ten of Cups

Title: Lady of Perfected Success

World of Yetzirah

Yetzirah is the archetypal world of air. In fire, we had inspiration, and water was the reflection of the inspiration in our feelings. Here, in the world of Yetzirah, is where the mind comprehends and decides. This is where the one becomes the many and we make choices and plans to determine the course of our lives. The powers of air can be quite useful, as the mind is a powerful tool for us to wield to shape our own reality.

Kether of Yetzirah

Kether of Yetzirah is the source of air: **will.** Kether of Yetzirah gives the power to know your True Will. It is invoked to initiate a project or to change your life to be more consciously aligned with your True Will, which is what you came here to do. This is very powerful when invoked to acquire more education.

Tarot Card: Ace of Swords

Title: Root of the Powers of Air

Chokmah of Yetzirah

Chokmah of Yetzirah is the power of air: **penetration.** The power of Chokmah of Yetzirah is to quickly resolve an issue by using the mind's ability to penetrate seemingly unsolvable situations to perceive the root of the issue at hand. It is invoked to quickly and decisively resolve a problem by direct action.

Tarot Card: Two of Swords

Title: Lord of Peace Restored

Binah of Yetzirah

Binah of Yetzirah is the form of air: **productivity.** Binah's limiting power focuses the mind to a fine point, allowing one to concentrate and accomplish great tasks. It is invoked for deadlines of a mental type, such as writing papers, programming or designing, and planning.

Tarot Card: Three of Swords

Title: Lord of Decisiveness

Chesed of Yetzirah

Chesed of Yetzirah is the love of air: **equality.** The benevolent forces of air act with fairness to judge all equally, with leniency. Chesed is invoked for legal situations when neutrality is needed. The scales of justice will be balanced in a way that is least disruptive.

Tarot Card: Four of Swords

Title: Lord of Rest from Strife

Geburah of Yetzirah

Geburah of Yetzirah is the will of air: **sterilization**. The will of air will banish all unneeded, disruptive elements, cleaning your life of negativity. It is invoked to remove all unhelpful elements from a situation. Be careful with this one. While it is very helpful, it will chase off people and situations that are not helping you to self-actualize. It can be a bit startling to see it work.

Tarot Card: Five of Swords

Title: Lord of Purification

Tipareth of Yetzirah

Tipareth of Yetzirah is the harmony of air: **synchronicity**. The solar consciousness of Tipareth in the realm of air allows us to see the subtle signs that we are on the right path and making the right choices. Synchronicities appear as noncausal coincidences that have spiritual meaning to us on our journey. It is invoked to see, sometimes literally, the path and choices before us.

Tarot Card: Six of Swords

Title: Lord of Earned Success

Netzach of Yetzirah

Netzach of Yetzirah is the emotions of air: **art**. The emotional expression of the mind is art in all of its manifestations. Artistic expression requires careful planning and skill to manifest well. Netzach is invoked for artistic skill, to come up with the ideas to express our inner emotions.

Tarot Card: Seven of Swords

Title: Lord of Creativity

Hod of Yetzirah

Hod of Yetzirah is the intellect of air: **science**. The intellect of Hod within the realm of air creates the method of science: careful planning and measurement to create predictable results. This allows us to anticipate future outcomes. Hod of Yetzirah is invoked for increased learning and to become more focused and methodical. This force can create powerful mental discipline.

Tarot Card: Eight of Swords

Title: Lord of Shortened Force

Yesod of Yetzirah

Yesod of Yetzirah is dreams of air: **insight**. Yesod of Yetzirah has the power to bring the contents of our subconscious mind into our awareness. Our shadows, dreams, and unconscious motivations are brought into the light of consciousness. It is invoked to gain a better understanding of these elements. Increasing this connection will make you a more powerful magician and meditator. The more we increase our internal communication, the closer we get to enlightenment.

Tarot Card: Nine of Swords

Title: Lord of Shadows

Malkuth of Yetzirah

Malkuth of Yetzirah is the manifestation of air: **influence**. Malkuth of Yetzirah provides power to manifest an idea or a thought in our social network or society in general. It is invoked to influence the thinking of a group or to manifest a zeitgeist.

Tarot Card: Ten of Swords

Title: Lady of Revolution

World of Assiah

Assiah is the archetypal world of earth. The world of creation is where we live and grow and make connections with the other people in our social groups. The powers of Assiah can bring many good things into manifestation, including health, security, and wealth, but we should note that all these things come into our lives through other people. All sentient beings are part of the flow of the life force of spirit, which animates the first three elements to create the element of earth.

Kether of Assiah

Kether of Assiah is the source of earth: **birth**. Kether of Assiah is the entry point of spirit into the material world. It has the powers of growth, well-being, and abundance. The spiritual essence creates wholeness and material perfection. It is invoked for beginning new projects of a material nature, such as starting a business. This force can also be invoked to increase vitality, to birth a child, or for a fresh start in life. This is the power of beginnings on the material plane.

Tarot Card: Ace of Pentacles

Title: Root of the Powers of Earth

Chokmah of Assiah

Chokmah of Assiah is the power of earth: **transformation.** The nature of existence is constant change and transformation, and the power of earthly existence is evolution. Chokmah is invoked to end a cycle and release the powers trapped within that manifestation. This power can allow you to make new choices available and viable that you would have never considered before.

Tarot Card: Two of Pentacles

Title: Lady of Harmonious Change

Binah of Assiah

Binah of Assiah is the form of earth: **civilization.** Earth energies manifest in ever more complex combinations. The most advanced is civil society—both for humans and the animal kingdom. Working as a group, bees, people, and other animals can accomplish seemingly impossible feats, such as building the great pyramids or landing on the moon. Binah of Assiah is invoked to gain access to social organizations and businesses and the advantages of working with people at scale. This power is good for advancing your career or for understanding culture.

Tarot Card: Three of Pentacles

Title: Lady of Material Works

Chesed of Assiah

Chesed of Assiah is the love of earth: **protection.** Chesed of Assiah powers the benevolent aspects of society, and its laws manifest to secure each person's rights and property. It influences the general goodness of people, the desire to create justice, and the urge to care for one another. It is invoked for protection and security from the correctly functioning laws and institution of a just and benevolent society. Its powers also push our courts and other institutions that we empower to protect us to work correctly.

Tarot Card: Four of Pentacles

Title: Lady of Material Power

Geburah of Assiah

Geburah of Assiah is the will of earth: **evolution.** All things manifested are flawed in some way, and each manifestation suggests its own improvement. In this way, all things are perfect; their flaws make them real and show the path to evolve slowly to perfection. Geburah of Assiah is invoked to cause change and improvement to cultures or organizations. It is also invoked to affect long-term change in the cultural zeitgeist.

Tarot Card: Five of Pentacles

Title: Lady of Material Trouble

Tipareth of Assiah

Tipareth of Assiah is the harmony of earth: **satiety.** This power represents finding a balance in one's life. Tipareth uses knowledge and intuition to solve issues and create long-term stability and financial growth. It assists in having what you need and having room to grow naturally. It is invoked to establish financial security and long-term rather than short-term growth.

Tarot Card: Six of Pentacles

Title: Lady of Material Success

Netzach of Assiah

Netzach of Assiah is the emotions of earth: **partnership.** Netzach of Assiah has the power to create emotional bonds that are enduring and deep. These heart-centered connections can be permanent, such as a marriage or a business partnership. It can also create a great deal of material wealth, as partnerships can build wealth over time. It is invoked to find or strengthen long-term partnerships or to understand why we are unable to do so.

Tarot Card: Seven of Pentacles

Title: Lady of Compromise

Hod of Assiah

Hod of Assiah is the intellect of earth: **luck.** Hod of Assiah assists in the ability to perceive the patterns of manifestation and take advantage of opportunities as they present themselves. What appears as luck to an outsider is simply paying attention to opportunities and seizing them, but often this requires courage or trust in the process. It is invoked to change your fortune and as a general tonic for any activity.

Tarot Card: Eight of Pentacles
Title: Lady of Prudence

Yesod of Assiah

Yesod of Assiah is the dreams of earth: **fun.** Yesod of Assiah is the manifestation of our inner desires and needs materially. This is the unstructured time that allows us to renew and enjoy ourselves, acting spontaneously and enjoying life, being in the moment. And the moment is joy. Yesod is invoked to manifest pleasure and fun, to take a break from the struggle of life and the grind of daily living. It also helps in manifesting a vacation or other diversion that can renew a love of life and sense of purpose.

Tarot Card: Nine of Pentacles
Title: Lady of Material Gain

Malkuth of Assiah

Malkuth of Assiah is the manifestation of earth: **nurturance.** This is the final evolution of the current of life force in the fourfold tree. While the Page of Pentacles (earth of earth) is the final manifestation of the Ace of Pentacles, the Ten of Pentacles represents the turning point of the flow of life force to a return to source. This is the power to nurture and heal physically and spiritually; it is invoked for all forms of healing. This power can also connect us with our ancestors and can be powerful for creating legacies and resolving issues with inheritance.

Tarot Card: Ten of Pentacles
Title: Lady of Wealth

• • • • • • •

There are several powers in the list that we use a lot. One of those is Yesod of Briah, or the dreams of water. It is a general wish-granting power that is very useful in group workings. Another one we often use is Chesed of Malkuth, which is a great protection power. Geburah of Yetzirah is fantastic for clearing out dead weight from your life. Sometimes it works too good. Hod of Assiah is a general luck power and always good to have. Make a talisman for this one and put it in your wallet. Malkuth of Assiah is great for physical healing.

Once you get the basics of the Pyramid of Power ritual down, you will be able to manifest all forty effects easily.

— CHAPTER 23 —
The Elemental Octagram

The Elemental Octagram is an eidolon ritual that uses two Greater Rituals of the Pentagram (GRP) built in opposition to each other. This creates an energy field that is vastly more powerful than the GRP and gives us sixteen effects rather than four. Once you become confident using it, it will become the power source for your workings.

Elemental Synergy

We can combine an element within another element to create a powerful, new elemental force. This elemental force, a double vortex, has the enduring power of the Rose Ankh (chapter 18) and the explosive force of the Pyramid of Power (chapter 21). Created as an energetic force, it has the impressive ability to wear away at the most difficult problems; however, if we create the vortex as an eidolon, we can then call in the spiritual intelligence of an Enochian angel to empower our rites and grant us its wisdom and emotional harmony.

An element within an element gives us a total of sixteen angelic powers, which correspond to the sixteen court cards in the tarot. For example, the fiery part of earth is the King of Pentacles. One might imagine this force to be like the slow burn of a compost heap breaking down matter into fertile soil. The power of the King of Pentacles is to create abundance by taking great care in matters and responsibilities. By comparison, the earthy part of fire would be the Page of Wands. The Page of

Wands could be imagined as possibly a healthy forest fire that clears away debris for new growth. All sixteen are defined in the following chapter, "The Concourse of Forces for the Elemental Octagram."

Sixteen powerful elemental angels direct and enliven the forces of creation that flow between the worlds of Yetzirah and Assiah. They are lower-ranking angels, to be sure, but very powerful and friendly ones. These forces can help you balance and become conscious of your emotional and mental universe in profound ways. By coming into contact with and scrying these forces, we become aware not only of the positive aspects of these forces flowing through our lives but also the shadow elements or hidden parts that are contributing to cognitive distortions and inhibiting us from our full potential.

Uses for the Elemental Octagram

The elemental energy created by the ritual is very useful by itself. For example, you can use your pore breathing skills to absorb the energy within yourself and open those mental and emotional channels. Meditation in the energetic field opens the channels in our nephesh, or lower mind nature, to these elemental forces, which are always there. We are just not conscious of them.

Our advice is to at first simply create the elemental vortex, pore breathe, and sit in mindful awareness of the field. Simply experience it and see what it brings up from your subconscious mind. Don't use this ritual for another purpose until you have tried it with all four elements and feel reasonably confident in your ability to perform it. You don't need to have it completely memorized, but you should be familiar with the flow and sequence of actions.

Some people do work with this elemental energy as a magical practice. The limitation is that this force is only elemental and can only act in simplistic ways. An elemental is intelligent in the same way you can say electricity is intelligent. Electricity is smart enough to follow Ohm's law; however, if not directed by a competent electrician, it can cause fires, electrocute people, and so on. That is why we invoke the angel. It raises the vibration of the field and makes it intelligent; it is the electrician that we call to direct our elemental force. This electrician can understand what we are trying to do, make suggestions and improvements, and offer wisdom. These angels are very wise in that they know absolutely everything about their particular elemental combination, though little about anything else.

For instance, if someone wanted to improve their health, they could create the elemental field earth of earth and invoke the angel ABALPT ARBIZ (Ah-Bal-Pey-Teh Are-By-Zod) into the field. This is one of our favorites, as she has a direct connection to the life force and is very grounding and energizing. She can create a sense of calm. For emotional insights, we would invoke water of water. NELAPR OMEBB (Nel-ah-Par Omeb-beh) can show you your emotional core. If we wanted more influence and friends, air of fire might be good; mind of inspiration can be very charismatic. There is a complete list in the following chapter, which includes all our notes on who is good for what.

The Flow of the Elemental Octagram Ritual

This is a longer ritual, using all of the skills we have discussed so far. Let's deconstruct it.

Introit

The inspiration for the intro to this rite comes from the book *Rebel in the Soul* by Bika Reed.[67] It is a very good translation of a sacred text given to initiates of Egyptian temples. In this book, the initiate is arguing with their soul. They find life depressing, people are liars, priests are hypocrites, politicians only want power, and so on. Sound familiar? The original text was written thousands of years ago. The initiate wants to sacrifice his flesh and go to the realm of the gods, to the field of reeds. His soul answers back and tells him that only through incarnation can he find illumination, and what he is asking for will doom him.

The living Nefa is the Egyptian model of the incarnated soul; it is like an egg with many layers. Only through incarnation can liberation be found. The intro takes us through the afterlife and into the hall of Osiris, where we will encounter many Egyptian gods.

The Base Vortex, Setting of the Four Directions

This is similar to the Greater Invoking Ritual of the Pentagram (GRP), but here we are creating a vortex with a node beneath the floor. Since the earth is masculine in Egyptian mythos, we invoke five male archetypes for the base vortex. This is the base element, so if we are creating air of fire, it would be fire, or if the intent is to create water of earth, then it would be earth.

The Modifying Vortex, Setting of the Four Angles

The modifying element is created by the same method as the base except inverted, like a mirror image at the top of the ritual space. We use the angels and move counterclockwise. Additionally, the pentagrams traced are inverted mirror images. We also use five goddesses, as the Egyptian heavens are female. The created effect is two swirling tornadoes of power with the open ends of the cones facing each other at the midpoint of the space.

67. Reed, *Rebel in the Soul.*

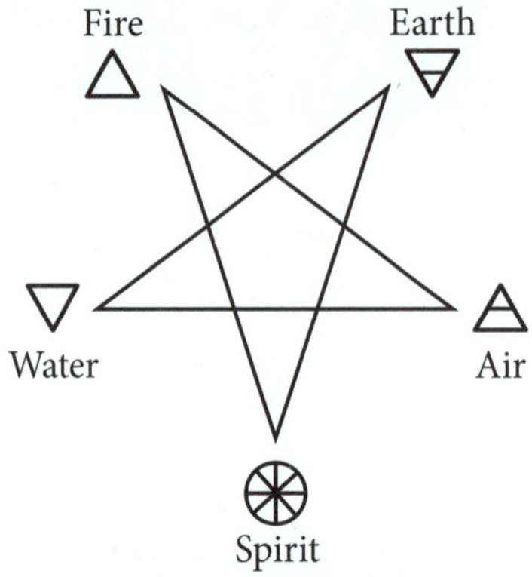

Obverse Pentagram
with Elements

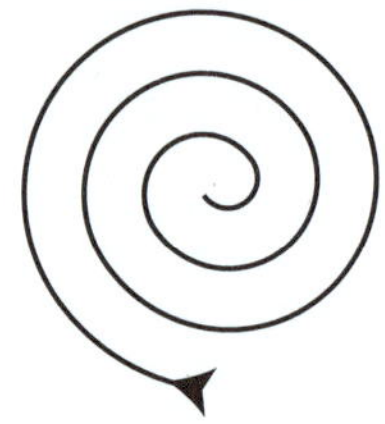

Invoking Spiral

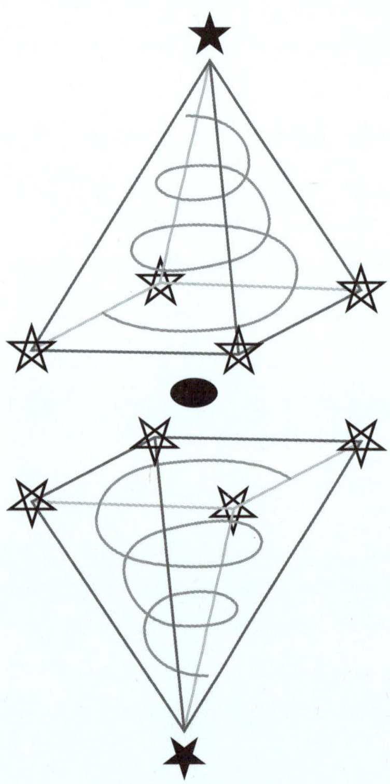

Double Greater Ritual
of the Pentagram

Fusing the Two Vortexes

Now we need to pull the two energy fields together with a third pass. To start, we draw an equal-armed cross and pull the energy to a central node. There we invoke the four royal sons of Horus, which are the figures on the canopic jars found in Egyptian tombs. These jars contained the mummified internal organs of the deceased and were considered very important to the afterlife.

Symbolically we are creating an energy body by fusing the vortexes and invoking the gods of the organs the Egyptians thought were vitally important. This is the eidolon, the symbolic energy body that our Enochian angel will manifest in. The final act of grabbing each node and pulling them through the center will fuse the fields. In our experience, it is very energetic and explosive in effect. At first, the form is like a double Pyramid of Power, rotated 45 degrees facing in opposition, like a mirror image.

Once the double vortex is fused, its form changes to resemble a torus field. It is similar to the magnetic fields of the earth and flows inward and outward around the temple space.

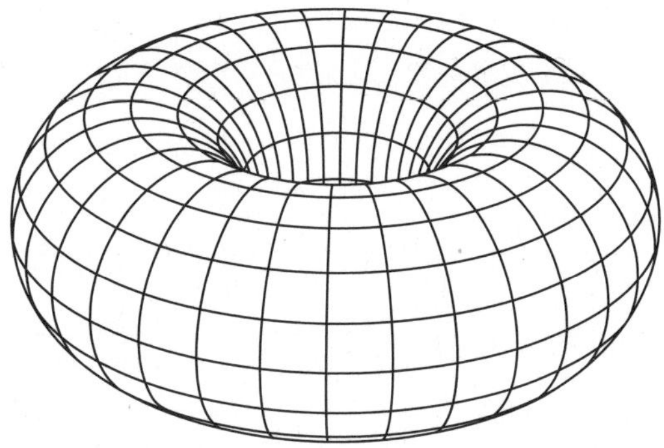

Final Form – Torus Shape

Invocations in the Elemental Vortex

Once the vortex is established, you can either simply pore breathe in the eidolon energy or you can invoke one of sixteen Qabalistic angels. To put it another way, you can focus on experiencing the electricity or call the electrician.

R•I•T•U•A•L
THE EGYPTIAN ELEMENTAL OCTAGRAM

Before beginning this ritual, decide if you are going to experience the energy field or invoke the angel. Either way, you should walk through the ritual flow and practice the pentagrams, mirrored pentagrams, and other shapes you will be drawing. Images are included to help prompt your memory. If you want to experience the angel, then look through the Concourse of Forces and select the angel you would like to experience. We suggest starting with Earth of Earth since it is very healing and grounding and brings prosperity. Then select Air of Air, Water of Water, and Fire of Fire in that order. You can then proceed to explore the more subtle combinations such as Air of Water and Water of Air. Each angel has either one or two calls listed in the Concourse of Forces. You should look up those calls up in the appendix. Read the calls over before the ritual, but you don't need to memorize the calls. Each angel listed also has a short invocation we have written after our experiences with the angels, and we have positive indications that each angel has approved our short invocation and its sigil. You can make your own copy of the sigil or use the one in the book. Marking these pages you will need to turn to beforehand will help things flow smoothly. We suggest using sticky notes to mark the pages you need to find quickly; they don't damage the pages.

Things You Need

Space for the ritual

Something pointy to draw the shapes in the air

Optional: The court card from a tarot deck that corresponds to the elemental force you are invoking; place this on a central altar or in the center of your space

Directions

Perform a Qabalistic Cross, the Temple Consecration, and optionally the Rose Ankh Vortex. Then, assume a godform, such as Thoth or Ma'at, if you wish.

The Rose Ankh and godform are not absolutely necessary, but they can boost the effect of the ritual. It depends on how much magical force you want to work with and your own time constraints, as you may want to also do a Pyramid of Power afterward to exteriorize the energy of the Elemental Octagram. When you first try this ritual, only do a temple consecration and then the Elemental Octagram. Just experience the energy the first time you do the ritual, then add an angel and increase the complexity as you feel comfortable. When you have performed this ritual for each element with an angel, then consider adding the Pyramid of Powers to the end.

Open with eight tolls of the bell or eight knocks. We like to move around the space and give one ring for each node around the circle; other people just give eight rings.

Introit

Face east and say:

Only through the living Nefa can the intellect reach the heart and become the haven for the upstream struggle. Then, by my hand it would arrive blissful at the beyond, like the one within their pyramid, who stood up, survivor of their own burial! I have come, and I have drawn nigh to see thy beauties. My two hands are raised in adoration of thy name both right and truth. I have come unto the place where the acacia tree growest not and where the tree thick with leaves exists not and where the ground yields neither herb nor grass, and I have entered unto the place of secret and hidden things.

The holy rulers of the pylons are in the form of the shining ones! Anubis spoke saying, "He knowest our cities and our paths, I have been pacified. Therefore, pass through the gate in triumph to the hall of Osiris."[68]

The Base Vortex, Setting of the Four Directions

Continue to face east. Vibrate *Eolis* (to make or create) while drawing the invoking pentagram of the chosen base element.

Vibrate *Exarp* while drawing an invoking spiral over the pentagram with yellow energy. Visualize Thoth and say:

I invoke thee, Thoth, ibis-headed scribe of the gods and keeper of the keys of wisdom. Thy knowledge spans all space and time, and you are the lord of balance and equilibrium. Hail unto thee!

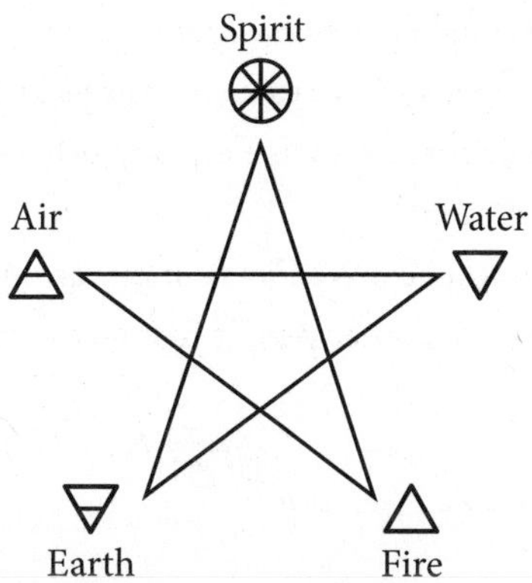

Pentagram with Elements

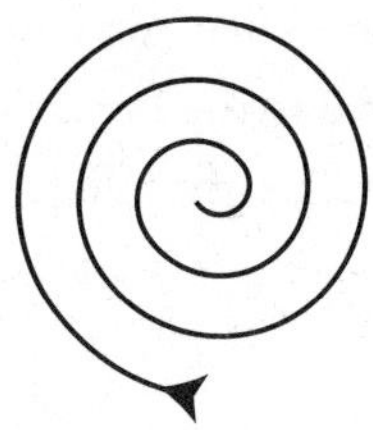

Invoking Spiral

Face south and vibrate *Ar* (the sun) while drawing the invoking pentagram of the chosen base element.

Vibrate *Bitom* while drawing an invoking spiral over the pentagram with scarlet energy. Visualize Horus the elder and say:

I invoke thee, Horus, lord of the raging flame, swift as the hawk in flight who swoops down victorious over his enemies and who rises with the golden disk forged in the fires of Edfu. Hail unto thee!

68. Reed, *Rebel in the Soul*, 35.

Turn to face west. Vibrate *Zorge* (love) while drawing the invoking pentagram of the chosen base element.

Vibrate *Hcoma* while drawing an invoking spiral over the pentagram with blue energy. Visualize Osiris and say:

> *I invoke thee, Osiris, lord of the two kingdoms and wearer of the white crown. You are risen from the corridors of the NeterKhet, triumphant over death and ruling in splendor over the western lands. Hail unto thee!*

Face north and then vibrate *Limlal* (a treasure) while drawing the invoking pentagram of the chosen base element.

Vibrate *Nanta* while drawing an invoking spiral over the pentagram with green energy. Visualize Anubis and say:

> *I invoke thee, Anubis, jackal-headed guardian of the Khersec-Shu, guardian of thy pylons and the pyramid who watches from the heights, unmoved amidst the swirling desert sand. Hail unto thee!*

Face center and vibrate *Paid* (the eternal) while drawing the invoking pentagram of spirit receptive to the infrapoint.

Vibrate *EHNB* while drawing an invoking spiral over the pentagram with black energy. Visualize Geb and say:

> *I invoke thee, Geb, lord of the earth. You are the provider of stability and form, the chief of the gods who watches the weighing of the hearts in the hall of judgment. Hail unto thee!*

Connect and finalize the structure by performing the Analysis of the Keyword. Say the keyword for each node while activating it again by sending energy to the node using the sword or other tool. *"Eolis, Limlal, Zorge, Ar, Paid."* Then say, *"ELZAP, the way of the initiate!"* Finally, the four watchtowers are drawn together through the infrapoint using the sword.

The Modifying Vortex, Setting of the Four Angles

Face the southeastern angle. Vibrate *Nazps* (the sword) while drawing the inverted invoking pentagram of the chosen modifying element.

Vibrate *OHOWOHAATAN* while drawing an invoking spiral over the pentagram with orange energy.

Visualize Sekhmet and say:

I invoke thee, Sekhmet, lady of fire's bright splendor. The illuminated lioness is poised to spring forth from the heart of Ra! Hail unto thee!

Face the northeastern angle. Vibrate *Oma* (understanding) while drawing the inverted invoking pentagram of the chosen modifying element.

Vibrate *TAHAOEIOJI* while drawing an invoking spiral over the pentagram with light blue energy.

Visualize Ma'at and say:

I invoke thee, Ma'at, resplendent vulture, lady of truth and balance, whose reed flower rests upon the scales of the universe. You wait in your hall with your forty-two assessors to weigh the heart of the initiate. Paneter Apu Ma'at. Hail unto thee!

Face southwestern angle. Vibrate *Vaul* (to labor) while drawing the inverted invoking pentagram of the chosen modifying element.

Vibrate *THAHEBYOBEEATAB* while drawing an invoking spiral over the pentagram with purple energy.

Visualize Nephthys and say:

I invoke thee, Nephthys, dark sister of Isis. Thou art the lady of the scorched sands of the desert which receive thy twilight charms and cool gentle night mists as a balm and a blessing. Hail unto thee!

Face the northwestern angle. Vibrate *Ap* (unchanging) while drawing the inverted invoking pentagram of the chosen modifying element.

Vibrate *THAHAAOTHAHE* while drawing an invoking spiral over the pentagram with ocher energy.

Visualize Isis and say:

I invoke thee, Isis, horned lady of the moon. You are queen of the fertile earth, and thy love is descended, flowing forth from sacred pools as tears of untold beauty upon the face of the maiden. Beloved of the gods and men. Hail unto thee!

Turn to face the center of the circle. Say:

I invoke thee, Nuit, lady of the starry night sky, whose body spans the heavens in a glimmering arch. Galaxies and nebulae rush forth from your infinite form in never-ending circles of time. Hail unto thee!

Connect and finalize the structure by performing the Analysis of the Keyword. Say the keyword for each node while activating it again by sending energy to the node using the sword or other tool. *"Vaul, Ananael, Oma, Ap, Nazps."* The say, *"VAOAN. The eternal truth is known through the will penetrating the mysteries."* Finally, the four watchtowers are drawn together through the ultrapoint using the sword or other tool.

Fusing the Two Vortexes

Stand in the center of the circle and face each watchtower in turn, moving clockwise to invoke the four sons of Horus, each bearing one of the four great powers from their resting place in Amenti. Once the invocation is complete, pull the energy from the fused field to the central point of the space. It will attach and the double vortex will be "pinched" at each of these four points. To draw the equal-armed cross, simply draw a large number four.

Face east and vibrate *ORO IBAH AOZPI* while drawing an equal-armed cross over the pentagram. Vibrate *Toh* (triumph) while drawing an invoking spiral over the cross.

Visualize Duamutef and say:

> *I invoke thee, Duamutef, lord of the east and royal son of Horus, unleasher of the winds and guardian and keeper of the wand and staff. Hail unto thee!*

Draw an invoking spiral around both the pentagram and the cross. Then draw both through the mezzo point.

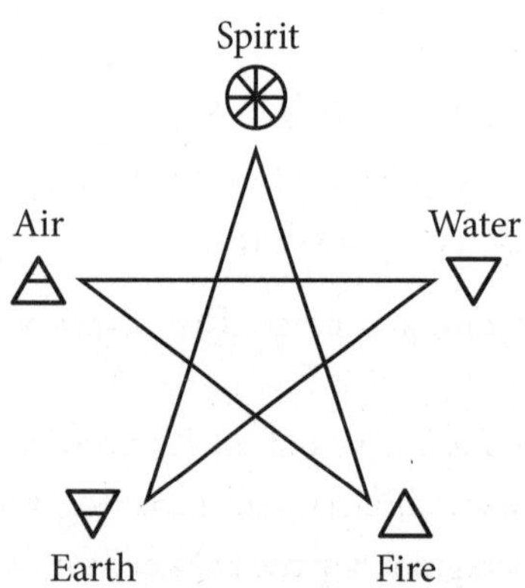

Pentagram with Elements

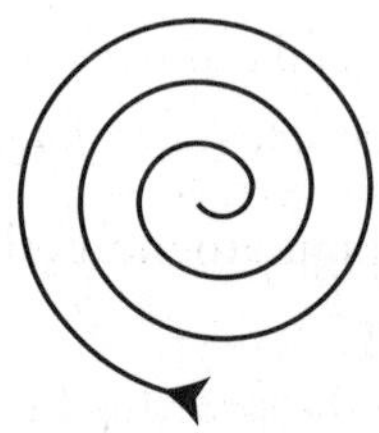

Invoking Spiral

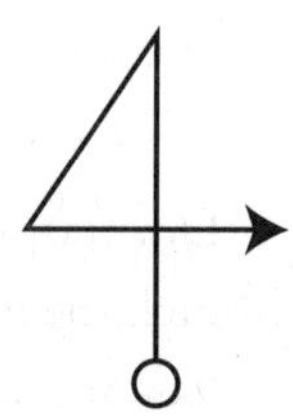

Cross

Face south. Then vibrate *OIP TEAA PDOCE* while drawing an equal-armed cross over the pentagram. Vibrate *Olprt* (the light) while drawing an invoking spiral over the cross.

Visualize Imset and say:

> *I invoke thee, Imset, lord of the south and royal son of Horus, keeper of the flame and wielder of the scimitar of righteousness. Hail unto thee!*

Draw an invoking spiral around both the pentagram and the cross. Then draw both through the mezzo point.

Turn and face west. Vibrate *MPH ARSL GAIOL* while drawing an equal-armed cross over the pentagram. Vibrate *Apia* (eternal life) while drawing an invoking spiral over the cross.

Visualize Qebehsenuef and say:

> *I invoke thee, Qebehsenuef, lord of the west and royal son of Horus. You preside over the rivers and seas and are the keeper of the sacred vessel of fulfillment. Hail unto thee!*

Draw an invoking spiral around both the pentagram and cross, and then draw both together through the mezzo point.

Face north and vibrate *MOR DIAL HCTGA* while drawing an equal-armed cross over the pentagram. Vibrate *Noib* (the affirmation) while drawing an invoking spiral over the cross.

Visualize Hapi and say:

> *I invoke thee, Hapi, lord of the north and royal son of Horus. You are the keeper of the dish that holds the treasures produced from the rich black lands, an infinite source of life. Hail unto thee!*

Draw an invoking spiral around both the pentagram and cross. Then draw both through the mezzo point.

Connect and finalize the structure by performing the Analysis of the Keyword.

Using the sword to draw and arc, connecting all the watchtowers and angles together, pausing to energize all eight nodes of the combined octagram, say the keyword for each node while activating it again by sending energy to each node. "*Toh, Olprt, Apia, Noib, Toz.*" Then say, "*TOANT. The divine love and union are the center wherein the secret awaits.*"

Perform the Assumption Sign (page 185) and unite the octagram within yourself.

Invocations in the Elemental Vortex

At this point, the rite is at a stage of completion. You have created the elemental vortex, and it can act as an eidolon. However, you have options. You can pore breathe the energy in and meditate mindfully in the space. You can also imagine the energy doing something for you, such as healing your body or bringing in luck and good fortune.

If you would like to progress to a more advanced working, you can invoke a Qabalistic angel. The eidolon is complete, and you can follow the instructions in the section Concourse of Forces for the Elemental Octagram. If not, you should shut down the elemental vortex.

Closing

Shutting down the elemental vortex is accomplished by drawing a banishing spiral to the nodes and the angels. Give thanks to the spirits you have invoked and to the guardians of the watchtowers. Complete the rite by stating a dedication of merit. Finally, with a long ritual we like to clap our hands three times and state, "The ritual is now complete."

• • • • • • •

Without a doubt, this is our favorite ritual. It acts as a power source for all our advanced workings. As mentioned before, you can combine this ritual with the Pyramid of Power for an enhanced effect, and the Elemental Octagram can also act as a power source for gate structures as well, as you will see in chapter 25, and much more that this book will not be able to cover. While some might think elemental magic is basic since it applies mainly to the microcosm, in truth, the elements flow in a fractal pattern throughout all of creation: four elements and a dual spirit nature repeating in near infinite combinations.

— CHAPTER 24 —

The Concourse of Forces for the Elemental Octagram

The following is a list of angelic forces that can be invoked into the eidolon created by the Elemental Octagram. It is a listing of the sixteen Qabalistic angels, or angels of the angels, as they are the rulers of the elemental sections of the watchtower tablets. It is true that you can invoke many angels from each elemental quarter; these are the rulers, or it can be said that they sum up each elemental quarter.

These angels are the connection between the planes of Yetzirah and Assiah. They focus and maintain the synergistic powers that the material world coalesces onto, like dew on a spiderweb in the morning hours. They are older than time and wiser than dreams, and they have a generosity that is embarrassing to encounter. And yet, they are low-ranking angels, creative forces that are close to reality. In harnessing their power, you will not only get to know your inner workings in a way that is impossible to describe but see how reality is mutable. You can wield this power using the Pyramid of Power.

In the following listings, there is first a section with general information on each group of angels by elements. Then each angel has its own approved sigil and a description on its personality and area of expertise and our experience with it. Since we need some method of knowing what the angel might be like before we encounter it, we consider both the court card it corresponds to and a hexagram from the *I Ching*. Using the *I Ching* may seem odd, but it goes back to Crowley, who had a very great interest in the oracle. Since the *I Ching* hexagrams have elemental attributions, such as

Hexagram 27, Earth of Fire, which corresponds to the Page of Wands, the keywords, in this example *Nourishment*, gives us a clue to what the energy will be like. We have included these traditional attributions so you can see how they correspond to our experiences. You can also look them up in the *I Ching* for more insight if you wish. This would be an example of Concordance. Each angel also has a short invocation to use after the Enochian Call(s). It is included in English and Enochian. Erich composed these, and each angel approved its invocation in a separate working.

How to Call the Enochian Angel

There are nineteen calls, or prayers, given to John Dee to open the storehouses of God. They are in the mysterious Enochian language, and when read, they produce very specific trance states. The version of the Calls we use are listed in the appendix. You should read them in Enochian. Pronounce the Calls to the best of your ability. They will sound largely like English, and you will need to add in what seems to be the most natural vowel sound if there are too many consonants. Back when Erich first started using this ritual, his instructions were to just read the specific call for the elemental combo he was working with. You can just read a single call, sit mindfully, and scry the angel.

These sixteen angels listed to work with are under the umbrella of the archangels of the elements you have been working with since the Lesser Ritual of the Pentagram. These are much closer to creation than even the elemental kings and have more to do with the fabric of reality than the kings, who are more like organizing principals. In the end, it's a bit like describing the flavor of a delicious meal; a person can't truly understand it until they taste it themselves.

Performing the Elemental Octagram and then a single Enochian call worked really well. Erich was able to commune with the Enochian angels, who turned out to be incredibly patient, wise, and very generous with their wisdom. Since that time, Erich has learned more about how the system is intended to work, and now his method, which we share, is more complex.

The primary elemental combo has one call. For example, fire of fire uses only call six. However, if you want to call water of fire, then you read call six and then call seventeen. The primary opens up the tablet, or elemental plane, and the second call opens up the subquarter, or it drills down a bit to the next level.

In addition, we have created a method to create sigils for each angel, and we place the sigil in the center of the space as an object of meditation. These sigils are the hieroglyphs of these forces. We have also written short invocations for each angel that should be read after the calls.

While we have had good results with only reading one call, adding in these additional parts does seem to increase the power level, especially for people who have not done this work before. We will put the salute before each section by element since it won't change for the four angels in each elemental section. You are saluting the higher-ranking angels, including the planetary angels we will work with later.

The salute follows this pattern:

Enochian: *Do a omaos de _____, ge hoath ge qaal.*

English: In the name of _____, we worship our creator.

My recommendation is you use one of two methods. You can first create the eidolon using the Elemental Octagram ritual and then just read the one call for the specific angel.

Or you can follow the more complete method:

1. Place the sigil of the angel to be called on the central altar. You can trace it out of this book onto paper or just use this book.
2. Read the calls for the angel, either one call or two as noted in the listing.
3. Read the correct salute by the element. This calls all the angel's supervisors and gets their attention. It is similar to copying someone's boss in an email.
4. Read the invocation we have for each angel and sit mindfully scrying.

Start simple, then go complex once you get your bearings.

In the following listings for each elemental combination, we will include the information we have based on our experience. Each angel has a two-part name, and it is said that the first name calls the angel and the second commands it. We have always thought it sounded very old-fashioned. In practice, the two-part name is more like balanced forces. Vibrating both brings an alignment with the intelligent energy that is balanced. We have included some notes on pronunciation as well.

Angels of Fire

These forces of fire bring clarity, excitement, and knowledge. They can be very visual, appearing for Erich as volcanic beings made of liquid metal. They also appear as spatial distortions, similar to the effect of heat rising on a hot road but more angular, like a stick figure just on the other side of reality. If that sounds scary, it's not; nothing in this book can or will harm you.

The fire angels bring tremendous light and insight into your mind. The hottest aspects of fire—the emotions of fire, the mind of fire, and the actions of fire—bring what some call knowledge, or intuition. It is more like an alignment with your True Will or best course of action. To contact these forces is to become aware of the fire within yourself and how you connect to the heat of inspiration that courses through the universe, tying all together in perfect action. It is hard to describe, but to refine is to burn, and burn you will—brightly.

The fire elementals relate to a very clear awareness of pure knowing, without words or any narration of the rational mind. It is a very pure and uncontrived state of awareness that reveals our true nature and real motivations.

Salute of Fire

Do a omaos de Oip Teaa Pdoke ge hoath ge qaal. (Secret Holy Name)
Do a omaos de Bitom ge hoath ge qaal. (Fire of Spirit)
Do a omaos de Edlprna ge hoath ge qaal. (Sun of Fire)
Do a omaos de Aaetpio ge hoath ge qaal. (Mars of Fire)
Do a omaos de Adoeoet ge hoath ge qaal. (Jupiter of Fire)
Do a omaos de Alndvod ge hoath ge qaal. (Moon of Fire)
Do a omaos de Aapdoce ge hoath ge qaal. (Venus of Fire)
Do a omaos de Arinnap ge hoath ge qaal. (Saturn of Fire)
Do a omaos de Anodoin ge hoath ge qaal. (Mercury of Fire)

Fire of Fire, King of Wands

God Name Pair: RZIONR NRZFM

Read the sixth call only. The *I Ching* hexagram number 51 is titled "Shock." The effect of this angelic force is to burn away any self-delusion and leave only the truth behind. Once it said to Erich, "Sit with this truth, and if it pains you, then find your medicine in the spagyric of the ashes of your illusions." A spagyric is a type of salt crystal extracted from the ashes of a plant that contains powerful medicine. Fire of fire is quite a serious force, but it is very useful.

The heat generated in the temple with this angel present really has to be experienced. It is invoked for inspiration and insight into any question.

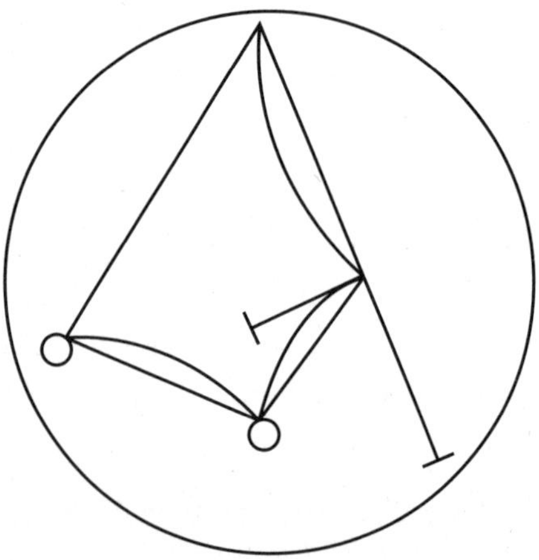

Fire of Fire Sigil

Call it to find your best path in life without the distractions and distortions of any shadow parts. Often, we do this for the New Year in our temple.

Pair this with the Ace of Wands for a very powerful fiery force that brings great inspiration.

INVOCATION FOR FIRE OF FIRE

Enochian: *Brita, nonca zir vaoan rlodnr. Niiso oecrima g luiahe.*

English: I have spoken of you; you are truth's furnace. Come and sing your song of honor.

Water of Fire, Queen of Wands

God Name Pair: VADALI OBAVA

Read the sixth call then the seventeenth call. The *I Ching* hexagram number 17 is titled "Following." Water of fire brings clarity to introspection and inner knowledge. It also provides a type of inner knowing and alignment with one's spiritual path. When invoked, it is easy to see the truth of any emotional conflict or quandary and to see the trash that surrounds it confusing you and creating doubt. Although fiery, it brings a certain peace and certainty.

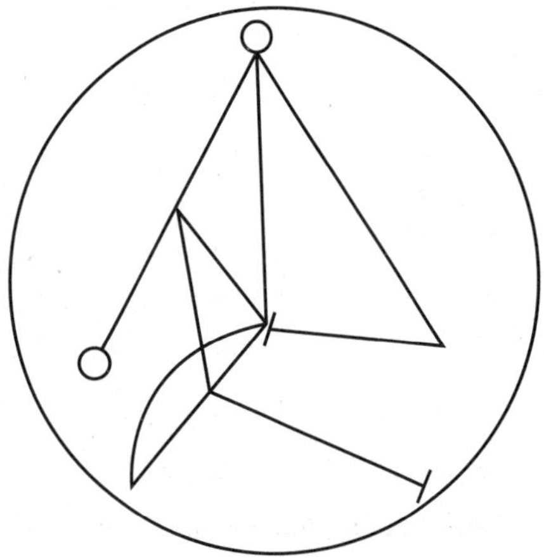

Water of Fire Sigil

This is the power of intuition, knowing things without knowing why, bypassing the narrator in your mind with great confidence.

Paired with the Two, Three, or Six of Wands, it brings great insight and a visionary quality to self-knowledge. Paired with the Eight of Pentacles, it can bring intuitive powers to know when to act. It is a very useful angelic force in general.

INVOCATION FOR WATER OF FIRE

Enochian: *Nonca zir a monoas ooanoan. Dlugar geh oma ag goho.*

English: You are the heart's eyes. Give us understanding without speech.

Air of Fire, Knight of Wands

God Name Pair: NOALMR OLOAG

Read the sixth call then the sixteenth call. The *I Ching* hexagram number 42 is called "Increase." The intellect of fire brings great charisma and influence. When you have inspiration in your mind, it is infectious and can bring people to your cause or way of thinking—not in a hypnotic way. It can be described as someone who looks like they swallowed the sun. This angel shows you your inner light and fire and brings confidence. It once told Erich, "No matter what you do, people will criticize you, so do what you will." Good advice, we think.

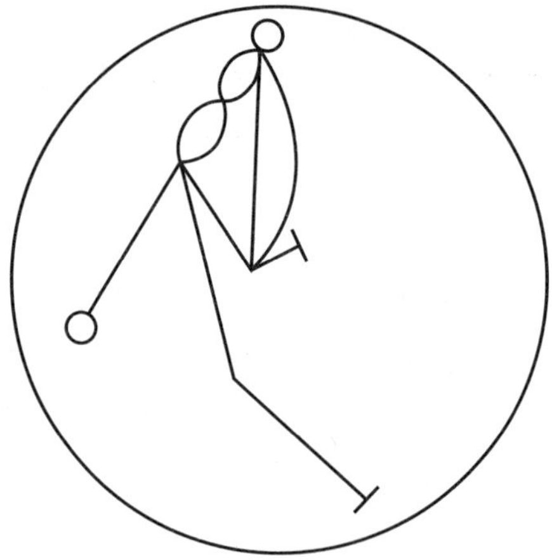

Air of Fire Sigil

Pairing it with the Seven or Eight of Wands brings the ability to be very convincing and influential. With the Ten of Swords, the effect is magnified in groups, creates influence in organizations, and helps to create movements of social change.

INVOCATION FOR AIR OF FIRE

Enochian: *Nonca, zir iaod bogpa. Zamran a noan de balt od bliorax.*

English: You who are the source of leadership, show us the way of justice and comfort.

Earth of Fire, Page of Wands

God Name Pair: VOLXDO SIOD

Read the sixth call then the eighteenth call. The *I Ching* hexagram number 27 is titled "Nourishment." Ambition, the closest word we can find in *The Complete Enochian Dictionary* by Donald Laycock is *Zilodarp*, to "stretch forth and conquer."[69] This matches the feeling of earth of fire. The nature of fire is to consume its boundaries as it expands. This angel gives the feeling of being unstoppable, providing great confidence and the ability to reorganize everything around you in a more efficient and

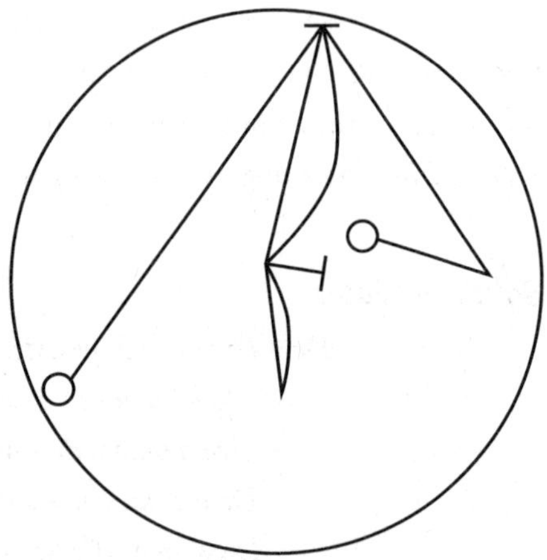

Earth of Fire Sigil

69. Laycock, *The Complete Enochian Dictionary*, 186.

focused way. It is invoked to overcome limitations. It is an "open the roads" force that can remove obstacles, and most often, these blocks are the ones we create for ourselves.

For a powerful banishing, pair it with the Five of Swords. Pairing it with the Four of Pentacles creates a powerful protection.

INVOCATION FOR EARTH OF FIRE

Enochian: *Geh lonsa zilodarp. Xirdo goholor te od chirlan ado nonca.*

English: Thou art the power to stretch forth and conquer. We are lifted up and rejoice with you.

Angels of Water

The angels of elemental water deal directly with the emotions and are very popular in our temple workings, as they can deliver insight and emotional healing. We get a lot of interest in Water of Water, or the Queen of Cups, because she can show you your emotional core. These angels are the most psychedelic, giving the most interesting visions. The visions can be very mysterious and dreamlike or so direct you feel punched in the gut. If asked, they can assume a humanoid form, very often like a mermaid (to Erich, at least), with a lot of deep-sea and sea cave imagery.

These are as introspective as the fire angels are expansive, but they are in many ways more important. We need to understand our emotional world before we can be effective in life and understand that emotions, like thoughts, are something that we have, not who we are. And like thoughts, emotions arise, exist for a while, and then fade.

These angelic forces provide emotional healing and understanding, so we invoke them often. Everyone needs more understanding and healing. Emotions are wonderful and fill life with joy and meaning, but they can also arise so unexpectedly when they come out of a shadow part that we are unaware of. These angels can show you those hidden parts, and much more.

Salute of Water

Do a omaos de Mph Arsl Gaiol ge hoath ge qaal. (Secret Holy Name)
Do a omaos de Hcoma ge hoath ge qaal. (Water of Spirit)
Do a omaos de Raagios ge hoath ge qaal. (Sun of Water)
Do a omaos de Lsrahpm ge hoath ge qaal. (Mars of Water)
Do a omaos de Saiinou ge hoath ge qaal. (Jupiter of Water)

Do a omaos de Laoaxrp ge hoath ge qaal. (Moon of Water)
Do a omaos de Slgaiol ge hoath ge qaal. (Venus of Water)
Do a omaos de Ligdisa ge hoath ge qaal. (Saturn of Water)
Do a omaos de Soaiznt ge hoath ge qaal. (Mercury of Water)

Fire of Water, King of Cups

God Name Pair: IAAASD ATAPA

First read the fourth call then the twelfth call. The *I Ching* hexagram number 54 is titled "Careful Affection." *Compassion* is the best keyword we can think of, and in Enochian, the best translation we have found is *Oquasbi Tliobn*, or "the destroyer of separation." The most active aspect of water is to dissolve substances and hold them in solution.

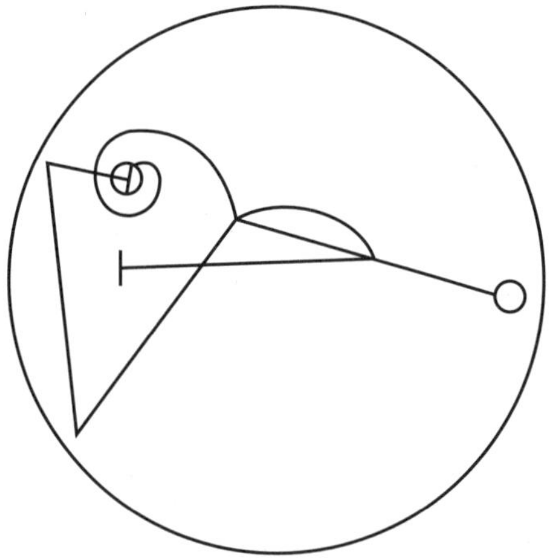

Fire of Water Sigil

The effect of the fiery part of water is to dissolve differences between people and all sentient beings. This is very important to our practice. Without the ability to connect with the universe with compassion, to form a connection that is not reactive but caring, then we are not going to accomplish anything with spiritual practice. It will be just an empty gesture. Fire of water is invoked to gain the experience of selfless compassion, spiritual understanding, and union with all.

Pairing it with the Three of Cups brings an experience of being connected to all. With the Eight of Cups, it can make allies out of difficult people.

INVOCATION FOR FIRE OF WATER

Enochian: *Nonci oquasbi givaoan de tliobn, na geh oma yadnah.*

English: You destroy the illusion of separation, that we may know the unity of being.

Water of Water, the Queen of Cups

God Name Pair: NELAPR OMEBB

Read the fourth call only. The *I Ching* hexagram number 58 is titled "Joy." Water of water gives the secret wisdom of dreams. One of the four primal combinations, water of water is the most psychedelic. It communicates with dreamlike images, some clear and some very cryptic.

In our temple, we have invoked this force many times, as her ability for emotional healing is amazing. Ages ago, when Erich first invoked her, he asked her for psychic powers, the response was immediate. A voice in his mind said, "Very well, then you will learn to trust," which he hated hearing at the time, but now it makes so much sense to him. How to trust is a skill you have to learn through living and paying attention or by listening to spiritual wisdom. It is a requirement for any sort of psychic development and emotional healing of an attachment injury. Many times, our group has received visions from this force that led to emotional insight and healing.

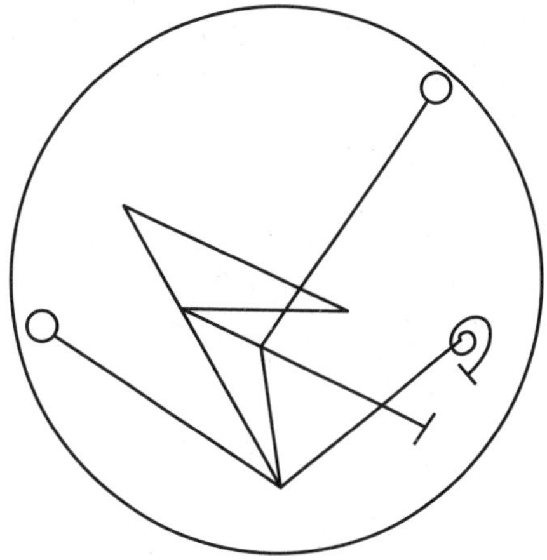

Water of Water Sigil

This is an extremely powerful and useful force when used alone for emotional healing. It can be paired with the Four of Cups for an even more powerful emotional healing effect.

INVOCATION FOR WATER OF WATER

Enochian: *Etharzi gah soba limlal noan brgda ananael, nonca brint grad nobloh.*

English: Peaceful angel whose treasure is the secret wisdom of dreams, you hold the moon in the palms of your hand.

Air of Water, the Knight of Cups

God Name Pair: OBGOTA AAABKO

Read the fourth call, then the tenth call. The *I Ching* hexagram number 61 is titled "Centering in Truth." The airy part of water brings up images of effervescence, the joy and enthusiasm that it implies. This force brings a connection between the thoughts and the mind so we may know what really brings us satisfaction and truth.

We have worked with this force a few times. It brings inner knowledge of our emotional life, what works and what doesn't, and clarity to the situations around us in our personal and emotional connections without the

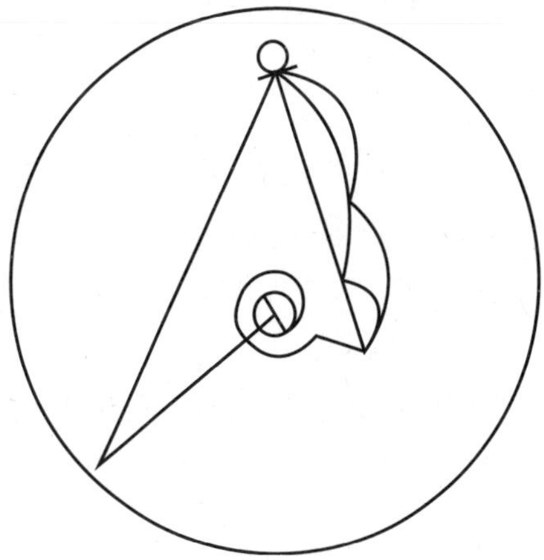

Air of Water Sigil

obscurations of our own prejudices and preconditioned patterns of expectations from ourselves and others. For example, when someone makes plans with us and then doesn't show up or call, we might think they don't care about us, but really, they are just a disorganized person doing the best that they can and need our compassion.

We often pair this with the Three of Cups, compassion, as a tonic to bring joy and clarity, though it can be used with any of the qualified powers to bring clarity and peace to a situation.

INVOCATION FOR AIR OF WATER

Enochian: *Lring moz ado ga na gi dorpal mirk qaan od chirlan.*

English: Stir up joy within us that we may look with gladness upon creation and rejoice.

Earth of Water, the Page of Cups

God Name Pair: MALADI OLAAD

First read the fourth call then the eleventh call. The *I Ching* hexagram number 41 is titled "Decrease." While the *I Ching* calls this decrease, to us, it is focusing on what you truly desire and manifesting it directly. It is discovering what you need rather than what you have been told you want by social programming. Consider the densest form of water, which is ice. It is a crystalline form of the life-giving fluid, or our emotional needs crystalizing into a solid form. This angelic force helps to clarify and manifest our deepest needs.

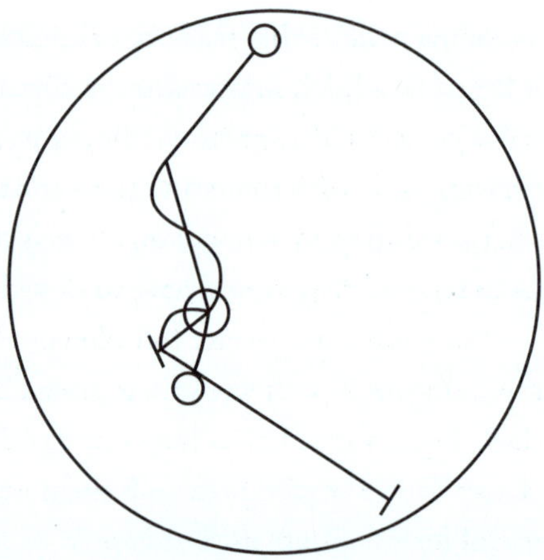

Earth of Water Sigil

We have called upon it often, pairing this force with the Wish Card, the Nine of Cups. This works well in a group where each person may have a different need to manifest. As a general ritual of manifestation it works wonders, literally.

INVOCATION FOR EARTH OF WATER

Enochian: *Childao gah a drilpa qaas ge gil panpir g lonsa pugo qaa pilada.*

English: Diamond angel of the mighty manifestation of our desire, pour down your power upon creation continually.

Angels of Air

The angels of elemental air deal directly with the mind. The mind is the aspect of ourselves that makes decisions and learns. Our thoughts are only the most visible part of the mind. Our inner narrator is only telling us what is happening in the mind, as thoughts arise seemingly out of nowhere, float around, and feel very important before vanishing when a more compelling thought occupies the inner screen of the mind.

Our inner narration is only keeping track of and organizing the complex activity of our mind. This is the Qabalistic plane of Yetzirah, the formative world where the one becomes the many and cause and effect are separated so we can make choices. This is where the forces set in motion by fire and water crystalize into a plan of action. This plan becomes a blueprint or framework for the manifest universe to coalesce upon like dew collecting on a spiderweb in the early morning.

In our encounters with these forces, they resist taking on a particular form, instead manifesting as complete ideas that we have to unravel later. This would seem more like a fire force, but we think it is just too much information to communicate at once, and we need time to process it. When we try to get a visual impression, they appear as classical images such as an architect working over their drawing table with rulers and tools and sometimes famous people who represent the stream of consciousness they are embodying. It feels to us as if these streams of sentience are moving too fast for us to see, and they would have to slow down for us to receive a vision.

More often, we receive full-blown realizations. We see connections between ideas that we never saw before or a complete idea is placed in our memory that we have to unpack over time. Approach these forces for practical how questions, such as "how can I get ahead in my job?" You will receive clarity. They can also help with memory, creativity, clarity of mind, focus, and so on. They are very useful forces to have in your corner.

Salute of Air

Do a omaos de Oro Ibah Aozpi ge hoath ge qaal. (Secret Holy Name)
Do a omaos de Exarp ge hoath ge qaal. (Air of Spirit)
Do a omaos de Bataivh ge hoath ge qaal. (Sun of Air)
Do a omaos de Abioro ge hoath ge qaal. (Mars of Air)
Do a omaos de Aaozaif ge hoath ge qaal. (Jupiter of Air)
Do a omaos de Htmorda ge hoath ge qaal. (Moon of Air)
Do a omaos de Ahaozpi ge hoath ge qaal. (Venus of Air)
Do a omaos de Hipotga ge hoath ge qaal. (Saturn of Air)
Do a omaos de Avtotar ge hoath ge qaal. (Mercury of Air)

Fire of Air, the King of Swords

God Name Pair: AOURRZ ALOAI

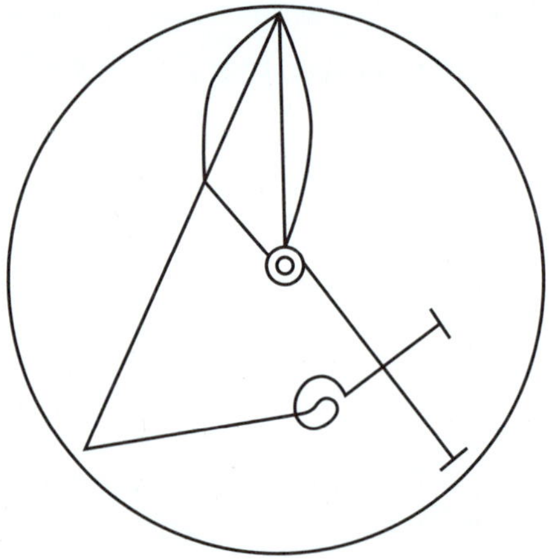

Fire of Air Sigil

First read the third call, then the ninth call. The *I Ching* hexagram number 32 is titled "Endurance." Fire of air is the power of understanding one's best course of action moment to moment, understanding your inner motivations, and acting on them. Lightning over wind, the two arise together naturally.

It is powerful to realize your life's purpose in any given situation and act upon it. If we understand our own inner motivations and trust them, then we can manifest the best possible outcomes through bold and decisive actions. Fire of air appears to Erich as a lightning flash, and he needs to work through the illumination for days after the vision.

This force pairs well with any of the sword cards as well as the Two, Three, and Four of Wands for prophetic insight.

INVOCATION FOR FIRE OF AIR

Enochian: *Olprit de omax g avavago matorb nothoa a oresa.*

English: Light of understanding, your thunder echoes through the darkness.

Water of Air, the Queen of Swords

God Name Pair: LLAKZA PALAM

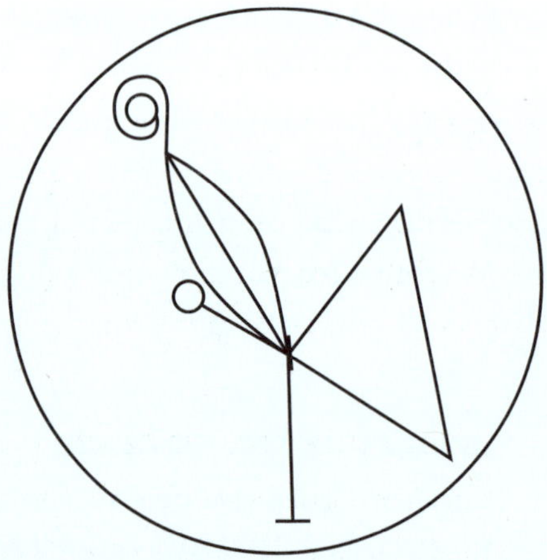

Water of Air Sigil

First read the third call, then the seventh call. The *I Ching* hexagram number 28 is titled "Preponderance of the Great." This is the angelic power of artistic expression, the emotional expression of the intellect. It is creative imagination expressed with skill and planning. To be an artist requires the mind to plan and create, to express the deepest emotions and sublime meanings of our experiences.

Water of air is invoked for artistic skill and inspiration. She appears to Erich in a form somewhat like Frida Kahlo except darker in aspect and wearing rich silks and jewelry.

One of Erich's favorite forces to invoke, she has given him many ideas on artistic projects that are ultimately practical, including the confidence to take up calligraphy, book binding, and more.

Water of air pairs well with Seven of Swords for artistic excellence. Pair it with the Two of Wands for inspiration and creativity if you are stuck.

INVOCATION FOR WATER OF AIR

Enochian: *Nonka dlugar ozien monons eolis vaul, niiso oecrimi moz.*

English: You who gives hands to the heart to create wonders, come sing your song of joy.

Air of Air, the Knight of Swords

God Name Pair: IDOIGO ARDZA

Read the third call only. The *I Ching* hexagram number 57 is titled "Gentle Penetration." *I Ching* would describe this force as gentle constant pressure. We agree, as this angel brings that feeling to mind when we are attempting to think through some problem to find a solution. Erich works with technology for a living, and often things break for no obvious reason and are difficult to solve. When he is faced with problems seemingly beyond his reasoning ability, he remembers this force. It brings a calm clarity, like a clear sky, and allows new ideas to form in the empty space.

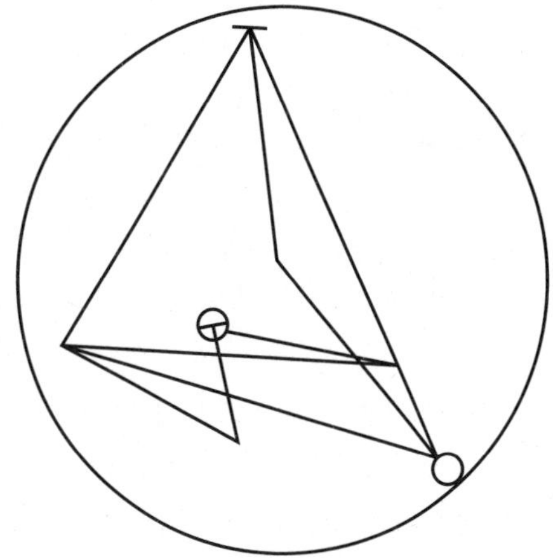

Air of Air Sigil

It is called a dispeller of illusion, but that does not mean that we are fooling ourselves. In this case, our illusion is a genuine attempt to solve a problem in ways that have worked in the past. When we look at the issue with a fresh mind, new solutions and ideas can form. If you can recall the experience of communicating with this force when you are stuck and feeling panicky or frustrated, you will find that behind those feelings is a solution waiting for you.

We don't often pair this angel with the qualified powers, as it has a simple profundity on its own that is well worth cultivating, but the Two of Swords will work as an amplifier if needed.

INVOCATION FOR AIR OF AIR

Enochian: *Geh a el ds izazaz a korselh ds vaoan; uniglag od imvamar plapli ananael.*

English: Thou art the one who squares the circle of truth; descend and apply yourself to the seekers of the secret wisdom.

Earth of Air, the Page of Swords

God Name Pair: AIAOAI OIIIT

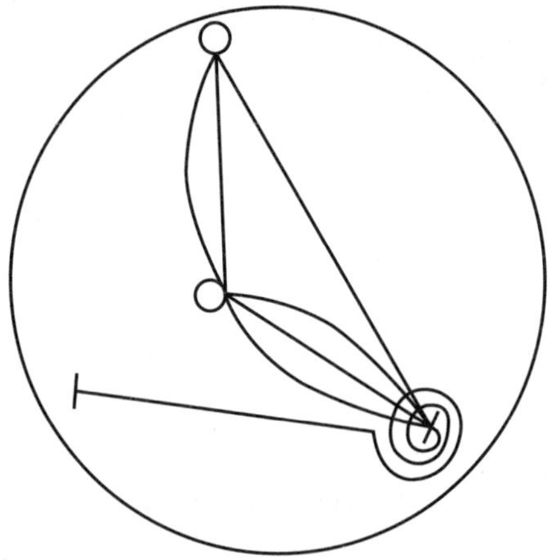

Earth of Air Sigil

Read the third call, then the eighth call. The *I Ching* hexagram number 18 is titled "Repair." Earth of air helps with repairing what has spoiled through lack of engagement and neglect. Here we have the image of a refocused effort to stabilize and enhance our responsibilities. This is an angel of discipline, the powers of the mind manifested materially. Strong in engagement and focus, this angel brings images of martial artists like Bruce Lee for Erich. There is a quiet nondramatic focus to the discipline it inspires.

We spend so much time getting in our own way by dreading and procrastinating and building goals up into impossible challenges in our minds. When we stop psyching ourselves out over nothing, we can achieve greatness with no effort at all. Behind those swirling thoughts when you are lost in the action is a clarity and calm. The *Tao Te Ching* says, "A truly good man does nothing. Yet leaves nothing undone. A foolish man is always doing. Yet much remains to be done."[70]

Discipline is a somewhat nasty word. Like bitter medicine, we all want it but flinch at the thought of it. In reality, when we get out of our own way, we can be free to get lost in our work, though it is not work or discipline at all—just joy. It is invoked for effortless focus to achieve your goals. Call it discipline if you will or the joy of structured action. Earth of air is useful when you are overwhelmed by tasks and need to get your ideas manifested in the world.

Pair it with the Three, Eight, or Ten of Swords.

INVOCATION FOR EARTH OF AIR

Enochian: *Umplif ugegi ado nonki od ol uran lo sonf vors ol.*

English: Our strength waxes strong with you, and I see that I reign over myself.

Angels of Earth

The angelic rulers of elemental earth deal with the manifestation of our material world, the flow of the life force in Assiah, the Qabalistic world of earth. These very helpful angelic intelligences deal

70. Geng and English, *Lao Tsu*, chapter 38.

not only with the manifestation of the material world and all its wealth and abundance but also with our connections we build to all sentient beings. They help us to understand how we are fed and in turn feed others—not just by food alone but the energy we exchange with one another.

All the complexity of the preceding twelve angels of fire, water, and air is contained and expressed through these rather generous and unassuming angelic forces. In Erich's visions with these forces, he usually finds himself in mountain forests with very large old trees and granite boulders, sometimes vineyards, or lush gardens. If he sees the angels at all, they usually take the form of dark and somewhat wild-looking people dressed in nature itself with clothes of leaves and rough jewelry with uncut stones.

Angels of earth are invoked for mostly practical purposes, such as money, advancement in life and society, and physical healing. The angels of air can tell you how, while these angels will simply manifest changes in what seems like luck. One can create a constant connection with the life force and nature by cultivating a connection to these angelic forces. They also tend to focus on long-term goals rather than quick changes, enduring lasting effects instead of quick flashy ones.

Salute of Earth

Do a omaos de Mor Dial Hctga ge hoath ge qaal. (Secret Holy Name)
Do a omaos de Bitom ge hoath ge qaal. (Earth of Spirit)
Do a omaos de Iczhhca ge hoath qaal. (Sun of Earth)
Do a omaos de Laidrom ge hoath ge qaal. (Mars of Earth)
Do a omaos de Aczinor ge hoath ge qaal. (Jupiter of Earth)
Do a omaos de Lzinopo ge hoath ge qaal. (Moon of Earth)
Do a omaos de Alhctga ge hoath ge qaal. (Venus of Earth)
Do a omaos de Liiansa ge hoath ge qaal. (Saturn of Earth)
Do a omaos de Ahmlicv ge hoath ge qaal. (Mercury of Earth)

Fire of Earth, the King of Pentacles

God Name Pair: AOURRZ ALOAI

First read the fifth call then the fifteenth call. The *I Ching* hexagram number 62 is titled "Attention to Detail." The hexagram tells us that we should focus on small things, and this is not bad advice. This angel is an initiator on the material plane. If you want to begin a business or some material endeavor, start small and get the beginnings right.

Fire of earth is invoked for new material beginnings. This force can advise on the best work for you and help you to understand how to find your place in the material world of work and responsibility. It is not super flashy but very helpful when you want to start a new career or bring your current one to a new level. Attunement with this force brings material establishment and a type of maturity when dealing with power and authority.

Combine it with the Eight of Pentacles for luck in new endeavors, and the Ace of Pentacles is good for new jobs and businesses.

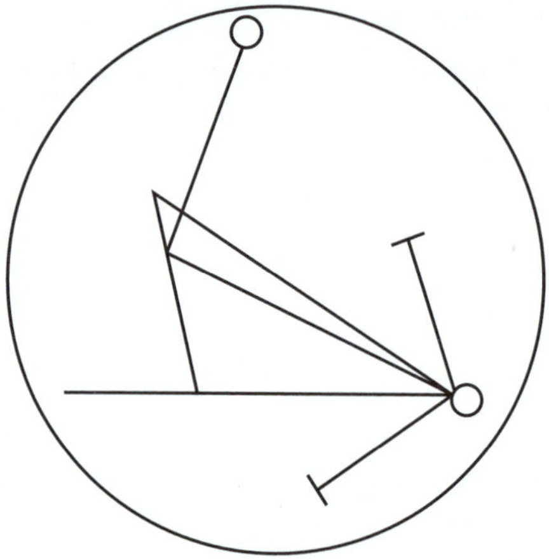

Fire of Earth Sigil

INVOCATION FOR FIRE OF EARTH

Enochian: *Els tabaan de aziagiar niis camliax a molasci od odo a emetgis iaiadix.*

English: O thou governor of the harvest, come speak the great name and open the seal of honor.

Water of Earth, the Queen of Pentacles

God Name Pair: NAEEM ILPIZ

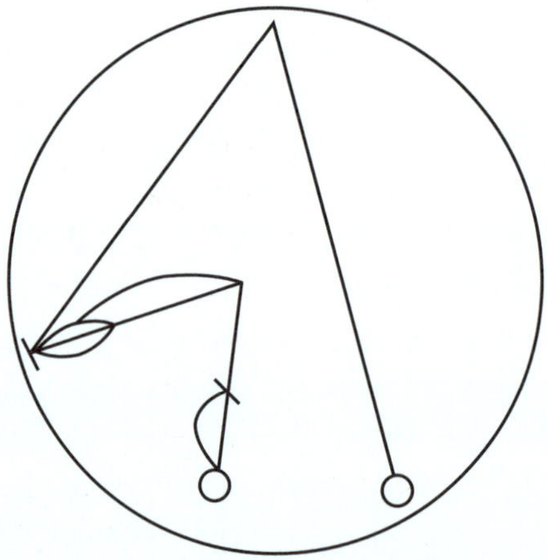

Water of Earth Sigil

First read the fifth call then the fourteenth call. The *I Ching* hexagram number 31 is titled "Influence/Wooing." This is the romance angel—our cupid, if you will. Water over earth represents the force of fecundity, nurturance, and giving of life. The creation of new life, incarnating spirit in the flesh, is the most sacred act possible, but even when we make love only for the goal of pleasure, we are imitating and get a preview of the experience of enlightenment.

A duality joins into a singularity, and for a brief moment, we can experience the total loss of ego, as at the moment of orgasm we dissolve into total bliss. If this is viewed as a sacred experience, then it can bring one close to enlightenment, and all magic is really sex magic, the combination of opposites in some fashion. The sacred marriage of a temple consecration is but one obvious example.

This angelic force brings the realization of the sacredness and profundity of love making. This force is also one of fertility for the land. If you had a farm or were raising animals, it would be a good force to be in tune with. We have only a simple backyard farm, but we do all right.

Invoke water of earth to revolutionize your feelings toward physical intimacy and to increase the fertility of your life. We have used this as a base for a love spell as well, but some caution here is warranted. Never target an individual, and before you do the working, make a list of the twelve most important qualities in a partner, putting them in order of importance. If you can't do that, then you are not ready for a relationship. Then invoke, commune, and exteriorize with the Ten of Cups.

INVOCATION FOR WATER OF EARTH

Enochian: *Nonci coazior a lorslq od levithmong de a coasg oali obeloce avabh mirk ge.*

English: You who increase the flowers of and cattle of the earth place your garland of hyacinth upon us.

Air of Earth, the Knight of Pentacles

God Name Pair: ANFPOI VNNAX

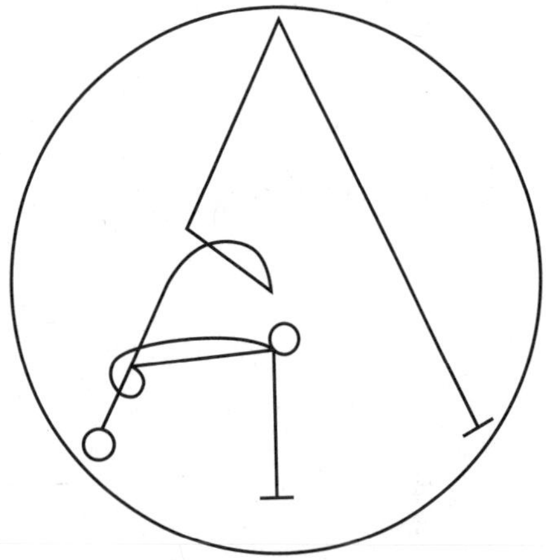

Air of Earth Sigil

Read the fifth call then the thirteenth call. The *I Ching* hexagram number 53 is titled "Gradual Development." This is a force of slow but steady progress, looking at the long-term plans and creating things that last. This force appears to Erich as a planner, an architect of a temple or cathedral, or a mason.

The ability to come up with a plan that may take years to bring to fruition is a very powerful ability. No plan ever survives its implementation without constant adjustment to the changing environment and obstacles with always the final goal in mind. Air of earth provides the ability to work daily and make progress, constantly building, and the calmness and certainty that comes with this power. It is as if it was already done; we just need to go through the motions to manifest all we desire.

We pair this force with the aces to make sure the beginning invoked becomes solid and manifested.

INVOCATION FOR AIR OF EARTH

Enochian: *Ado zuraah ge vavale de ge isro, nisso micma ge ca ge ugegi g iaiadix.*

English: With humility we work to our promise. Come witness us as we grow strong in honor.

Earth of Earth, the Page of Pentacles

God Name Pair: ABALPT ARBIZ

Only read the fifth call. The *I Ching* hexagram number 52 is titled "Keeping Still." Earth of earth is Erich's favorite elemental angelic force, and he communes with her daily. She is at once the physical healer and grounding and centering personified. The *I Ching* hexagram is two mountains facing each other in silence and meditation.

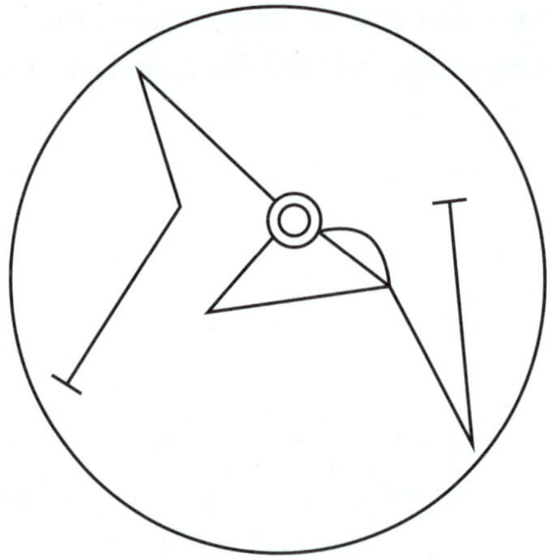

Earth of Earth Sigil

When Erich invokes this force in the informal way, he feels a flow of healing energy, a life force that he can use to heal physical pain and injury. In the formal ritual, she has great power to ground and to manifest what people need. Here is a connection with the source of all life and manifestation, the ability to create and preserve.

When we achieve the stillness expressed by the *I Ching* hexagram, we allow the natural life force to flow and fill the emptiness created. The enlightenment of this angel is that our connection with the life force is passive. If we create space for it, it will naturally flow and fill that space to overflowing.

The uses of this power are almost endless. Combined with the Four of Cups, it can be emotionally healing in a gentle way. With the Ten of Pentacles, it can be used for manifesting things we need. With the Six of Cups, it makes a serenity that is most profound. Really, it can enhance any of the qualified powers, and this is one you should be able to manifest in your daily life. The body feeling is quite blissful and serene.

INVOCATION FOR EARTH OF EARTH

Enochian: *Nonci ds zlika a caosg od toltorg od fonts a lukiftian od pild bliorax, iaial ge ednas zorge.*

English: You, who waters the earth and her creatures that we may dwell in brightness and continual comfort, include us as receivers of your love.

Angels of Spirit

The fifth element, spirit, acts as a glue and a grease holding the elements together and keeping them separate enough that they retain their uniqueness. When we performed the pore breathing exercise, we experienced the element of spirit both passive and active (chapter 10). When we looked at the

Enochian system, we mentioned the Table of Union that separates and joins the four elemental tablets together. This is where the real goodies are as far as enlightenment goes. In chapter 7, "Enochiana," there is a description of the Table of Union and details on how it is created and what angels are listed there. Please review this chapter if you need a refresher.

r	Z	i	l	a	f	A	y	t	l	p	a	e	T	a	O	A	d	u	p	t	D	n	i	m
a	r	d	Z	a	i	d	p	a	L	a	m		a	a	b	c	o	o	r	o	m	e	b	b
c	z	o	n	s	a	r	o	Y	a	u	b	x	T	o	g	c	o	n	x	m	a	l	G	m
T	o	i	T	t	z	o	P	a	c	o	C	a	n	h	o	d	D	i	a	l	e	a	o	c
S	i	g	a	s	o	m	r	b	z	n	h	r	p	a	t	A	x	i	o	V	s	P	s	N
f	m	o	n	d	a	T	d	i	a	r	i	p	S	a	a	i	x	a	a	r	V	r	o	i
o	r	o	i	b	A	h	a	o	z	p	i		m	p	h	a	r	s	l	g	a	i	o	l
t	N	a	b	r	V	i	x	g	a	s	d	h	M	a	m	g	l	o	i	n	L	i	r	x
O	i	i	i	t	T	p	a	l	O	a	i		o	l	a	a	D	n	g	a	T	a	p	a
A	b	a	m	o	o	o	a	C	u	c	a	C	p	a	L	c	o	i	d	x	P	a	c	n
N	a	o	c	O	T	t	n	p	r	n	T	o	n	d	a	z	N	z	i	V	a	a	s	a
o	c	a	n	m	a	g	o	t	r	o	i	m	i	i	d	P	o	n	s	d	A	s	p	i
S	h	i	a	l	r	a	p	m	z	o	x	a	x	r	i	n	h	t	a	r	n	d	i	L
m	o	t	i	b			a	T	n	a	n		n	a	n	T	a			b	i	t	o	m
b	O	a	Z	a	R	o	p	h	a	R	a	a	d	o	n	p	a	T	d	a	n	V	a	a
u	N	n	a	x	o	P	S	o	n	d	n		o	l	o	a	G	e	o	o	b	a	u	a
a	i	g	r	a	n	o	o	m	a	g	g	m	O	P	a	m	n	o	v	G	m	d	n	m
o	r	p	m	n	i	n	g	b	e	a	l	o	a	p	l	s	T	e	d	e	c	a	o	p
r	s	O	n	i	Z	i	r	l	e	m	u	C	s	c	m	i	o	a	n	A	m	l	o	x
i	z	i	n	r	C	Z	i	a	M	h	l	h	V	a	r	s	G	d	L	b	r	i	a	p
M	o	r	d	i	a	l	h	C	t	G	a		o	i	P	t	e	a	a	p	D	o	c	e
O	c	a	n	c	h	i	a	s	o	m	t	p	P	s	u	a	c	n	r	Z	i	r	z	a
A	r	b	i	z	m	i	i	l	p	i	z		S	i	o	d	a	o	i	n	r	z	f	m
O	p	a	n	a	l	a	m	S	m	a	P	r	d	a	l	t	T	d	n	a	d	i	r	e
d	o	l	o	P	i	n	i	a	n	b	a	a	d	i	x	o	m	o	n	s	i	o	s	p
r	x	p	a	o	c	s	i	z	i	x	p	x	O	o	D	p	z	i	A	p	a	n	l	i
a	x	t	i	r	v	a	s	t	r	i	m	e	r	g	o	a	n	n	P	A	C	r	a	r

Great Table Black Cross

Originally, Erich sought to open the Table of Union to gain insight into those four holy names as well as EHNB. He thought that if he experienced communion with these forces when he used those names in rituals, he would be able to better channel those spiritual forces. What he found were beings of unimaginable vastness. They are the presences of the four worlds of the Qabalah.

The following image shows the Black Cross if it were folded up like a carpenter's ruler to reveal the names of powerful angels that rule over or summarize the powers of the four watchtowers and the Great Table itself—four mighty angels who correspond to the aces of the tarot and one more who is the Enochian Tetragrammaton.

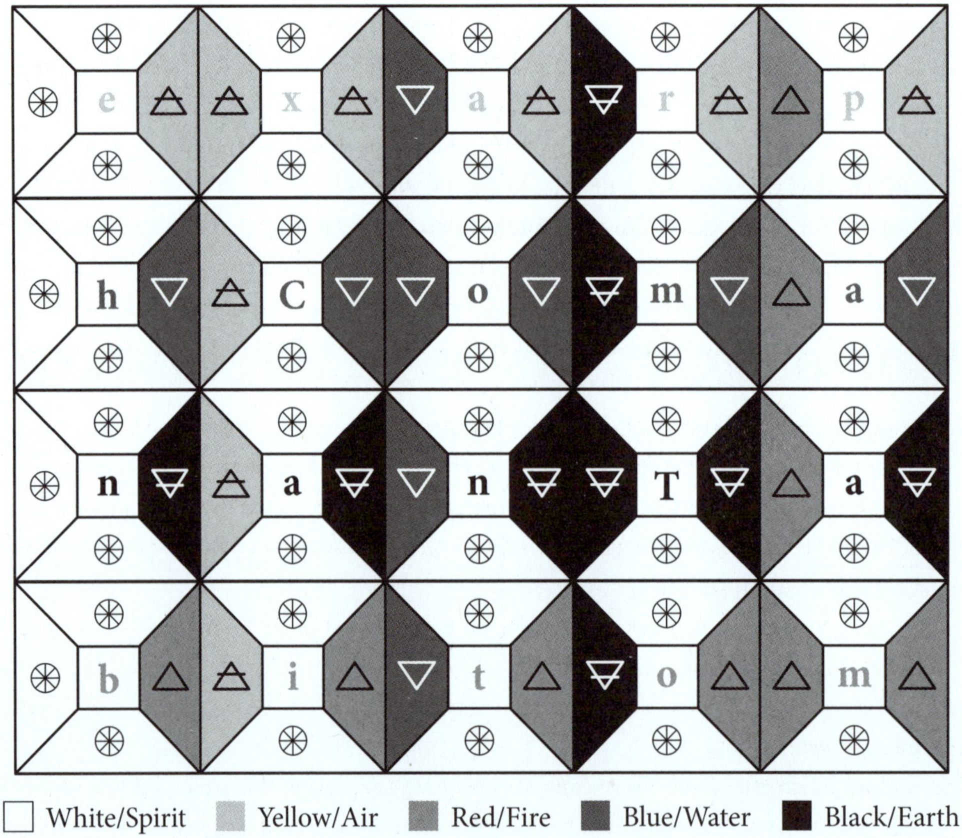

Table of Union with Elements

We call these angels presences because of the feeling of vastness and expansiveness of consciousness Erich encountered when he made contact. He was completely unprepared for the level of consciousness he was suddenly jolted into when the final veil fell. When he has performed invocations of the archangels, such as Raphael, there is an experience of heightened consciousness and power as well as the awe you might encounter if you met with your favorite rock star, living or dead, and they turned their entire attention to you and were sincerely interested in you and your well-being. But there is a sense of a concentration of power with the archangels.

Methods to Opening the Table of Union

At this point, we find ourselves wanting to blather on about how powerful and kind and wonderful these forces are, but we don't think that is helpful. Instead, we will describe two ways to open the Table of Union, one complex and one simple, and tell you what we were able to find within. These spirits were difficult to contact, but they freely gave us great insights into magic and ourselves. Now when we are performing rituals and we vibrate their names, we can recall the feeling of being in their presence and channel the wave of sentient force quite naturally.

The methods for opening the Table of Union are straightforward if you have mastered the Elemental Octagram. First invoke all sixteen elementals or at least the main four rulers: fire of fire, water of water, air of air, and earth of earth. Invoking and creating an authentic connection with all sixteen angels will attune you to the elemental energies so you will have a better experience, but it is not required.

You proceed as before. First, perform a temple consecration and the Elemental Octagram, using spirit active or passive as the base element and the element of the union angel as the modifier. When Erich invoked Hcoma, he used spirit passive as the base and water as the modifier. This created the eidolon for that force. For Bitom, he used spirit active as the base and fire as the modifier. Once the eidolon is created, you can go one of two ways.

To start, read the Enochian Calls for the selected angel. The standard way to invoke the angels of spirit would be to read the first and second calls followed by the call of the element (fire-six, water-four, air-three, earth-five). You would then, for example, meditate on the concept of the watery part of spirit and its meaning.

The method Erich chose was more complex, as he was exploring the Great Table and invoking all of the elemental angels. When he was working with the air angels, it was revealed to him that he could invoke all four angels of an element, fuse them to a single expression using a gate structure, and then read the standard calls. The gate ritual follows this section. This worked very well, but when he completed the calls, a final veil remained. Erich had to intuit how to open this final barrier, but he has already told you how in the section on pore breathing (chapter 10). The final visualization for each element is how he broke through. He will cover that in his descriptions of each angel.

The Great Seal of the Elemental Tablet of Fire

Fire of Spirit, Ace of Wands

God Name: BITOM

Read calls one, two, and six. Use spirit active for the base element and fire for the modifying element. After Erich invoked all four fire elementals and fused them to a single expression with the Gate Ritual, he read the calls and sat in contemplation of fire. There was only emptiness. Erich thought will was the final key to the last barrier, so he envisioned an entire universe of fire and forced it backward to creation to a single point in space. The vision started with a very clear image of a single candle flame in the dark with all the colors of the rainbow visible in the flame. Erich relaxed into the vision, and it expanded. He saw an Asian dragon flying through the eye of a hurricane and a world of fire where golden twins, male and female, embraced in union.

The plane of Atziluth is said to be beyond polarity, and Erich supposes he was at the limits of his spiritual attainment that he was not able to get more information from Bitom. He plans to explore it more in the future. Still, there was much that he felt that is hard to put into words—that fire cannot burn itself, the knower cannot know itself, and this is the reason for creation. The universe and all that is in it was created by an act of relaxation of release; the unfolding complexity was allowed, not willed. Creation was allowed to happen as the Creator contemplated itself—mind observing mind. The continual unfoldment of the universe that we are all a part of is the answer to the question of "Who am I and what is my nature?" Fire is the force of expansion that unveils and breaks down the singularity into all the permutations of what it contains.

The Great Seal of the Elemental Tablet of Water

Water of Spirit, Ace of Cups

God Name: HCOMA

Read calls one, two, and four. Use spirit passive for the base element and water for the modifying element. After a lengthy ritual, Erich sat to contemplate the watery part of spirit and was confronted with a highly energized void full of potential. He intuited that love was the key to the final veil. Erich imagined all the people and pets and things he felt real love for, until he had a very strong feeling in his body and heart center. He focused on the body feeling and also the emotion without any target of that love. That is when the final veil was rendered. At once he was flying through an old growth forest, through huge trees on a mountain side. His awareness was expanded in a way he did not realize was possible.

Erich could see the morning sunlight reflecting on every drop of dew on every leaf in the entire forest. It was as if he was using 10,000 percent of his brain. Still, if he tried to think, the vision began to fade, so he had to stay in the experience. Erich searched for Hcoma, but he could not find her. He could not think of how to find the target of his ritual, so he had to call by desire.

He received a brief view of a woman's hair in the sun, and he ached for her. He was able to think of his question "Who are you and what is your nature?" He received an answer in a thousand voices. "You know me. I am love and all things respond to me. Those are your words." Erich was able to eek out, "Please grant me your wisdom." The reply was "We have granted you our wisdom, but you don't believe any of it. Well, now you can." At that moment, he had the realization of how protective of his emotions he really was, and it was as if a boil in my heart was lanced, and it began to flow freely.

The cynicism Erich was using as a protective shield was limiting his ability to feel, and now it was gone. The vision changed as well, from the forest to a series of images of fibers—hair, spiderwebs, then roots—and then deeper images in a fractal pattern, deeper and deeper into creation. Next appeared a sort of five-lobed blue heart that was beating slowly. This seemed to take forever. Finally, Erich wanted one more thing: an image of Hcoma. He felt it was important to have something to visualize when he invoked this force. She finally granted him a vision of her.

First, he saw a wooden table, as if the watchtowers were divided into squares. The wood was very old and sun aged, like a dock that has been in the elements too long, gray and cracked. Then a woman's face rose from the tablet, as if it was water. She had mahogany skin and high cheekbones. When she opened her wide eyes, they were like dragonfly wings. This and the vision of the sunlight on the trees come up for Erich when invoking the divine name Hcoma now.

This was one of those occasions where you enter the temple as one person and come out a different one. The empowerment of Hcoma was like the removal of a layer of shadow self Erich had relied on for protection of his feelings and sense of his emotional self. She released that bond, and now Erich can be more of who he is.

The Great Seal of the Elemental Tablet of Air

Air of Spirit, Ace of Swords

God Name: EXARP

Read calls one, two, and three. Use spirit active for the base element and air for the modifying element. After a long ritual, Erich finally sat and tried to view Exarp only to be greeted with a deafening silence. He tried everything he could think of. Still nothing. Finally, he created an image of himself, put his mind in that image, and projected it into the Table of Union.

The vision began immediately. First, Erich saw a yellow candle in a chandelier that was large and blocky. He was at the ceiling of a huge chamber made of light blue-gray stone. This stone was covered in some sort of spidery writing that he could not read. Erich explored the chamber, looking for Exarp. He found him sitting against a wall in a sort of throne. He looked really old; had white, dry-looking skin; was wearing a robe of some sort of white and blue fur; and wore a crown made of silver metal shaped sort of like a pinecone with layers or sections. His eyes had huge pupils, and in many ways, he looked a lot like one of those Assyrian statues with the beard and huge irises. Erich was not able to communicate with this being. He was only able to watch him move about the chamber and then approach a sort of table in the center of the room before Erich lost the trance.

Erich repeated the ritual because his first attempt was tantalizing, but he was unable to communicate with Exarp. As he finished the calls for his second attempt, the vision started immediately. The being he took to be Exarp appeared in his vision in the temple, as if he was busy before but now was ready to fully focus on Erich and his questions. Erich felt it was a bit odd to have this being suddenly staring at him, but he asked his questions. The being replied that he was Exarp and that his function was to "separate cause and effect so the universe would be intelligible." Erich thought this was a very strange answer, so he asked, "Are you time?" Exarp seemed to think this was an inaccurate statement but eventually answered, "Yes, you could see it that way." Erich was given a vision of timelines dividing into multiple versions based on choices. The plane of Yetzirah was where the one becomes the many, duality divides into a multiplicity. Erich then asked if Exarp could show him other times and places, and he answered yes. Erich was then able to have visions of ancient times, the building of the pyramids, and his own birth. But then Erich felt as if he was abusing this gift since he didn't have a reason or plan for what he was seeing. He thanked Exarp and ended the ceremony.

The Great Seal of the Elemental Tablet of Earth

Earth of Spirit, Ace of Pentacles

God Name: NANTA

Read calls one, two, and five. Use spirit receptive for the base element and earth for the modifying element. After completing the ritual, Erich sat and contemplated the earthy part of spirit. What he began to see was the social network that sustains him—and all of us. This network is made up of all the people who support us and includes work friends, family members, partners, and even just acquaintances. Then further out, he began to see the trees that make air, the plants that make food, and how we are connected to all the world in ways both subtle and obvious. These are the relationships we have that connect us to all sentient beings.

Nanta appeared to Erich as a pale woman with red hair. She was wearing rich jewels and silks, and she seemed very vulnerable yet powerful as well. There was not a verbal communication, but Erich could feel that what he was supposed to understand is that as a part of this world, it is in his hands, that he is responsible for caring for the world and for the beings within it.

Erich could also see the restraints placed upon him by his social conditioning. As if he was in a maze, he could only see certain options for choices and behaviors in any given situation. It was a bit terrifying, as he could see how completely he had accepted the programming. Some of it *is* necessary for civilized life, but much is not helpful and only serves to hinder us.

The cure is to be conscious and aware of ourselves and who we are and to come from an authentic, heart-centered place. When we are centered in our authentic selves, we can be clear and uncontrived and kind to one another. Does this action bring peace and relaxation? Or tension and unhappiness? These are the questions to ask ourselves before we act or speak.

John Dee's Symbol from Monas Hieroglyphica, Representing All Knowledge

Spirit of Spirit

God Name: EHNB

Read call one only. Use spirit receptive for the base element and spirit active for the modifying element. This force sums up the entirety of the Great Table. It is the Enochian Tetragrammaton, or four-letter name of god. The first time Erich invoked this force, he called all four of the presences and fused them to a single force, then he read the first call. Each time thereafter, he simply did the Octagram and read the first call.

Having read Lon Milo DuQuette's *Enochian Vision Magick*, Erich had certain expectations in invoking this force. It did not appear to him the same way as it did to DuQuette, but it did live up to his expectations. After exploring the Great Table and the other angels of the Table of Union, this force appeared to Erich immediately. It appeared first as Thoth, the ibis-headed god of wisdom, and then more often as a sort of Eastern master, similar to the ones found in old kung fu moves—think the bad ones from the 1970s. When Erich asked why it chose such odd images, it told him that it didn't want to appear as he was expecting so Erich knew it was him.

Erich has invoked this force many times, and it is always friendly and immediate. It can answer pretty much any question, but it excels at answering questions related to past lives. Once Erich asked about his birth family and ancestry, since he was adopted, and it gave him some useful information. Within a week, Erich was contacted by his biological uncle. We have also invoked this force for our group, and everyone is able to get insight into issues they have. We could see having a practice focused solely on this one force, but it is our nature to explore, and there is so much more magic to experience.

• • • • • • •

Once again, we stress that the listing is our own experiences with these forces and how we have learned to use them. The sigils we have included for the Enochian spirits are of our own design and are not part of the original material collected by John Dee. If your experiences or point of view is different from ours, then good; you are your own best teacher. Your Higher Self will be your source of information and the angels your teachers.

— CHAPTER 25 —
The Gate of Transformation

Initially published in Frater Barrabbas's *Mastering the Art of Ritual Magick,* the Gate of Transformation fuses all of the ritual work done in a space to a single expression, then you enter that unified field. While the final pass in the Elemental Octagram fuses all of the work you did *within* the Elemental Octagram, this fuses the *entire ritual* into a single expression. The Gate of Transformation is far more versatile and subtle than the forced fusion of the Elemental Octagram, allowing the fusion of multiple rituals. You could, for instance, invoke several Enochian angels and then fuse them into a more powerful angelic force. They don't mind. In fact, we don't think they even notice. The way the tables work is that each letter is an angel, which then group up to spell the names of more powerful angels, and so on. The Gate of Transformation will work with any sort of ritual work, and this pattern is also used in our method of Rising on the Planes, or exploring the Enochian ethers, and extensively in planetary magic.

As we mentioned in chapter 24, you can invoke the angels of the Tables of Union by invoking the four elemental angels and fusing them together. This is the method we use to first make contact, and the initial contact is often very difficult to accomplish. We sometimes use more elaborate rituals at first, then simplify after we have an authentic connection.

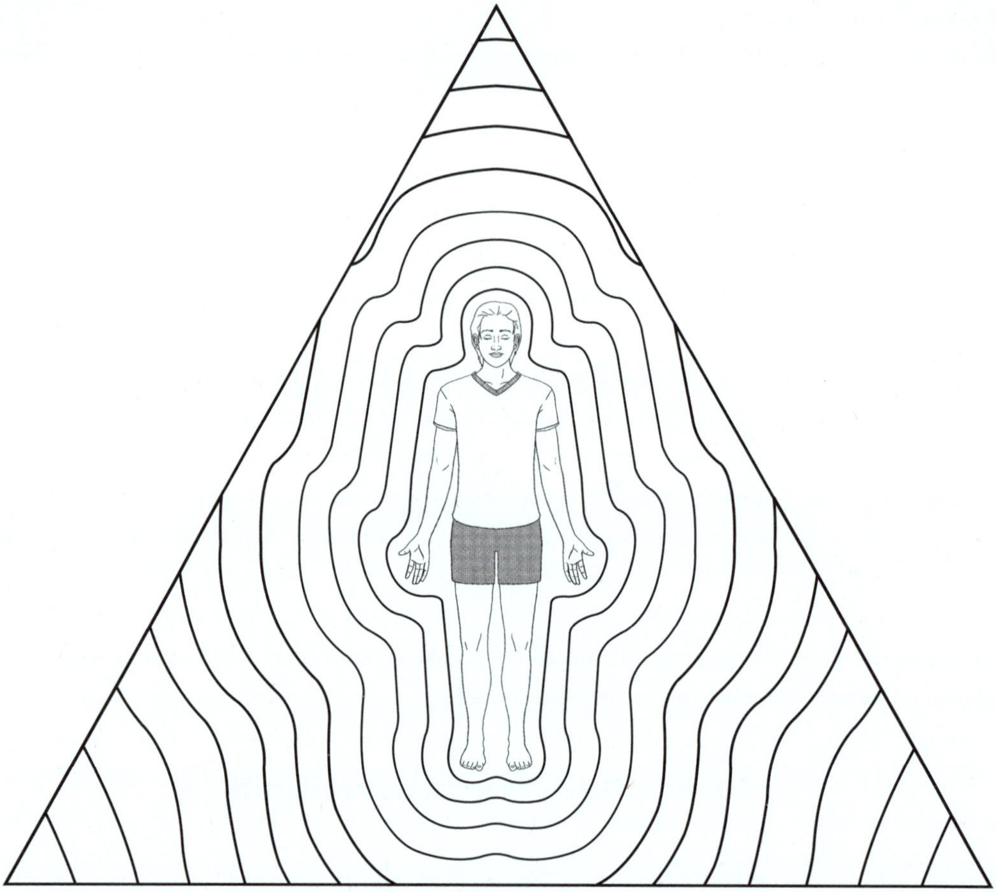

The Gate

The Gate itself is a simple ritual, one you can even ad lib once you know the underlying meaning and pattern. It is three-fold, a triangular gate like those used to manifest spirits in so many systems. The triangle is the simplest and most solid shape. We have three nodes to invoke and then open the gate and step through.

The Hero's Journey in Ritual

The design of this rite is taken from the Hero's Journey, which, as mentioned in chapter 4, is an archetypal journey that we all take repeatedly in our lives. In *The Hero with a Thousand Faces*, Joseph Campbell proposes that there is a metamyth, or monomyth, that is repeated cross-culturally and across time, and this is the human story—our story.[71] Basically, the hero is called, they meet a guide, leave their local society, face challenges in some sort of other world, and then are transformed by the experience. The hero finally receives a boon, a solution to their problems, that they must bring back to their normal life to solve the problem that initiated the journey to begin with.

Magic is about the journey to the other side to gain a boon from supernatural beings. Once it is received, we return and apply the wisdom and gifts to transform and revitalize our lives, and a revitalized person transforms the world. The Bill Moyers interviews of Joseph Campbell are on YouTube; you need to watch them if you haven't and read his books too.

As Frater Barrabbas points out, there are twenty-two stages in the Hero's Journey and twenty-two major arcana cards in the tarot, so if you have a tarot deck, you can use it in this small rite.[72] You can also look at chapter 9, "The Tarot," for an overview of the connection between the major arcana and the Hero's Journey. We don't need to use all twenty-two stages. We can sum up the gate with just three nodes: the guide, the guardian, and the ordeal. There is a gate for return as well, where the hero (you) needs to face another similar set of challenges in order to bring the gained boon back and use it universally.

The rite itself is very simple. This is the version we use, and we are sure you can rewrite it in your own words. Using the major arcana cards is optional, so do not worry if you do not use the tarot. Erich uses a set of large cards that he painted himself.

The Two Gates: There and Back Again

There are two gates. The first goes deeper into the ritual structure, and the second is the gate of return. When you go deeper into the underworld, you will summon the spirit guide to help you, the fierce guardian that challenges you, and finally the ordeal that you go through to gain the boon of insight that you seek. The High Priestess tarot card is the spirit guide that appears in stories as a teacher or helper who often gives some gifts to the seeker, such as a magic sword or talisman. The fierce guardian is a figure in storytelling that blocks the hero and is often but not always the cause of the situation that necessitates the journey. The fierce guardian is usually at the edge of what society considers acceptable and so here is represented by the Hermit. In Arthurian legends, a hermit-like figure often challenges the knights on their journey to find the Grail. The hero must overcome facing the fierce guardian to cross over the threshold from normal life to the magical underworld of the subconscious. It is there that the real adventure begins. In practice, these two figures cancel each

71. Campbell, *The Hero with a Thousand Faces.*

72. Barrabbas, *Magical Qabalah for Beginners*, 129–39.

other out, leaving the hero to face the ordeal on their own with only the teachings of the guide to help them. The ordeal is represented by the Tower card. This is the stage called In the Belly of the Whale. In this stage the hero enters into the collective unconscious and begins the transformation of the self.

The Gate of Return, Coming Forth by Day

Once the journey is complete, the hero must return and heal the mundane world with the boon they acquired on their journey. The return journey is structured similarly to the journey to the underworld, but it might seem less familiar. First, we have the Emperor card representing the stage Rescue from Without. In this stage of storytelling, the hero is off in some other world or communing with the spiritual world in some state such as a coma. The hero needs to be called back to the waking world. In this stage, a guide appears and heals the hero or calls their name, awakening the hero for the return journey. This is the guide for the return. The Moon card represents the stage the Magic Flight. In this stage, the hero makes a perilous return and must face the same crossing of the threshold they faced on the inward journey. Here there are obstructions and opportunities for self-betrayal, as the hero must separate truth from illusion and insight from ego. The Moon card perfectly reflects this challenge. Finally, the hero must face the ordeal of the return journey. Here it is represented by the stage the Reoccurrence of the Boon. The boon granted on the journey must be translated from a personal experience to something universal; this challenge is represented by the Temperance card. When translated from the personal to the universal, something is lost; the experience can't be transmitted completely. This necessitates the initiation of a new journey.

R•I•T•U•A•L
GATE OF TRANSFORMATION: JOURNEY TO THE UNDERWORLD

In the Gate of Transformation ritual, you will combine all the energies in a space to create a doorway or gate into the heart of the ritual. Once inside the gate, you will experience a space that is the summation of all your ritual work. This new space can be used to do further magical work, such as communing with spirits or traveling in the spirit vision or pathworking.

Things You Need

The High Priestess tarot card (to represent the stage Meeting with the Spirit Guide)
The Hermit tarot card (to represent the stage Meeting the Fierce Guardian Stage)
The Tower tarot card (to represent the ordeal, the Belly of the Whale stage)
A wand, crystal point, or something else pointy for drawing shapes

Directions

Entering the underworld begins by standing in the east, facing west. Say:

> *The journey within has begun by the crossing of the first threshold, opening the gate. That is transformed what was once established here.*

Place the tarot card the High Priestess in the southeastern angle of the space. Draw an invoking spiral over the High Priestess (or in that direction). Say:

> *I open the gate between worlds. I invoke thee Anubis, jackal-headed guardian of the underworld and helper of the lost. Open the ways and be our teacher and protector in the trials before us.*

Place the tarot card the Hermit in the west, draw an invoking spiral over it (or in that direction) and say:

> *I open the gates between worlds. I invoke thee Sekhmet, lion-headed lady of life, lady of death as the fierce guardian. My desire to see knowledge is challenged. Courage shall open the door and fear shall end my journey forever.*

Place the tarot card the Tower in the northeast angle. Draw an invoking spiral over it or toward that area and say:

> *I open the gates between worlds. I invoke thee Apophis, serpent enemy of Ra. You represent all that is outside the ordered universe. I invoke you as the ordeal, the enemy in my heart that I strive to overcome.*

Face west, make the opening of the portal gesture (use both hands; mime that you are opening heavy curtains), and say:

> *I open the gates of mystery. Odo a aiyon de cicle.*

Take three steps forward and turn, facing the east. Make the closing of the portal gesture (mime that you are closing heavy curtains).

You are now within the fused ritual expression and can work further magics, such as the calling of another angelic force or a Pyramid of Power.

R•I•T•U•A•L
GATE OF RETURN: COMING FORTH BY DAY

Having ventured into the underworld and gained the boon, the hero (you) must make the return to waking life and apply the boon to renew the world. Once you have completed your ritual work after having performed the Gate of Transformation, use the Gate of Return as a way to symbolically come back from your adventure in the other world.

Things You Need

The Emperor tarot card (to represent the Rescue from Without stage)

The Moon tarot card (to represent the Magic Flight stage)

Temperance tarot card (to represent the Reoccurrence of the Boon stage)

A wand, crystal point, or something else pointy for drawing shapes

Directions

When you have finished with your inner workings, it is important to open a gate of return. We must symbolically unwind the ritual and return so we are grounded again and also to provide a finality to the working. We must return transformed, ready to apply our new wisdom and insights to our lives.

Stand in the west, face east, and say:

The return journey has begun, we will come from the darkness and into the light. Going forth by day.

Place the tarot card the Emperor in the southwest. Make an invoking spiral over it (or in that direction) and say:

I open the gates between worlds. I invoke thee Kephra. As you arise from the void, so shall I. My new role and purpose I will define and awaken to my True Will and glorified destiny.

In the east, place the tarot card the Moon. Draw an invoking spiral over it (or in that direction) and say:

I open the gates between worlds. I invoke thee Khonsu, god of the moon, as the fierce guardian of return. I will separate truth from illusion as I reintegrate with the world.

In the northwest, place the tarot card Temperance. Draw an invoking spiral over it (or in that area) and say:

I open the gates between worlds. I invoke thee Osiris, as the ordeal. I will translate the boon from the inner world into a symbol that will transform the whole world. As above, so below, as within, so without.

Face east, make the opening of the portal gesture (use both hands; mime that you are opening heavy curtains), and say:

I open the gates of return. I shall come forth by day.

Take three steps forward and turn, facing the west. Make the closing of the portal gesture (mime that you are closing heavy curtains).

Close the rite by drawing banishing spirals over the watchtowers and expressing gratitude to any spirits invoked. Then offer a dedication of merit.

• • • • • • •

The Gate of Transformation is structured to summarize the Hero's Journey. Using the Gate of Revealing, you can enter and return from the heart of any ritual or series of rituals you wish. This allows you to create more complex eidolons for ever more profound experiences. By reenacting myth, we come in contact with the ineffable truths, and then we must return to our normal waking lives with those truths and use them to revivify and inspire our lives.

— CONCLUSION — Final Thoughts

The practice of modern Hermetism is about developing yourself to awaken and become conscious of your own innate divine nature. There is no difference ultimately between your nous and the nous of the Creator. But this must be experienced; it can't really be told. When the hero returns from their journey and translates the boon for everyone to benefit from, something is lost. Each person must make their own journey to the otherworld to find the boon that will heal and revivify their world, their microcosm.

When you develop your own practice of magic, you will explore the utter vastness of you and all that you are capable of learning and being. We hope that you have learned not just to command the elements of the universe but also how to design your own rituals. We wanted to share with you just how the sausage is made. Every ritual and practice in this book is one that we personally use, and most are modified from decades of usage. We hope you can see that process so that you too will make the Hero's Journey and return to translate what you have discovered into something other people can benefit from as well. It is this process of journey and return that rejuvenates the world. Just as you are renewed, so is the whole world.

— APPENDIX —
Enochian Calls

These are the prayers received by John Dee and Edward Kelley that activate the various letter squares, and more importantly, they create very specific states of trance that allow us to tune into specific frequencies of creation and contact the spiritual intelligences that vibrate on a similar wavelength.

Much has been written about Enochian pronunciation. We find it best simply to try to pronounce the words as you would in English, inserting a natural vowel sound when needed. Finding your own pronunciation is part of the attunement of this form of magic, so make it your own. There are many copies and versions of the calls, some are written phonetically. This is the version we use, except we have it written out in Enochian letters in a book we made just for the calls.

First Key, Used for EHNB Alone and for the Angels of the Table of Union

OL SONF VORSG, GOHO IAD BALT	I reign over you, sayeth the god of justice,
LANSH CALZ VONPHO. SOBRA	In power exalted above the firmaments of wrath. In whose
ZOL ROR I TA NAZPSAD, OD GRAA	hands the sun is as a sword, and the moon

TA MALPRG- DS HOLQ QAA	As a through-thrusting fire; which measured your garments
NOTHOA ZIMZ, OD COMMAH TA	In the midst of my vestures, and trussed you together as
NOBLOH ZIEN. SOBA THIL GNONP	The palms of my hands. Whose seats I garnished with
PRGE ALDI DS VRBS OBOLEH	The fire of gathering and beautified your garments
GRSAM; CASARM OHORELA TABA PIR,	With admiration; to whom I made a law to govern the holy ones,
DS ZONRENSG CAB ERM IADNAH.	And delivered you a rod with the ark of knowledge.
PILAH FARZM OD ZNRZA ADNA	Moreover you lifted your voices and swore obedience
OD GONO IADPIL DS HOM OD TOH, SOBA	And faith to him that lives and triumphs, whose
IAOD IPAM OD UL IPAMIS; DS LOHOLO	Beginning is not nor end can not be; which shines
VEP ZOMD POAMAL OD BOGPA	As a flame in the midst of your palace and reigns
AAI TA PIAP BALTOH OX VAOAN	Among you as the balance of righteousness and truth!
ZACAR CA OD ZAMRAN ODO CICLE	Move therefore and show yourselves! Open the mysteries
QAA ZORGE LAP ZIRDO	Of your creation! Be friendly to me for i am
NOCO MAD HOATH IAIDA	The servant of your God a true worshiper of the highest!

Second Key, Used for the Angels of the Table of Union

ADGT VPAAH ZONG OM FAAIP	Can the wings of the winds understand your voices
SALD VIV L SOBAM IALPRG	Of wonder? O ye, the second first: whom burning flames
IZAZAS PIADPH CASARMA ABRAMG	Have framed in the depths of my jaws; whom I have prepared
TA TALHO PARACLEDA Q TA LORSLQ	As cups for a wedding, or as flowers
TURBS OOGE BALTOH GIVI CHIS	In their beauty for the chamber of righteousness. Stronger are
LUSD ORRI OD MICALP CHIS	Your feet than the barren stone, and mightier are
BIA OZONGON LAP NOAN	Your voices than the manifold winds. For you are become
TROF CORS TA GE OQ MANIN IAIDON	A building such as is not, except in the mind of the all-powerful.
TORZU GOHEL ZACAR CA CNOQOD	Arise, saith the first, move therefore unto his servant!
ZAMRAN MICALZO OD OZAZM VRELP	Show yourselves in power and make me a strong seething,
LAP ZIR IOIAD	For I am of him that lives forever.

Third Key, Calls Exarp and Activates the Whole of the Table of Air

MICMA GOHO IAD ZIR COMSELH AZIEN	Behold, says your God, I am a circle on whose hands
BIAB OS LONDOH. NORZ CHIS OTHIL	Stand twelve kingdoms. Six are the seats
GIGIPAH UNDL CHIS TA PUIM Q	Of living breath; the rest are as sharp sickles or

MOSPLEH TELOCH QUIIN TOLTORG	The horns of death, wherein the creatures of earth
CHIS I CHISGE M OZIEN DS BRGDA	Are and are not except my hands, which sleep
OD TORZUL ILI EOL BALZARG	And shall rise. In the beginning I made you stewards
OD AALA THILN OS NETAAB DLUGA	And placed you in seats twelve of government, giving unto
VOMSARG LONSA CAPIMALI VORS CLA	Every one of you power successively over 456,
HOMIL COCASB FAFEN IZIZOP	The true ages of time, to the intent that, from your highest vessels
OD MIINOAG DE GNETAAB VAUN NANAEEL	And the corners of your governments you might work my power:
PANPIR MALPIRGI PILD	Pouring down the fires of life and increase continually
CAOSG. NOAN UNALAH BALT OD VOOAN.	Upon the earth. Thus you are become the skirts of justice and truth.
DOOIAP MAD GOHOLOR, GOHUS, AMIRAN!	In the name of your God, lift up, I say, yourselves!
MICMA IEHUSOZ CACACOM OD DOOAIN	Behold his mercies flourish and his name
NOAR MICAOLZ AAIOM CASARMG GOHIA	Become mighty among us! In whom we say:
ZACAR, UNIGLAG, OD IMUAMAR PUGO	Move, descend, and apply yourselves to us as unto
PLAPLI ANANAEL QAAN	Partakers of the secret wisdom of your creation.

Fourth Key, Calls Hcoma and Activates the Whole of the Table of Water

OTHIL LASDI BABAGE OD DORPHA	I have set my feet in the south and looked about me
GOHOL: GCHISGE AVAVAGO CORMP	Saying: are not the thunders of increase numbered
PD, DS SONF VIV DIU CASARMI OALI	Thirty-three which reign in the second angle? Under whom I have placed
MAPM SOBAM AG CORMPO CRIP L;	9639 whom none have numbered but one;
CASARMG CROODZI CHIS OD UGEG;	In whom the second beginning of things are and wax strong;
DS T CAPIMALI CHIS CAPIMAON, OD	Which also successively are the numbers of time, and
LONSHIN CHIS TA LO CLA. TORZU	Their powers are as the first 456. Arise,
NOR QUASAHI OD F CAOSGA! BAGLE ZIR	You sons of pleasure and visit the earth! For I am
ENAY IAD, DS I OD APILA! DOOAIP	The lord your God, which is and liveth! In the name of
QAAL, ZACAR OD ZAMRAN OBELISONG	The creator, move and show yourselves as pleasant deliverers
RESTEL AAI NOR MOLAP	That you may praise him among the sons of men.

Fifth Key, Calls Nanta and Activates the Whole of the Table of Earth

SAPAH ZIMII D DIV OD NOAS	The mighty sounds have entered the third angle and are become
TA QANIS ADROCH: DORPHAL	As olives in the olive mount: looking with gladness

CAOSG OD FAONTS PERIPSOL	On the earth, and dwelling in the brightness of the heavens
TA BLIOR CASARM AMIPZI	As continual comforters. Unto whom I fastened
NAZ ARTH AF OD DLUGAR ZIZOP ZLIDA	Pillars Of gladness nineteen and gave them vessels to water
CAOSGI TOLTORGI OD ZCHIS ESIASCH	The earth with all her creatures. And they are the brothers of
L OD VIV OD IAOD THILD,	The first and the second, and the beginning of their own seats,
DS PERAL HUBAR PEOAL	Which are garnished with continual burning lamps 69636
SOBA CORMFA CHIS TA LA ULS OD	Whose numbers are as the first, the ends, and
QCOCASB CA NIIS OD DARBS QAAS	The contents of time! Therefore come ye, and obey your creation!
F ETHARZI OD BLIOR IAIAL EDNAS	Visit us in peace and comfort! Conclude us as receivers
CICLES BAGLE IAD I L!	Of your mysteries. Why? Our lord is all one!

Sixth Key, Calls Bitom and Activates the Whole of the Tablet of Fire

GAH S DIV CHIS EM MICAOLZ	The spirits of the fourth angle are nine, mighty
PILZIN SOBAM EL HARG	In the firmament of waters: whom the first hath planted as
MIR BABALON OD OBLOC SAMVELG	A torment to the wicked and a garland to the righteous;
DLUGAR MALPRG AR CAOSGI OD	Giving unto them fiery darts to fan the earth, and

ACAM CANAL SOBA ELZAP F BLIARD	7699 continual workmen whose courses visit with comfort
CAOSG OD CHIS ANETAB OD MIAM	The earth, and are in government and continuance
TA VIV OD D DARSAR SOLPETH	As the second and the third. Wherefore, hearken
BIEN BRITA OD ZACAM	Unto my voice: I have talked of you and I move you
GMICALZO SOBA HAATH TRIAN LUIAHE	In power and presence, whose works shall be a song of honor
OD ECRIN MAD QAAON	And the praise of God in your creation.

Seventh Key, Invokes the Angle of Water of Air

RAAS I SALMAN PARADIZ OECRIMI AAI	The east is a house of virgins singing praises among
IALPIRGAH QUIIN ENAY BUTMON	The flames of first glory: wherein the lord hath opened his mouth,
OD INOAS NI PARADIAL CASARMG	And they are become twenty-eight living dwellings in whom
UGEAR CHIRLAN OD ZONAC	The strength of men rejoices. And they are appareled
LUCIFTIAN CORS TA VAUL ZIRN	With ornaments of brightness such as work wonders
TOL HAMI SOBA LONDOH OD MIAM CHIS TA	On all creatures. Whose kingdoms and continuance are as
D OD ES UMADEA OD PIBLIAR	The third and fourth, strong towers and places of comfort,

OTHIL RIT OD MIAM CNOQUOL RIT,	The seats of mercy and continuance. O you servants of mercy,
ZACAR ZAMRAN OECRIMI QAADAH OD	Move, appear singing praises of the creator, and
OMICAOLZ AAIOM	Be mighty among us!
BAGLE PAPBOR IDLUGAM LONSHI	For to this remembrance is given power,
OD UMPLIF UGEG BIGLIAD	And our strength waxes strong in our comforter!

Eighth Key, Invokes the Angle of Earth of Air

BAZME LO I TA PIRIPSON OLN	The midday, the first is as the third heaven: made of
NAZ AVABH OX CASARMG URAN CHIS UGEG	Pillars of hiacynth twenty-six, in whom the elders are become strong.
DS ABRAMG BALTOHA GOHO IAD	Which I have prepared for my own righteousness, sayeth the Lord,
SOBA MIAM TRIAN TA LOLCIS ABAI	Whose long continuance shall be as bucklers to the stooping
VOVIN OD AZIAGIER RIOR	Dragon, and like unto the harvest of a widow.
IRGIL CHIS DA DS PAAOX BUSD CAOSGO	How many are there which remain in the glory of the earth?
DS CHIS OD IPURAN TELOCH CACARG	Which are, and shall not see death until
O SALMAN LONCHO OD VOVINA CARBAF	This house fall and the dragon sink?
NIISO BAGLE AVAVAGO GOHON NIISO	Come away! For the thunders have spoken! Come away!
BAGLE MOMAO SIAION OD MABZA	For the crowns of the temple and the coats of

IADOIASMOMAR POILP	Him that was, is, and shall be crowned are divided.
NIIS ZAMRAN CIAOFI CAOSGO OD BLIORS	Come, appear to the terror of the earth, and to our comfort
OD CORSI TA ABRAMIG	And of such as are prepared!

Ninth Key, Invokes the Angel of Fire of Air

MICAOLI BRANSG PURGEL NAPTA IALPOR	A mighty guard of fire with two-edged swords flaming,
DS BRIN EFAFAFE P VONPHO OLANI OD	Which have vials eight of wrath for two times and
OBZA SOBA UPAAH CHIS TATAN OD TRANAN	A half, whose wings are wormwood and the marrow
BALYE ALAR LUSDA SOBOLN OD CHIS	Of salt, have settled their feet in the west and are
HOLQ CNOQUODI CIAI UNAL ALDON MOM	Measured with their ministers 9996. These gather up the moss
CAOSGO TA LAS OLLOR GNAY LIMLAL AMMA CHIIS	Of the earth as the rich man doth his treasure. Cursed are they
SOBA MADRID ZCHIS OOANOAN CHIS AVINY DRILPI	Whose iniquities they are: in their eyes are millstones greater
CAOSGI OD BUTMONI PARM ZUMVI CNILA	Than the earth, and from their mouths run seas of blood.
DAZIZ ETHAMZ A-CHILDAO OD MIRC OZOL	Their heads are covered with diamond, and upon their heads
CHIS PIDIAI COLLAL ULCININ A-SOBAM UCIM BAGLE	Are marble sleeves. Happy is he on whom they frown not: for why?

IAD BALTOH CHIRLAN PAR NIISO OD IP	The God of righteousness rejoices in them! Come away! And not
EFAFAFE BAGLE COCASB I CORS TA UNIG BLIOR	Your viols: for the time is such as requires comfort!

Tenth Key, Invokes the Angel of Air of Water

CORAXO CHIS CORMP OD BLANS	The thunders of judgment and wrath are numbered, and are harbored
LUCAL AZIAZIOR PAEB SOBA LILO-NON	In the north in the likeness of an oak, whose branches
CHIS VIRQ OP EOPHAN OD RACLIR MAASI	Are nests twenty-two of lamentation and weeping laid up
BAGLE CAOSGI DS IALPON DOSIG OD BASGIM	For the earth. Which burn night and day,
OD OXEX DAZIZ SIATRIS OD SAL-BROX	And vomit out the heads of scorpions and live sulfur
CINXIR FABOAN UNAL CHIS CONST DS DAOX	Mingled with poison. These are the thunders which 5678
COCASB OL OANIO YOR EORS MICAOLI	Times in the twenty-fourth part of a moment roar with a hundred
OL GIXYAX OD MATB COCASB PLOSI MOLUI	Mighty earthquakes and a thousand times as many surges.
DS PAGE LARAG OM DROLN MATORB COCASB	Which rest not, neither know any echoing time
EMNA L PATRALX YOLCI MATB NOMIG	Here. One rock brings forth a thousand even as
MONONS OLORA GNAY ANGELARD OHIO OHIO OHIO	The heart of man does his thoughts: woe, woe, woe,

OHIO OHIO OHIO NOIB OHIO CAOSGON	Woe, woe, woe, yea, woe to the earth!
BAGLE MADRID I ZIROP CHISO DRILPA	For her iniquity is, was, and shall be great!
NIISO CRIP IP NIDALI	Come away! But not your noises!

Eleventh Key, Invokes the Angel of Earth of Water

OXIAYAL HOLDO OD ZIROM O CORAXO DS	The mighty seat groaned and they were five thunders which
ZILDAR RAASY OD VABZIR CAM-LIAX OD	Flew into the east: and the eagle spake and
BAHAL NIISO	Cried with a loud voice: come away!
OD ALDON SALMAN TELOCH	And they gathered them together in the house of death,
CASARMAN HOLQ OD T I TA ZCHIS	Of whom it is measured and it is as they are
SOBA CORMF I GA NIISO BAGLE ABRAMG	Whose number is thirty-one. Come away! For I have prepared
NONCP ZACAR CA OD ZAMRAN ODO CICLE	For you! Move, therefore and appear! Open the mysteries
QAA ZORGE LAP ZIRDO NOCO MAD	Of your creation! Be friendly to me, for i am the servant of God,
HOATH IAIDA	The true worshiper of the highest!

Twelfth Key, Invokes the Angel of Fire of Water

NONCI DS SONF BABAGE OD CHIS OB	O you which reign in the south and are twenty-eight,
HUBARO TIBIBP ALLAR ATRAAH OD EF	The lanterns of sorrow: bind up your girdles and visit us!

DRIX FAFEN MIAN AR ENAY OVOF	Bring down your train 3663, that the lord may be magnified
SOBA DOOAIN AAI I VONPHO	Whose name among you is wrath!
ZACAR GOHUS OD ZAMRAN ODO CICLE	Move, I say, and appear! Open the mysteries
QAA ZORGE LAP ZIRDO	Of your creation! Be friendly to me, for I am
NOCO MAD HOATH IAIDA	The minister of God, the true worshiper of the highest!

Thirteenth Key, Invokes the Angel of Air of Earth

NAPEAI BABAGEN DS BRIN VX OOA-ONA	O ye swords of the south, which have forty-two eyes
LRING VONPHO DOALIM EOLIS OLLOG ORSBA	To stir up wrath of sin, making men drunken
DS CHIS AFFA MICMA ISRO MAD	Which are empty: behold the promise of God,
OD LONSHI TOX DS IVMD AAI GROSB	And the power of him which is called among you a bitter sting!
ZACAR OD ZAMRAN ODO CICLE QAA	Move and appear! Open the mysteries of your creation!
ZORGE LAP ZIRDO NOCO MAD	Be friendly to me, for I am the minister of God
HOATH IAIDA	The true worshiper of the highest!

Fourteenth Key, Invokes the Angel of Water of Earth

NOROMI BAGIE PASBS OIAD DS	O you sons of fury (and) the daughters of the just: which
TRINT MIRC OL THIL DODS TOL HAMI	Sit upon twenty-four seats, vexing all living creatures
CAOSGO HOMIN DS BRIN OROCH QUAR	Of the earth with age; which have under you 1636;
MICMA BIAL OIAD AISRO TOX DS IVMD	Behold the voice of God, the promise of him which is called
AAI BALTIM	Among you fury, or extreme justice!
ZACAR OD ZAMRAN ODO CICLE QAA	Move and appear! Open the mysteries of your creation!
ZORGE LAP ZIRDO NOCO MAD	Be friendly to me, for I am the minister of God,
HOATH IAIDA	The true worshiper of the highest!

Fifteenth Key, Invokes the Angel of Fire of Earth

ILS TABAAM L IALPRT CASARMAN	O thou the governor of the first flame, under whose
VPAAH CHIS DARG DS OADO CAOSGI ORSCOR	Wings are 6739 which weave the earth with dryness;
DS OMAX MONASCI BAEOVIB OD EMETGIS	Which knowest the great name righteousness, and the seal
IAIADIX ZACAR OD ZAMRAN ODO CICLE QAA	Of honor; move and appear! Open the mysteries your creation!
ZORGE LAP ZIRDO NOCO MAD	Be friendly to me, for I am the minister of God,
HOATH IAIDA	The true worshiper of the highest!

Sixteenth Key, Invokes the Angel of Air of Fire

ILS VIV IALPRT SALMAN BALT DS BRIN	O thou second flame, the house of justice: which has
ACROODZI BUSD OD BLIORAX BALIT DS	Thy beginning in glory and shall comfort the just; which
INSI CAOSG LUSDAN EMOD DS OM	Walks the earth with feet 8763 that understand
OD TLIOB HAMI DRILPA GEH ILS	And separate creatures; great art thou
MADZILODARP	In the God of stretch-forth-and-conquer!
ZACAR OD ZAMRAN ODO CICLE QAA	Move and appear! Open the mysteries of your creation!
ZORGE LAP ZIRDO NOCO MAD	Be friendly to me, for I am the minister of God,
HOATH IAIDA	The true worshiper of the highest!

Seventeenth Key, Invokes the Angel of Water of Fire

ILS D IALPRT SOBA VPAAH CHIS NANBA	O thou third flame whose wings are thorns
ZIXLAY DODSIH OD BRIN FAXS HUBARO	To stir up vexation, and hast 7336 living lamps
TUSTAX YLSI SOBA IAD I VONPOVNPH	Going before thee; whose God is wrath in anger;
ALDON DAXIL OD TOATAR	Gird up thy loins and harken!
ZACAR OD ZAMRAN ODO CICLE QAA	Move and appear! Open the mysteries of your creation!
ZORGE LAP ZIRDO NOCO MAD	Be friendly to me, for I am the minister of God,
HOATH IAIDA	The true worshiper of the highest!

Eighteenth Key, Invokes the Angel of Earth of Fire

ILS MICAOLZ OLPIRT OD IALPRG BLIORS	O thou mighty light and burning flame of comfort;
DS ODO BUSDIR OIAD OVOARS CAOSGO	Which opens the glory of God to the center of the earth;
CASARMG LAIAD ERAN BRINTS CASASAM	In whom the secrets of truth 6332 have their abiding;
DS IVMD ACLONDOH MOZ OD MAOFFAS	Which is called in thy kingdom joy, and not to be measured:
BOLP COMO BLIORT PAMBT	Be thou a window of comfort unto me!
ZACAR OD ZAMRAN ODO CICLE QAA	Move and appear! Open the mysteries of your creation!
ZORGE LAP ZIRDO NOCO MAD	Be friendly to me, for I am the minister of God,
HOATH IAIDA	The true worshiper of the highest!

Recommended Reading

The Book of Solomon's Magick by Carroll Poke Runyon

Poke was an expert on Solomonic magic. The real interesting part is his discoveries of methods of scrying with a black mirror using your reflected face.

The Chicken Qabalah of Rabbi Lamed Ben Clifford: A Dilettante's Guide to What You Do and Do Not Need to Know to Become a Qabalist by Lon Milo DuQuette

The best introduction to the Qabalah out there; this is a great place to start if you are new to Qabalah. Next, look at books such as *The Mystical Qabalah* by Dion Fortune, *Ladder of Lights; Or, Qabalah Renovata: A Step by Step Guide to the Tree of Life and the Four Worlds of the Qabalists* by William G. Gray, and *A Practical Guide to Qabalistic Symbolism* by Gareth Knight.

Enochian Vision Magick: A Practical Guide to the Magick of Dr. John Dee and Edward Kelley by Lon Milo DuQuette

Simply the best book out there to get introduced to the Enochian system and its basic history. We believe no one has published a book that covers so much ground and is yet approachable and practical.

The Essential Golden Dawn by Chic Cicero and Sandra Tabatha Cicero

An excellent resource for the basic rituals of our practice in their standard, traditional forms, it includes the Lesser Ritual of the Pentagram along with the Qabalistic Cross.

Feeding Your Demons: Ancient Wisdom for Resolving Inner Conflict by Tsultrim Allione

You need this book. If the method we described for working with your shadows seems useful, then you want this. The author also has videos on YouTube and a website for her institute: https://www.taramandala.org/.

The Hero with a Thousand Faces by Joseph Campbell

Read this and watch the Bill Moyers interviews with Joseph Campbell on YouTube. It will change your life.

Initiation into Hermetics by Bardon Franz

A wonderful book full of useful exercises and a complete system of magic not directly tied to the Golden Dawn or Crowley.

The Magick of Aleister Crowley: A Handbook of the Rituals of Thelema by Lon Milo DuQuette

An excellent resource into the basic rituals of both Crowley and the Golden Dawn. It is very useful to see the rituals side by side.

Mastering the Art of Ritual Magick, Spirit Conjuring for Witches: Magical Evocation Simplified, and *Magical Qabalah for Beginners: A Comprehensive Guide to Occult Knowledge* by Frater Barrabbas

Frater B. is Erich's initiator, and his books are wonderful. If you can get a copy of *Mastering the Art of Ritual Magick,* then do so. You will have the original versions of the rituals in this book and much more.

The Middle Pillar: The Balance Between Mind and Magic by Israel Regardie

This is the book that got Erich started; the Ciceros have extended it a lot.

Rebel in the Soul: An Ancient Egyptian Dialogue Between a Man and His Destiny by Bika Reed

A fantastic look at Egyptian mythology about the plight of the soul during a spiritual crisis.

Tarot of Ceremonial Magick: A Pictorial Synthesis of Three Great Pillars of Magick: Enochian, Goetia, Astrology by Lon Milo DuQuette

Another excellent resource for ritual design, this deck shows how the many systems of Hermeticism are interwoven and fit together like a jigsaw puzzle; it is very useful to see the big picture.

Bibliography

Al-Kindi. *On the Stellar Rays.* Translated by Robert Zoller and edited by Robert Hand. The Golden Hind Press, 1993.

Allione, Tsultrim. *Feeding Your Demons: Ancient Wisdom for Resolving Inner Conflict.* Little, Brown, 2008.

Bardon, Franz. *Initiation into Hermetics; A Course of Instruction in Ten Stages: Theory and Practice.* Merkur Publishing, 1956.

Barrabbas, Frater. *Magical Qabalah for Beginners: A Comprehensive Guide to Occult Knowledge.* Llewellyn Publications, 2013.

Barrabbas, Frater. *Mastering the Art of Ritual Magick.* Megalithica Books, 2013.

Barrabbas, Frater. *Spirit Conjuring for Witches: Magical Evocation Simplified.* Llewellyn Publications, 2017.

Bolton, Chelsea Luellon. *Lady of Arrows: An Anthology for Neith.* Published by the author, 2023.

Budge, E. A. Wallis. *The Book of the Dead.* Gramercy, 1999. Originally published in 1895 by Harrison and Sons.

Budge, E. A. *The Gods of the Egyptians; or, Studies in Egyptian Mythology.* Vol. 1. Dover Publications, 1969.

Bulwer-Lytton, Edward, and Lon Milo DuQuette. *Zanoni Book One: The Musician*. Weiser Books, 2012.

Campbell, Joseph. *The Hero with a Thousand Faces*. New World Library, 2008.

Cicero, Chic, and Sandra Tabatha Cicero. *The Essential Golden Dawn: An Introduction to High Magic*. Llewellyn Publications, 2003.

Cicero, Chic, and Sandra Tabatha Cicero. *Golden Dawn Magic: A Complete Guide to the High Magical Arts*. Llewellyn Publications, 2019.

Crowley, Aleister. *777 and Other Qabalistic Writings of Aleister Crowley: Including Gematria & Sepher Sephiroth*. Weiser Books, 1986.

Crowley, Aleister. *The Law Is for All: An Extended Commentary on the Book of the Law*. Edited by Israel Regardie. Llewellyn Publications, 1975.

Crowley, Aleister. *Little Essays Toward Truth*. New Falcon Publications, 1996.

Crowley, Aleister. *Magick Without Tears*. Edited by Israel Regardie. Falcon Press, 1982.

Davies, Owen. "The Hermetic Order of the Golden Dawn and the Origins of Wicca." *Yale University Press*. October 31, 2023. https://yalebooks.yale.edu/2023/10/31/the-hermetic-order-of-the-golden-dawn-and-the-origins-of-wicca/.

DuQuette, Lon Milo. *Enochian Vision Magick: A Practical Guide to the Magick of Dr. John Dee and Edward Kelley*. Weiser Books, 2019.

DuQuette, Lon Milo. *Low Magick: It's All in Your Head, You Just Have No Idea How Big Your Head Is*. Llewellyn Worldwide, 2010.

DuQuette, Lon Milo. *The Magick of Aleister Crowley: A Handbook of the Rituals of Thelema*. Weiser Books, 2022.

DuQuette, Lon Milo. *Understanding Aleister Crowley's Thoth Tarot*. New Edition. Weiser Books, 2017.

The Editors of Encyclopaedia Britannica. "Aleister Crowley." *Britannica*. Updated August 16, 2024. https://www.britannica.com/biography/Aleister-Crowley.

Ferris, Timothy. *Coming of Age in the Milky Way*. HarperCollins, 2003.

Fowden, Garth. *The Egyptian Hermes: A Historical Approach to the Late Pagan Mind*. Princeton University Press, 1993.

Gordon, Richard. "*Charaktêres* Between Antiquity and Renaissance." *Academia*. https://www.academia.edu/13925134.

Hanegraaff, Wouter J. *Western Esotericism: A Guide for the Perplexed.* Guides for the Perplexed. Bloomsbury Academic, 2013.

Hargrave, John. G. "Paracelsus." *Britannica.* Updated September 20, 2024. https://www.britannica.com/biography/Paracelsus.

Holy Bible: New Revised Standard Version. American Bible Society, 1997.

Jung, Carl G. *Man and His Symbols.* Bantam Books, 2023. Originally published in 1964 by Doubleday.

Jung, Carl G . *Synchronicity: An Acausal Connecting Principle.* Vol. 8 of the Collected Works of C. G. Jung. Translated by R. F. C. Hull. Princeton University Press, 2011.

Laycock, Donald C. *The Complete Enochian Dictionary: A Dictionary of the Angelic Language as Revealed to Dr. John Dee & Edward Kelley.* Weiser Books, 2023.

Leitch, Aaron. *An Encyclopedic Lexicon of the Tongue of Angels.* Vol. 2 of *The Angelical Language.* Llewellyn Publications, 2010.

Leitch, Aaron. "What Is Enochian Magick? (The Two Mystical Traditions of Enoch the Prophet.)" September 13, 2012. https://www.llewellyn.com/journal/article/2321.

Lévi, Éliphas, *Transcendental Magic: Its Doctrine and Ritual.* Translated by Arthur Edward Waite. George Redway, 1896. Made available through the Internet Archive in alliance with the University of Toronto as part of the Open Content Alliance. https://archive.org/details/transcendentalma00leviuoft.

"The Emerald Tablet of Hermes Tristmagistus." *The Cabinet.* June 2018. https://www.cabinet.ox.ac.uk/emerald-tablet-hermes-trismegistus.

Paracelsus. *Four Treatises of Theophrastus Von Hohenheim, Called Paracelsus.* Translated by C. Lilian Temkin and edited by Henry E. Sigerist. Johns Hopkins University Press, 1996.

Pearson, Carol S. *Awakening the Heroes Within: Twelve Archetypes to Help Us Find Ourselves and Transform Our World.* HarperOne, 2015.

Peterson, Joseph H, ed. *John Dee's Five Books of Mystery: Original Sourcebook of Enochian Magic: From the Collected Work Known as* Mysteriorum libri quinque. Weiser Books, 2008.

Pinch, Geraldine. *Egyptian Mythology: A Guide to the Gods, Goddesses, and Traditions of Ancient Egypt.* First Edition. Oxford University Press, 2004.

Reed, Bika. *Rebel in the Soul: An Ancient Egyptian Dialogue Between a Man and His Destiny.* Inner Traditions International, 1997.

Regardie, Israel. *The Golden Dawn*. Vol. 2. Llewellyn Publications, 1982.

Regardie, Israel. *The Middle Pillar: The Balance Between Min and Magic*. Edited by Chic Cicero and Sandra Tabatha Cicero. Llewellyn Publications, 2002.

Runyon, Carroll Poke. *The Book of Solomon's Magick*. Church of the Hermetic Science, 2021.

Salaman, Clement. *The Way of Hermes: New Translations of the Corpus Hermeticum and the Definitions of Hermes Trismegistus to Asclepius*. Inner Traditions, 2004.

Shakespeare, William. *Henry IV, Part 1*. MIT. Accessed January 2, 2025. http://shakespeare.mit.edu/1henryiv/full.html.

Shakespeare, William. *The Life and Death of Richard the Second*. MIT. Accessed January 2, 2025. https://shakespeare.mit.edu/richardii/full.html.

Shakespeare, William. *The Life of King Henry the Fifth*. MIT. Accessed January 2, 2025. https://shakespeare.mit.edu/henryv/henryv.1.0.html.

Shakespeare, William. *A Midsummer Night's Dream*. MIT. Accessed January 2, 2025. https://shakespeare.mit.edu/midsummer/midsummer.2.1.html.

Shakespeare, William. *Titus Andronicus*. MIT. Accessed January 2, 2025. https://shakespeare.mit.edu/titus/titus.2.1.html.

Skemer, Don C. *Binding Words: Textual Amulets in the Middle Ages*. Pennsylvania State University Press, 2006.

Turner, Robert. *Elizabethan Magic: The Art of the Magus*. Element Books, 1989.

von Worms, Abraham. *The Book of Abramelin: A New Translation*. Edited by Georg Dehn and translated by Steven Guth. Ibis Press, 2025.

Wang, Robert. *The Qabalistic Tarot: A Textbook of Mystical Philosophy*. Weiser, 1983.

Yang, Jwing-Ming. *Qigong Meditation Embryonic Breathing: The Foundation of Spiritual Enlightenment*. 2nd ed. YMAA Publication Center, 2022.

Notes

Notes

Notes

Notes